Paths from a White Horse
A Writer's Memoir

PETER VANSITTART

Paths from a White Horse

A Writer's Memoir

Quartet Books
London Melbourne New York

To Justine, and to all my friends,
who have heard it all so often.

First published by Quartet Books Limited, 1985
A member of the Namara Group
27/29 Goodge Street, London W1P 1FD

Copyright © 1985 Peter Vansittart

British Library Cataloguing in Publication Data

Vansittart, Peter
    Paths from a white horse : a writer's memoir.
    1. Vansittart, Peter—Biography   2. Novelists,
    English—20th century—Biography
    I. Title
    823'.914   PR6072.A76Z/

ISBN 0-7043-2457-1

Typeset by MC Typeset, Chatham, Kent
Printed and bound in Great Britain
by Mackays of Chatham Ltd, Kent

Author's Note

Any writer worth his salt knows that only a small proportion of literature does more than partly compensate people for the damage they have suffered by learning to read.   *Rebecca West*

I know of no person so perfectly disagreeable and even dangerous as an author.   *King William IV*

Only one person in a thousand is a bore, and he is interesting because he is one person in a thousand.

Harold Nicolson

Autobiography implies self-satisfaction, and to record my own imaginative growth is a gamble that may prove reckless and may only confirm Graham Greene's suggestion that, for the novelist, the compost of the imagination is not what he remembers but what he forgets. I myself find all people interesting, though too few give proof of it, and find that the apparently trivial may be a slow fuse. Slow fuses, unfreezing a too stolid imagination, is my theme. Some write in order to give the answers; myself, because I want to know the answers, to questions which, admittedly, no one has asked me. I write to record this growth without too many details of income and domesticity, and, indeed, I have never for long had very much of either.   P.V.

Acknowledgements

Early drafts of sections of this book have appeared in *Tribune*, *Vogue*, the *Spectator*, *Time and Tide*, the *Bookman*, the *London Magazine*, the *Listener*, and on BBC Radio 3. Poems and lines of poems are reprinted by kind permission of Faber and Faber Ltd from *The English Auden, Collected Poems* by W.H Auden, *Collected Poems* by Stephen Spender and *Collected Poems* by George Barker. The author is grateful to the Executors of the Estate of C. Day Lewis, Jonathan Cape and the Hogarth Press for permission to use C. Day Lewis's poem 'Newsreel' from *Collected Poems* 1954.

One

A stone's throw out on either hand
From that well-ordered road we tread,
And all the world is wild and strange.
                                    Rudyard Kipling

1

1923. I was three. A White Horse lay bare and solitary, cut
into a hillside. It changes whenever I return to it, like a book,
painting, friend, but remains fixed in my imagination, a
reminder of the multiple transformations that enthuse life. All
is provisional. Memory contracts and enlarges as if in a dream
that does not cease in the morning.

Adults seemed strangely unaware of the White Horse or
reluctant to mention it. Here, already, was the first of the
countless secrets that helped to awaken me. The Horse,
existing without breathing or eating, though, in days of
shadow and sun, it sometimes appeared to move, seemed
mysteriously more real than an actual white horse assiduously
cropping the pastures.

Such feelings, of course, are commonplace. A little girl, at
Wellington's funeral, seeing the Duke's boots dangling from
his horse, asked whether all people got turned into boots. A
small boy, he could have been me, seeing the statue of General
Gordon on a camel, eventually asked the name of the man
sitting on Gordon. Children can weep, not for joy at the
Prodigal Son's return, but in grief for the fatted calf. They
speak for moods into which adults too can periodically relapse

and which dictators may cynically understand, though understand little else. Absolute power demands the childish, occasionally the child-like.

Childhood was a ballad, beginning with the White Horse, reaching towards Troy, a headless rider, the rustle of trees on a windless day. With giants. With silver Essex ponds, where light sharpened beyond reed and bullrush and children seem forever stooping for sticklebacks, tadpoles, minnows. Bright light wavers, then stills, as if something is about to break surface. There, outside Loughton, I would see two suns, one in the clear sky, one both in and on the clear water and travelling faster, so that, tremulously, I awaited its collision with the bank, at which it soundlessly dissolved, to lie smudged on grass or, at a cloud, scattered in brilliant chips.

Water provoked imagination, as it does the world over, particularly the sea, moody and restless alongside Broadstairs, gnawing at Frinton and Dunwich; heavy and brutal in yellowing pictures where Steerforth lay dead on the sand, or flat and curled and tempting as young Ralegh watched a brown hand point westwards.

A cottage, crooked as if wounded, was perched on Dunwich cliff, almost the last of a great medieval town, soon to topple and join those long at one with rock and fish and tide.

A woman's voice reads aloud, and Henry Newbolt's verse makes a chant running with the summer waves.

> Effingham, Grenville, Ralegh, Drake,
>   Here's to the bold and free,
> Benbow, Collingwood, Byron, Blake,
>   Hail to the kings of the sea.

Newbolt was a stalwart of traditional patriotic values — courage, devotion, loyalty — and I was recently surprised, and glad, to hear from Patric Dickenson, that, in old age, threatened by Modernism, he gave praise, perception, sometimes practical support, not only to de la Mare, Yeats and Hardy's *The Dynasts*, but to Herbert Read, T.S. Eliot, Ezra Pound.

2

1926. We are now living in Southsea, at Fairlee, Florence Road, which still stands; down the road, in Portsmouth, Nelson had slept his last night in England. The *Victory* lay in dry dock and I could feel myself young Rodney Stone, agog to serve him. As a preliminary, I squashed my grey, ribboned sun-hat to a naval cock and intoned 'Nelson's peerless name', imagining him wantonly deprived of pears.

Such devotion, of course, is very natural. Freud so deeply identified himself with Hannibal that he long refused to visit Rome. He named a son Oliver, after Cromwell. We are lived, he would say.

Admirals enthralled me, they enlarged the world. Admirals with spy-glasses examining distant masts and doomed coast-lines, pacing quarter-decks, ordering floggings and cannon-ades, standing in blues, golds, whites against the sky, pillars of a life surely within reach. T.E. Lawrence would have shocked me on board ship, mocking officers by referring to the bridge as 'the veranda'. Jesus, walking on waves in an off-hand way, though lacking cocked hat and braid, was merely the perfection of admirals. I would certainly have saluted the epitaph, at St Mary's, Bromley-by-Bow, to the sailor, William Dean:

> He now at Anchor lies amid the Fleet
> Awaiting orders – Admiral Christ to meet.

Through dreams, the sea hummed and lamented, becoming the Cape, Spanish Main, Downs, flogged by Nor-East Trades, fluttered by a Nor-Wester, soothed in the Tropics. The sea, endlessly protean, had hearkened to the Israelites fleeing from Pharoah, neatly dividing to display, as if through the windows of Handley's Department Store, on separate levels the fish and the galleons, sea-chests, surly crabs, gothic barnacles, respect-able mermaids and touchy, blue-green gods.

Once, aged seven, angered by the injustices of home, I 'ran away to sea', like the young heroes of Ballantyne, Marryat and

Percy F. Westerman who provided an exchange that I have remembered, not quite perfectly, for fifty years.

'I say, Cain, he's dead.'
'Quite a logical statement, Pengelly, supported by circumstantial evidence.'

On that occasion in 1927, I fled adult folly and injustice in search of a ship, but only found myself alone on a pebble-bound beach, facing a dense, coarse sea. Where further? I slunk back, pretending I had never left the garden. I was too timid, needing my hero and protector, John Armitage, whom, in the dramatic reversals of dream, I nightly saved from quicksands, cannibals, the whirlpool.

Over forty years later, in a *London Magazine* extract by Dr Dannie Abse, with whom I have exchanged many books, I read that such fantasies may merely represent, symbolically, unconscious desires to save our mothers from the cruel embraces of the men they married. In general, this may deserve scrutiny but, for myself, the recollection of my mother and stepfather rebuffs it.

Daytime was still too dangerous. Had not Hansel and Gretel found a gingerbread house whose delights deceived?

Beyond the garden, beyond the beach, much was indeed astir, 1925–29, though, had I known it, it would have meant little. Jack Hobbs was overtaking Dr Grace's record of centuries, Bruno Taut proposing to redesign the Alps, and President Coolidge announced that, when many are out of work, unemployment results. Hitler now led 27,000 Nazis, Sacco and Vanzetti were executed, the Kellog Pact outlawed war, the Irish politician, Kevin O'Higgins, was murdered. Post-war confusion witnessed and sometimes seemed to necessitate dictators: Pilsudski in Poland, Primo de Rivera in Spain, Stalin, Mussolini, ultimately Hitler. Shocked by the mass casualties, endlessly seeking new solutions, Europe was experimenting. Outside Britain parliamentary democracy had at best shallow roots, save in France; though even there, since the Jacobins of 1792–94, the traditions were largely authoritarian, with anarchist undertones. Economic democracy was

4

probably the more desired. With their cruelty and fitful glamour, the dictators were to become an inescapable part of my imagination which I did not always wish to escape until 1973, when I wrote a book about them and their hold largely withdrew.

Stories, secrets, they were everywhere to hand, asking to be uncovered. I hummed a song:

> Polly, put the kettle on. . .
>
> and we'll all have tea
>
> Suki, take it off again. . .
>
> they've all gone away

But where had they gone? What had occurred? A sadness here, a hint of menace. Life was already filling with gaps, which needed stories to plug them.

The woman's voice reads on. Miss Ida Howe, young nursery governess, a title now obsolete as Padishah. Her voice slides open panels, disclosing Blind Pew on the winter road. *The Coral Island* induced fears of a tidal wave that would crack the South Parade Pier, shatter the Portsdown Hills, split the sky and reveal wrathful angels. This did not happen, but I was left oppressed by all the unwanted of the Twenties – beggars, unemployed, Bloody Bolshies, Lower Classes, cads, Irish, miners, strikers – being forced at bayonet-point under the sea, where cities were being built, hive-shaped, smooth, soundless, like the strange forts in the Solent. In silver masks and black repellent tights, the dispossessed would vanish forever, wailing, imploring, leaving behind only eerie bubbles. Through November gales their cries made us all wicked.

Wickedness was evident. On the beach with Miss Howe, I see motionless smudges and diagonals that become blazers, straw hats, long skirts, flowered brims, and beneath them, smoking, a man sitting on stones, bleakly isolated, grey face very still under a peakless cap. The crowd's silence is watchful, the waves creep away, the gulls hang as if painted. Concealed by a towering breakwater, I pluck Miss Howe's sleeve.

'What is it?'

'A German.'

'What has he done?'

'Hush.'

I dare ask no more.

Germans I associated with germs, from which, or from whom, little good came. They were also linked, criminally, with the beggars that roamed the streets, waylaying me, menacing my walks, offering matches, bootlaces, playing barrel-organ or hurdy-gurdy, often with a glum monkey or a dog, drowsy, perhaps dead, lying beside a cap with a penny in it. Many were armless, legless or blind. Their medals and ribbons were almost as florid as those of the Picture Palace Commissionaire: they had won the Great War but their gauntness, shabbiness, their eyes both cringing and aggressive, seemed to deny this, as if their victory had been shameful. One I particularly dreaded had a solitary tooth surrounded by a lot of grimy face: he would come to our door, selling notepaper, put his foot inside and refuse to go until we bought some. Secretly, I would weep for him, within my fear. Tears came easily, even when people switched off the wireless, for I felt the broadcaster's feelings must be irredeemably hurt. It showed a generous disposition unaccompanied by marked intelligence.

Behind the beggars, unseen but never quite concealed, lurked the Germans, not mentioned in the Bible, presumably because their deeds were unmentionable. Simultaneously, it was perplexing that my toy soldiers, castles, ships, gadgets, all seemed to be 'Made in Germany', as though that racked and ruined country was a cornucopia of presents for English children.

The Great War lingered on in the wounds, the cripples, the parades and tall stories. It is curious that in 1980, two of the Serbian participants in the Sarajevo murders were still alive: a professor, a curator, blandly proud of those millions of deaths, rich life becoming rich meat, for had they not produced Yugoslavia!

One early memory is that of my mother lighting a gas-geyser and setting her hair alight. For years, 'Geyser' denoted fire and horror and merged with 'Kaiser', a further

6

manifestation of 'German', often spoken of by adults, a dangerous presence, a ghost, a disease, but never actually explained.

Of public life I of course knew nothing, save that a Mr Ramsey Mac was liable to be hanged, very properly. Phrases, names, were exchanged across the breakfast table, from behind the tall walls of newspapers, or at dinner, during my brief visit 'for dessert'. I would ponder over 'Trouble in the Pits', 'General Strike', 'Foodpad', 'Rotters'. Rotters seemed worse than cads, much worse than bounders. A few years later, 'Haig Dying'. I see well-dressed people heads bowed, expressions doleful, but from a certain street where cads, bounders, rotters and Bolshies all lived together, there sounded cheers.

3

At home, there never seemed to be enough money: 'Tin', 'Chink', 'Sponduliks', 'The Ready'; secretly I craved Treasure, Pieces-of-Eight, Doubloons. 'No more money in the bank', the dance bands were soon to be playing, 'What's to do about it? let's turn out the lights and go to sleep.' My mother's investments in 'Mexican Railways' predictably paid nothing. One remedy, apparently, was 'The Irish Sweep', with powers inexplicit, always mentioned impersonally, but presenting me with an image sooty, violent, ruthless, his alleged riches helping no one. Solemn and silent, I had my questions, seldom asked, never satisfactorily answered, forcing me to spin my own fancies. Imagination throve on misunderstandings and my own reticence. With mute distress I assumed that the long, steel skewers regularly glinting in that tedious and prolonged phenomenon, the Sunday joint, had been driven into the doomed animal to prevent it struggling. Red squat cars sped past, 'Royal Mail'. Did King George really have so many letters? A particular house, absolutely forbidden me, was sometimes unnaturally hushed, sometimes raucous with songs and laughter. Each door, each green, mottled window, had inscriptions, arcane, vaguely alluring. 'Public Bar', 'Private Bar', 'Saloon', 'Bottle and Jug', 'Gentlemen', 'Wines from the Wood', 'Spirits'. *Spirits*! They surely explained my exclusion. But were they really there, hovering six inches above the floor, breakfasting on the ceiling, drinking 'Stout', tempting us to bring May into the house?

Once a bluejacket lurched out, touched my arm, his voice thick and shapeless: 'She don't give it me. Thinks 'erself God. God Almighty! Rotting bitch.' This last phrase interested me, and, back home, I repeated it aloud, without encouragement to do so again.

Warnings accumulated. Life had traps. The gingerbread house, the deceiving promise. It could wilt very suddenly. We had a gardener, Mr Friend, whom I assumed worked long hours in all weathers out of friendship. Then, one day, I was shocked to see a few coins change hands, unwillingly counted, glumly accepted. My trust in people began to narrow, drastically.

Tiny dramas were interlocked, which adults ignored and might not always have seen. On the pier was a row of glass cases, each containing a fixed, staring tableau. I drop in a penny, a click, a whirr, a tense pause, then the rope tautens on Charley Peace, Dr Crippen; a neat house gushes with fire, a fire engine swerves forward, dolls drop down a ladder but one is forgotten, left beating frantically on a window; the axe falls very slowly on the black-dressed Queen of Scots, always reminding me that behind a certain door at home, never, never opened, was almost certainly a scaffold.

Some years later, I was shocked to find in *The Wind in the Willows* that Mr Toad, in prison, passed 'the private scaffold'. In such a book this had no place. Today, when I encounter Kipling's 'faces that opened and shut their mouths horribly', I am instantly back on that pier, waiting to be beheaded, or burned to a cinder.

Less exacting was the summer beach astir with hymn-singers, picnics, balloons, flags, cricketers, Punch and Judy. At night, that noisy pair would be packed in their chest but, deep in their darkness, free at last, what antics did they perform together? Above, on the *Esplanade*, the El Dorado man, Stop Me and Buy One, was selling ices, another link with Ralegh. I had yet to learn that El Dorado was not an exotic land but a ruler, the Gilded Man.

I wandered, too rarely alone, along the creamy Southsea front where pearled gorgons and blazered commanders sipped on balconies or at small, coloured tables. I recognize the grimaces of Captain van Butte, who has never recovered from a blow he inflicted on his head while swatting a fly. I smile at Mr Moncrieffe, who, despite smashing a leg in the Great War, was either 'running' for office or 'standing' for Parliament, and remember that, appositely, his wife was considered 'fast'. Ahead, jutting into the sea, under another sky ripped by gulls and as if soiled by the breath of all the world's shantymen, was dirty Gosport, its beckoning masts, cranes, rusty funnels, shabby ensigns, warehouses crammed with Indiamen's loot, with prize packets, swag, dead men's spoils; and in taverns sailors were exchanging rattling good yarns, picking their teeth with cutlasses and remembering victims walking the plank. Gosport, like my nursery ceiling made of wedding cake, was always a little too far away, but like 'Orinoco', 'El Dorado', 'Pension Fund', 'Mexican Railways', was hung with the lures of the unknown.

Sometimes the streets flowered with naval bands, flags, processions, the beggars were hustled away: the Duke and Duchess of York were leaving for Australia, the King of Afghanistan was arriving, gun salutes banged against the sky, the trumpets blared, the Prince of Wales might come.

4

An only child, I had to invent many companions. Girls existed, but only as oddly dressed outlines, at their fullest and most dangerous at parties. Sheila and Bunty, Paddy, Pat and Cordelia, by now they all share an identical face, quite mute. I craved a Best Friend, which John Armitage, in all his grandeur, never quite became. Michael Batt was too ferocious, Wonky Maynard too wonky. My shyness, my fear of dancing, of being addressed, made parties occasions of dread. Once the eating ceased, games began, Hide and Seek, Sardines, Charades, at all of which I was (and remain) direly incompetent, once wrecking a considerable proportion of an expensive apartment, goaded into miming *Sense and Sensibility*. Once, by my mother's mistake of a date, I arrived an hour late for an ordinary tea-party wearing fancy dress, an object of ridicule and censure; horrible children elbowed me into reach of the candle flames, for the costume was of white, frilly paper in which I could move only gingerly, regarding candles and cigarettes with terror. My social shortcomings, of which even my closest friends endlessly remind me, can perhaps be traced to this. The costume was that of a clown.

One party was given annually by Dr Golder, who seemed born some millennia ago, considerably East of Eden. He always had a large pool filled with silver coins, we had only to pick one out, then keep it. Gleaming, real treasure lay in the water, but the water was electrified. You had to keep one hand on the rail, dip with the other. Groping, you felt the little shock running up your arm and the longer the shock, the larger the pain, the more money you got. We would laugh, rather hysterically. Dark and smiling, Dr Golder watched us dipping and crying out, unable to desist. Methodically, he increased the electric current, dropping in florins, half-crowns, eventually golden sovereigns, and adults joined in, greedily pushing us aside, going wild, snatching and quarrelling.

I can see Dr Golder now, rubbing his hands, watching us grovel. Who was he? I never knew. I can never remember asking my mother or stepfather a serious question. I imagined Dr Golder curling up in his own ear and falling asleep. As I write, I wonder whether he really existed. Could he have been, like some demon king, damaged hero, green man or centaur, a figment of night thoughts, psychic shorthand, ritual groove – and the more powerful because of it? Only one set of parties was enjoyable. At Christmas, children related to officers were rowed through Solent mists to clamber aboard some great warship: *Rodney*, *Hood*, *Renown*, *Repulse* . . . so many of which were to be sunk by Japanese in 1941, dragging with them three centuries of British sea power, the resonance of Admirals.

On board were mammoth celebrations, so large that no

shyness mattered. Another world, fragile, but with the fragility of moonlight that affects all and endures, leapt into being under the masts, the great guns, the moon, 'under hatches': amiable sailors, dressed as earringed pirates, pistols at the belt, and Regency tars in rough kerseys – today I live in Kersey itself – with swinging pigtails; officers' cabins transformed to shops where parcels were handed out; ranked torpedoes, inch thick in oil; scores of tables laden with cakes, jellies, trifles, ices; a gigantic Tiger Tim with eyes rolling like Catherine Wheels; Robin Hood, Dick Whittington, Humpty Dumpty, Red Riding Hood stalking past, a rival history more convincing than that in which I was starting to have lessons; a film show, Felix the Cat, Laurel and Hardy, marvellous zanies whose grave *non sequiturs*, shocked bewilderment and slow-burning explosions made the round world rounder. Grey tyrannical ships blazed with good humour on the rocking sea.

Those great ships were already obsolete; though, in 1927, none knew it. I myself was destined for the Royal Naval College, Dartmouth, which I was young enough to envisage romantically. In those days careers, like schools, were given to you like clothes. Few would have been worse than myself on the watch, none more likely to confuse the bridge with the veranda. In crisis, I have lasting inability to know left from right, I dislike giving and receiving orders. Meanwhile, however, I foresaw marvellous voyages, bright islands, unluckier fellows walking the plank watched by an approving shark.

5

Within such a regular frieze of people and ritual, alternately dark and gaudy, I was happy. Left unexplained, the most mundane had glamour. 'Explanation kills life,' Henry Green (I think) has written. A hole in the road revealed a choice entanglement of wires, tubes, metal caskets, rods, spoilt only when some busybody listed the workings. Streets throve on characters, not only beggars and hucksters but the knife-grinder behind his wheel, flower girls, messenger boys with tiny pill-box hats, dainty naval officers, naval and Marine processions and bands, tinkers, trams like genial mythical beasts, odds and ends men with small packed carts, scrap metal dealers, each with his high or croaking cry – I believed 'any old iron' was an euphemism for unwanted children. There was the Muffin Man with his bell, his tray balanced on his head, the Lamplighter with his long pole, very possibly guilty when the stars where shut and the moon was black, suggesting some lapse on his part or even 'sudden death', liable to be heard often enough, though on occasions oddly dissimilar. The Sweep would come, probably a spy, black faced, with donkey cart bristling with gollywog brushes. And the Man with Trombone, the Salvation Army with tunes shaken over me like confetti, French Onion-boys in berets, their goods on long pinkish strings. My mother remembered dancing bears and, presumably like Ancient Britons, the Blue Hungarian Band. Sometimes a juggler performed outside the fishmonger's, itself a toy circus: sea life in all hues, glistening, radiant, pallid, rainbow, the ovalled and circular, wiry and oblong, the gaping mouths and surprised eyes, piled in splendid profusion amongst hillocks of ice, parsley, lemon. I preferred glass flowers to the real. The most beautiful artefact I have ever seen was a sugar rose, given me at Christmas, 1927: a pink mass of lustred petals, folded, in tight pointed buds, curling outwards, gleaming with promise of delight; flame-like whorls, glistening cavities, small twists of sugar like pinnacles upon this tiny, enticing fane. I gloated over it for some weeks, then, overwhelmed by greed, tortured by embryo lust, recklessly crammed it into my mouth and crunched it to bits, my horror and guilt making it taste disgusting.

6

Words had begun to matter, falling like rain, then solidifying, building steps into the world or out of it. Without sufficient of them to know it, I was inwardly watching and waiting for enchantment to lapse, so that meaning could fill them to the brim. Words, jabs from the unknown, sips of the world.

'Summerhouse', symbol of pure, simple pleasure, 'Esplanade', of course, gemmed with the splendours of the Indies and leading to the Spanish Main, 'Pendragon Hotel', 'Mrs Copenhagen', 'Secret Society'. Certain words inevitably thrill me to this day. 'Troika', 'Charcoal-burner', 'Burgundian'. I brooded in silence, examining my scraps not of information but intuition. 'Overdraft' must mean death from cold, a conviction reinforced by the dismal tone in which it was always uttered. Many words, like the activities they signified, have dwindled almost to nothing 'drayman', 'pieman', 'cooperage'. 'Unless you wake up,' voices threatened, 'you will end up as a "crossing-sweeper"!' And who now remembers the *linkman?* Certain words, apparently ordinary, were charged with further, more baleful meanings, as adult voices switched between anger and alarm, amazement, caution, horrible politeness, as they said 'Business', 'Shares', 'Slump', 'The Huns', 'The Conservatives' (secret societies both) and 'Mussolini'. The last had vague but obvious grandeur: to have known that it meant 'muslin-maker' would only have enhanced it. Winston Churchill hailed the *Duce* in 1927: 'the expression of Roman genius, the great lawgiver among mankind, has shown every nation that may be harried by Socialism or Communism that there is a way out' and, rather later, conceded that Adolf Hitler might yet join those who have 'enriched the story of mankind'.

Presumably, as the twenties ended, news became more suggestive, more sinsister. Words continued to flow into me. 'Brokers', surely, broke people's hearts, like Richard the boy king. 'Tramp' seemed little better than 'Ladies of a Certain Class'. 'You're no better than a "Street Arab"' rang in my ears but so glamorous did this sound that I feared I was very much worse. I wished to be 'natty'; 'Catching a Tartar' was to be avoided, likewise 'The Army', for there, John Armitage asserted, men were compelled to eat soap and indeed his father, a major, with his smooth pink skin, must have been compelled very frequently. I loved every word in Captain Hook's 'rich, damp, green cake'. Darker words lay in ambush. 'Kidnapped', emitting anguished blindfoldings in a valley darkened by the wings of the terrible Crookback, crowned and merciless, shaped like a lightning flash, yet lonely, mute, despairing. Moreover, I was a kid, thus most likely to be napped. 'Hindenburg', 'Kenneth de Wattville', 'Hades' swiftly developed stronger profiles. 'Lantern' hung red at crossroads, outside smugglers' inns, or from the carved, gilded stern of a galleon.

Grown-ups had their own language, suggestive, sometimes poetic, but too often implying unfavourable comments on life. 'Swell', 'Toff', more rarely 'Knut', 'Jew-boy', 'Lounge-lizard', 'Burlington Bertie', 'Not out of the Top Drawer', 'Touch of the Tar', 'Dago': grades of being, cards of identity to be scrutinized but not, it seemed, to be punctiliously exchanged. 'You're a "Real White Man",' Colonel Higgins remarked, though to Paul Robeson. Despite the absence of Money in the Bank, there was constant talk and practice of 'Drinkies'. The social difference between 'Cad' and 'Bounder' I still find interesting. In a few years I was hankering to be a Vernon-Smith, the tough, erratic 'Bounder' of Frank Richards' fictional school, Greyfriars, stalking-place of Billy Bunter, to be found in the weekly *Magnet* (ostensibly for children but read by all age-groups throughout the Empire until wartime shortages compelled its closure).

7

By the time I was seven, Miss Howe had taught me to read, and I vividly remember lying in bed with a book under a window with a green glass circle, ever watching, the eye of God. Suddenly I realized that I was no longer spelling out words aloud but reading silently. Books — I did not yet imagine authors but sensed, not altogether foolishly, that books wrote themselves — allowed me to ride through the banal and the extraordinary, inextricably mingled, creating dimensions where, like an Other World from myth, the unusual was obvious and the normal was very, very strange. New friends entered me and took up residence, as if by right, though not always absolutely acknowledging me. Horatius, Mowgli, Rodney Stone, Mr Murdstone, and the waifish, awful

Christopher Robin whom my mother wished me to like. I replied that he 'stank like a fishwife', one of her own expressions, which she appeared not to enjoy hearing. Her irritation forced me to wonder whether I too was 'not out of the Top Drawer'.

Little Women still intrigues me. It contains more bores to the square inch than any work I know except *Cymbeline*, yet remains memorable. I read it often – indeed I read all I could find, enjoying everything, without discrimination, with the exception of 'Pleasant Work for Busy Fingers', which would have to wait some years before suggesting a more agreeable interpretation, unintended by the author. Though a constant rereader, I have always read too fast and too carelessly, never pausing long enough on a word to learn to spell consistently, endlessly confusing words – for many years I used 'vicarious' in the belief that it was a synonym for 'vicious' – and long imagining that the 'William' books were written, not by Miss Richmal Crompton but by Mr Richard Cromwell. I read *Chatterbox*, *Playbox*, *Tiger Tim's Weekly*. I had *The Blue Fairy Book*, *A Staircase of Stories* (in which a girl, locked in an attic for misbehaviour, unstitches her vest to make a ball, which I tried, unwisely, to imitate), *The Pedlar's Pack* containing the German 'Conrad of the Red Town' – red walls, red streets, red people – impelling me in 1947 to name the hero of *Enemies* (my first real novel) Conrad. This tale added a more engaging atmosphere to Germans, hitherto touched only with the sinister lights of war and fairytales. *Christie's Christmas*, Marryat's *Poor Jack*, *The Queen who Flew* (which only in 1980 did I discover was written by Ford Madox Ford), old red-bound volumes of *Chums*, with such stalwarts as Hangdog Dick. Before me is a slim green *Treasure Island* given me by Miss Howe. Pieces of Eight, Pieces of Eight, and tap tap tap as Pew seeks my door. A wise girl, Miss Howe showed me books, told me stories, encouraged me to browse and borrow, seldom interfering, and never making me associate reading with 'lessons'. She seemed to value the random, incidental, throw-away, and would have agreed with Thomas Mann: 'Education is a matter of atmosphere: nothing more.' She provided atmosphere, uttering lines that beckoned me beyond walls and over hills.

Hark! I hear horses.

Here I have a pilot's thumb
Wracked as homeward he did come.

By the pricking of my thumbs,
Something wicked this way comes.

I was one day to declaim, on stage, the most treacherous, if
scarcely the most complex line in Shakespeare:

DOCTOR   Well, well, well.

I never knew the inner relations between Miss Howe and my
mother who, like all her friends, paid, I dare say very stingily,
to have me kept away from her as much as possible, yet
simultaneously grumbled that she never saw me. After a
tedious day trailing round with her on the Great Saltings Golf
Course she told me irritably that but for me, she could have
afforded a small car. Foolishly, I offered to go and live in a hut
with Miss Howe. Later, after I had gone to bed, there was a
furious row downstairs and muted ferocity lingered for days,
during which I contemplated getting a job as a messenger boy,
crossing-sweeper or hangman's assistant, despite having
perhaps to pick up the torn-off head. I had heard, in the
kitchen, of Mrs Edith Thompson dragged screaming and
terrified to the gallows.

I connected my mother chiefly with 'Bridge', which had
somehow got detached from the main, rather enthralling
business: bridges led into the unknown, yet in my mother's
hands were muddled up with boring cards, late-afternoon
ill-will, little heaps of coin, bits of cigarette floating in
unfinished cups of tea, the drawing room rancid with smoke
through which drift sharp, tired voices: 'I'm getting tired of
Winston. The man's a chatterbox.'

In 1928, Miss Howe vanished, as if from a spell cast by that
long promised, much threatened 'School'. She married a sailor
and I think was killed by German bombs on Portsmouth. I

owe her much and I am sad never to have heard from her again. I still had immense obstacles to overcome or circumscribe before I could understand the growing complexity of words and books. Part of me is always literal-minded and stolid. How could gin, sherry, wine be dry? Another part is convinced that I, I alone, have seen incidents and glances, overheard murmurs, of the utmost importance and which I need to impart, to share. Strangers, trees, parks, skies, possess secrets lying like a coin on a carpet, obvious but often unseen, perhaps for years.

I began to write plays, acting them when the house was empty, then stories in lemon-juice so that the words were invisible until held before a fire. These I attempted, vainly, to sell to passers-by, forecasting what, essentially, I have been doing ever since. 'This author,' a reviewer commented severely in 1970, 'writes for himself alone, his meanings as if wrapped in invisible ink.'

Like all children I had imagination, but it was deeply flawed. I could not wholly separate fact and symbol. Misunderstandings fenced me about. That the Duke of Norfolk lived in Sussex was against natural law. The Prince of Wales should never leave Wales nor the King even for an instant remove his crown. Mr Friend should have dispensed the utmost friendliness. Our cook and Captain Cook must be directly, if surreptitiously, linked. 'Fifteen men on the Dead Man's Chest;' the dead man must have been a giant. I was perplexed by Good King Wenceslas looking *out* on the Feast of Stephen, for why should Stephen feast in the cold snow and the cruel wind? I was long unable to understand that a word could have several meanings. 'We've won', cried Tom, but I was puzzled by Tom's tears, like the Scarlet Poppies Crying in Flanders Fields. Marghanita Laski has told me of her youthful perplexity on hearing that her father was 'at the Front', imagining only the local sea-front. 'Barbed wire' suggested the Great War occurring in a field just outside a Manchester suburb. At ten, Eddie Marsh, entering Westminster School on an Exhibition worth £30 annually, believed, as his biographer Christopher Hassall put it, that 'the word meant that he must hold himself in readiness for exhibition to visiting parents as an exceptionally clever boy.'

Children still sang in the late twenties:

> Old Kaiser Bill went up the hill
> To see the terrible slaughter,
> He fell down and broke his crown
> And so he bloody well oughter.

The double meaning of 'crown' escaped me. 'Cracking a joke,' people said. This made no sense: 'releasing' a joke would have done, until long afterwards I realized that from a crack might emerge opposites whose collision could cause the shock that induces laughter. 'Invisible Menders' were a palpable fraud. At the lines:

> Golden lads and girls all must
> As chimney-sweepers come to dust —

I saw solid gold children abruptly corroded by soot. Only very slowly did I unfreeze sufficiently to adjust to metaphor, symbol, image, transmutation. I have not yet wholly succeeded. (In 1972, I was excited to read in Hugh Kenner's *The Pound Era* of a Warwickshire countryman remarking, as he blew away the grey head of a dandelion, 'We call these golden boys chimney-sweepers when they go to seed.')

I was reading the stock poems of current children's anthologies:

> Great praise the Duke of Marlbro' won,
>   And our good Prince Eugene.
> 'Why 'twas a very wicked thing'
>   Said little Wilhelmine.
> 'Nay . . . nay . . . my little girl,' quoth he,
>   'It was a famous victory.'
>
> And everybody praised the Duke
>   Who this great fight did win.
> 'But what good came of it at last?'
>   Quoth little Peterkin.

'Why that I cannot tell,' said he,
'But 'twas a famous victory.'

'Battlefield' suggested a neat, squared meadow where, after carnage, bishops under thick outflung banners ceremoniously counted the dead to decide who had won.

Myth thrives on such minor error. The ballad, wrote Edwin Muir in the sixties, grew perfect by a kind of forgetting. Medieval peasants, familiar with a statue of Ovid standing on a book, revered his ability to read through his feet. I myself similarly watched the grown-ups, and, like the young Bertrand Russell − in no other way comparable − I kept 'complete silence about everything that interested me', while my imagination grew fat, not on rubbish but often on nonsense. The small white posts around the cricket pitches I assumed nailed down the neat green squares to prevent them exploding and flying into the sky. Mrs Fisk always had her spectacles perched on her sharp, gold hair, convincing me that, by some uncanny talent or wound, she saw not through her eyes but through the top of her head. And Mr Friend, chewing the tobacco that others smoked, was surely liable to burst into flame at any moment. Reading *The Jungle Book* I was scared of touching certain pictures lest Nag, the cobra, bit me from the page. Once, after a quarrel with Miss Howe, I thrust her hand down on one of them and, understanding me well, she appeared next day with a bandaged hand. Hilaire Belloc's lines sounded convincing:

C stands for Cobra,
And when a Cobra bites an Indian Judge
The Indian Judge spends restless nights.

For me, anything in print was axiomatically true. The raw cut feet danced into the forest on their red shoes, the witch's lip hung to her waist, the dog's eyes were large as the round tower of Copenhagen. All were as natural as cottage pie.

I was easily frightened. Guy Fawkes night, lurid, throbbing, bizarre, had the beauty that scares. Miss Howe had read me the old story: 'for though there be no appearance of any stir they shall receive a terrible blow this Parliament, and they shall not see who hurts them'. Once, at a window, I saw a giant in the darkened garden, limned with blue, flickering light. Even as I approached my eighth birthday, I would sometimes crouch on a table, scared of the wolf, lean and grey, tinged with smoke, enlarging as the shadows grew and the sky shrivelled. The wolf might be dastardly King John who, in legend, roamed the land as a werewolf. I have always respected losers and I had some affection for John, and was glad to read Churchill's verdict: 'King John possessed an original and inquiring mind and to the end of his life treasured his library of books.' My novel, *The Death of Robin Hood*, published in 1981, largely derived from John and the wolf.

9

Awkwardly, I encountered other children on the Ladies' Mile where nannies under one tree, governesses under another, gossiped about their employers. Here I collected new lore, never wholly unexpected but often startling. A poem, Laforgue remarks, concerns an experience which has not hitherto existed. Something of this was happening, though without poems to show for it. Apparently, to rush in front of moving cars ensured immortality if the wheels touched our shadows. Useful, though for myself, academic. Existence was more varied than I had expected. Unpleasant events, I was assured, occurred in woods: as a reader of Grimm, I did not need to be told this but my friend Reggie Thompson was unpleasantly explicit. All trees had once been living people and sometimes followed you down a lonely road. I had indeed noticed that, at dusk, trees acquired outlines vaguely human, and only in 1983 I discovered a Somerset belief about willows following people after sunset, 'muttering'.

Life itself, we agreed, was solid, packed in tubes and bottles. Ladies sat at mirrors rubbing life into themselves, so that by ransacking dressing-tables we could shorten their lives. Provokingly, my mother remained unimpaired, eagerly playing bridge, golf, tennis, departing to Monte Carlo in that unreal place, 'Abroad'. Yet the theory appeared sound. The rich, Mr Baldwin, Montagu Norman, Queen Mary, Penelope Dudley Ward, lived longer because the life sold at expensive chemists was more powerful. Similarly, 'to give the wine time to breathe' showed that each bottle imprisoned an imp, destined to flee from one gullet into another.

A certain word could make people disappear forever, a most useful asset, but what was it? My informant smirked, then looked doubtful, unconvincingly secretive. At nights, I tried to track it down, irritating the adults I particularly disliked by addressing them with marked emphasis, continually experimenting with 'Leper', 'Mazurka', 'Plantagenet', 'Insurance', 'Noel Coward', 'Zam-buk', 'Zeppelin', 'Board School', 'Horndean Light Railway'. I had hopes of 'Passchendaele' or 'Jutland', so often followed by silence, sigh or horrid tale. Like a king in a story I whispered them into a hole in the ground, then filled it up and, through the summer, awaited some deadly growth, and indeed it did produce a toadstool of very telling scarlet.

Furthermore, everyone knew that each sigh entailed the loss of a drop of blood, so that by endlessly repeating these solemn words, I could spread wholesale destruction. Adults seemed curiously indifferent to the dangers through which they moved with so much swagger.

Once, much earlier, in Harpenden, perhaps in 1924, I was lying in bed in a third-floor room and saw my stepfather, quiet, kindly, inarticulate, staring at me from outside the window. That he was standing on a ladder did not occur to me: more obviously, at certain times he transformed himself to a giant, so that for many weeks I regarded him with suspicion, even dislike – and indeed until his death in 1972, I remained awkward and taciturn with him, after an easy beginning.

Less disturbingly, I hovered on the fringes of bridge tables, coffee tables, tea tables, absorbing hints of the wide world, much of it from a sparkling, pre-war London that few of the speakers would actually have known. There, where young Guards officers might attend some six parties in a night, the Russian Ballet initiated flamboyant fashions, tables glittered with brilliant wines and gloved hands gave unfailing service;

Eddie Marsh deplored 'the negrification of society' and, from ragtime, J.B. Priestley had sensed the emergence of new powers, the end of confidence and security, the start of frenzy and despair. My eyes, not my ears, had to absorb the marks of a darker world which, for so many, made the Great War a release, a stampede to the sunlight. There was urbane cruelty in those voices chattering above the teacups. Elsewhere, the writer Winifred Foley heard another voice, 'Isn't it quaint!' and saw a jewelled finger pointing at a woman of less than average income. Two twenties phrases recurred in my mother's set: 'she's pushing out the boat', and 'when my ship comes in' – appropriate to a naval town, but unexplained, surely improbable, and usually accompanied by disconsolate looks.

Two far-off potentates joined the Kaiser in grown-up talk. The Prince of Wales, always circling the world, always about to marry, without ever quite doing so, from whom miracles were expected which never occurred, a uniformed, friendly, inescapable presence, glimpsed on squash-courts, golf links, night-clubs, warships, landing from aeroplanes, born to be King and make his people live for ever. The other was more arcane. GBS, often mentioned, usually irritably or with reluctant laughs. Who was he? What was it? Circus clown? Patent medicine? Secret password? A very unusual pleasure? None of these were wholly inaccurate, but to discover more I would have to wait.

10

My artistic insticts were rudimentary. Certain pictures I relished but scarcely imagined that painting had any importance. The only paintings at home were my stepfather's mild watercolours of rural Hertfordshire and the Middle East; the English, Bernard Shaw asserted, mistake love of landscape for love of art. Street hoardings were more insistent: advertising Insurance, a cigarette lay red on a table and, behind, a house was drenched with flame; for a confectionary firm, a bottle of milk was poured into a block of chocolate. Another placard might prove useful: 'Royal Navy, Men and Boys wanted.' I might still become a powder-monkey.

I wanted pictures to reveal the obvious, in bold colours; history books contained the best. 'When the Danes came up the Channel a Thousand Years Ago.' 'The Death of Nelson.' Napoleon, solitary on a rock, gazing over a grey, blind sea:

> How far is St Helena from the Beresina Ice?
> An ill way – a chill way – the ice begins to crack.
> But not far for gentlemen who never took advice
> (*When you can't go forward you must e'en come back!*)

Theatrical posters were unfinished romances. *The Desert Song*, *The Count of Monte Cristo*, *The Scarlet Pimpernel*, flaunted figures of extraordinary brilliance, astride camels, leaping over chasms, smiling contemptuously at a guillotine, duelling by moonlight in a ruined castle. Of Christmas pantomimes I remember only *The Windmill Man* from 1928, forgotten now, but of some poetic fantasy within subtle variations of green, which must have had some unconscious part in my Robin Hood novel. I think theatres must have disappointed me and they could be frightening. At the Royalty Theatre I saw a brutal audience, mostly from the Fleet, hoot off Jack Smith, the Whispering Baritone, and his stricken, imploring face follows me to this day.

Serious music too had to wait its turn, though I had a few tiny records and was, and remain, helpless against tunes. 'Killarney', 'A Room with a View', 'The British Grenadiers', 'Bells Across the Meadows', 'In a Monastery Garden'. My mother's attempts to teach me the piano failed as emphatically as had dancing lessons; I would nevertheless listen, rapt, to her and her friends playing songs from *Show Boat*, *Hit the Deck*, *Good News*, *Lady Be Good*, on piano, violin, swanee whistle and, occasionally, a golden, mooing saxophone which I assumed was borrowed from heaven itself.

To this day I enjoy simple fifties Westerns, happy as a schoolboy playing truant as I sit alone, on some rickety seat, in a cinema ignored by the critics and barely surviving, with a bottle of whisky which I lift in unison with John Wayne, Lee Marvin, Robert Ryan, increasingly feeling part of the action as

23

the swingdoors swing, the piano honky-tonks, the bottle glides down the counter. I would swap much of the Marx Brothers for the exhilarating craziness of Spike Jones and his City Slickers in *Fireman Save my Child*. In twenties silent films, 'The Flicks', past and present, fantasy and reality were grandly confused, as they had been in a country fair where, amid dazzling gorse, Regency costumes mingled with those of the twenties, as they had at the battleship Christmas parties. Like print, film — *The Flag Lieutenant*, *The Keeper of the Bees* — recorded exact truth; that actors were involved was inconceivable. I saw talking cats, shoes moving without feet, a skyscraper toppling, and the world's store of wonders increased. A missionary film, in which eight Christian Ugandan boys were 'kidnapped' and burnt alive trailed my nights with horror.

Far less enticing were itinerant waxwork shows, though waxworks too had their own eerie lives, like Punch and Judy. This was confirmed a little later when, by some adult mistake, I saw the German film *Waxworks*, starring Emil Jannings, Werner Kraus, Conrad Veidt. Closing my eyes, I still see Ivan the Terrible, half glimpsed through shadows — 'Thou hast shed the blood of righteous men, O Tsar' — Jack the Ripper hovering behind a shed, Haroun al Raschid looming at the window, like Fagin: soundless creeping offshoots of an evil moon, encouraging my ambiguous fascination with Germany and leaving in my imagination very much more to unfreeze.

Yet the fantasies were less absurd than they would have seemed to my mother and Miss Howe. Across the sea, another youth was growing up. Listen:

> Among his most outstanding characteristics were strict attention to duty, unselfishness, love of nature, sentimentality, even a certain helpfulness and kindliness, simplicity, and finally a marked hankering after morality, an abnormal tendency to submit himself to strict imperatives and to feel authority over him.

Thus Joachim C. Fest, on Rudolf Höss, Commandant of Auschwitz extermination camp.

I accepted everything like a tip, with the fluctuating double vision of crowds endlessly assembling throughout history, ecstatic, thundering and waving as Caesar, Charlemagne, Wallenstein, Napoleon, Lenin, Mussolini, ride by, as the SS enter Paris, as Mao appears on the steps. Daniel Defoe remarked that 100,000 men were always ready to fight popery, without knowing whether this was man or horse. A thing is, and is not, like the bend of a stick thrust into water. Human credulity underpins history, together with desires to appease, surrender, flatter. The *Duce* was once told that incense is the weapon most fatal to rulers. Myth can convince more than fact. W.B. Yeats accepted the tale of a Japanese artist so skilled that his horses, painted on a temple wall, slipped away at night and trampled the rice fields. An early worshipper once saw them still wet from dew and now 'trembling into silence'. I myself would not have questioned it and regret having to do so now.

Congruity had glazed over my life from the start. The most abnormal might transform to the most commonplace. Dr Johnson speaks of hidden resemblances in things apparently unlike. Accidents were only apparent; coincidences were so regular, in adventure books, dreams, on pavements, as scarcely to deserve comment; prayers were invariably answered, though from unforeseen angles and by someone of ironic temper. I was not surprised to read in 1948 that Marshal Erwin Rommel was wounded in the Norman village, Saint Foy de Montgomerey, birthplace of the medieval ancestors of his most celebrated opponent.

More mundane intelligence was soon to be demanded.

'I expect you're looking forward to school?'. Vulpine, raddled Mrs Carey grins, shows fangs sticky with cream cake.

'Not perishing likely.'

A quote from Richmal Crompton's innocuous 'William' books, uttered with goodwill, received with disfavour.

School, like death, was inevitable but had always seemed unlikely. John Armitage, however, had already gone, never to reappear. He must have been ironed into mindless perfection at Winchester, scored prolifically for the Hampshire Hogs, never put a foot wrong and, perhaps, died imperturbably at Dunkirk, Alamein or Monte Cassino, without once giving me a thought.

In September 1928, a wooden playbox appeared, a red and blue cap and blazer, blatant targets for the jeers and worse of the less privileged. I was eight, going to school. Boarding School, Board School? Were they identical? Another unspoken question.

There was another change. My stepfather accepted a new position and departed with my mother to Abadan, on the Gulf. This was interesting rather than heartrending, which would have disappointed my mother, and indeed Freud. I was learning that there are few situations so critical as to be impossible to turn, in due course, to my advantage. A knowledge cool, perhaps callous, but undeniably useful.

Two

I am for getting a boy forward in his learning; for that is a sure good. I would let him at first read *any* English book which happens to engage his attention; because you have done a great deal when you have brought him to have entertainment from a book. He'll get better books afterwards.

Dr Johnson

Children are always cruel . . . Pity is acquired by the cultivation of reason.

Dr Johnson

Sir, while you are considering which of two things you should teach your child, another boy has learnt them both.

Dr Johnson

1

School, not parents, was the real challenge of my inner life. I was to be amazed at Freud's assertions of domestic rivalries and vendettas. That a busy, conventional, self-absorbed child could be, not overstimulated by parents, but merely mildly bored and determined to retain independence, seemed foreign to his middle-class, Central European mind. School life never seriously threatened my independence, which I have always valued above money, status, and even, at times, love.

Nevertheless, my inborn shyness was reinforced in the first ten minutes of boarding school life. On arrival, I found a tall, rather burly boy, later a distinguished naval officer and war casualty, standing in a corridor. From politeness rather than desire, I approached him and suggested we talked about whatever interested him. He at once knocked me down – he was the school bully – and to this day I spontaneously recoil when introduced to a stranger. All are guilty, until they prove themselves innocent.

Marlborough House School stood in the Drive, Hove, where Queen Victoria's statue still gazes seawards. Her presence was appropriate, for the school was Victorian in principles, methods, routine. The buildings, grey, severely functional, lacking any hint of the personal and inconsequential, might have been designed by a bored pupil with pencil and ruler, though to be fair, my schooling, with all its shortcomings, never once in my recollection induced boredom.

The small, tight back garden had grass but no flowers, as if they had been conscripted for lessons elsewhere. Photographs of our predecessors hung at all levels, the staff unbelievably young as they receded towards the Jubilee, almost, it seemed, to the Indian Mutiny. Prominent were individual photos of Old Boys killed in the Great War, rather too obviously our superiors, but scarcely to be envied. To get 'mentioned in despatches' was a gift to be avoided.

Colour, variety, experiment, nonconformity were lacking, but the place was rampant with vigorous, predictable, commonsensical personality, ultimately that of an Alice not in Wonderland but in a no-man's-land between holidays; competitive, harsh, sometimes cruel, but with regular truces for stretcher-bearers to ply their trade.

2

Marlborough House had been founded, probably as a Dame's School, in 1874, era of sailor suits, knickerbockers, and the straw hats, 'bashers', which still survived in 1928 and which, for the very smart, were attached to the lapel by elastic, as precaution against the wind. It was ruled, like a principality, by the founder's two daughters, Gertrude White and Mrs

Edith Bullick, and by her husband (nominally headmaster), the Revd Thomas Bullick, 'Baal', a quiet, friendly, humorous man. I saw little of him save at Morning Prayers and scripture lessons, in which I read, with voyeuristic concern, that the prophet Isaiah was placed in a hollow tree which was then sawn in two. His prophetic powers, I felt, must have been feeble.

Tom Bullick had some parish work, not, I suspect, very exacting, and, in the domestic power-game, had long since surrendered. Edith, 'Flash', shy, gentle, taught art though not to me, and did a bad job in charge of the kitchen. Her nickname, I had always imagined, derived from her swift, gliding movement down long corridors, up mysterious stairs, as if endlessly pursued by, perhaps, a fox, but Professor Peter Self assured me in 1976, that it actually commemorated the Whitsuntide appearance of the Holy Ghost. Peter, on matters of fact, I have never nerved myself to contradict.

We sang, never at full strength:

> Once upon a Time when Baal was Swine
> And Gertie chewed tobacco,
> Flash laughed to see such fun
> And Piché cried quack quacko.

From Miss White, always called 'Gertie', though not to her face, I swiftly sensed the importance of the individual in history. Gertrude Wolsey White! It has the resonance, the absolute weight, of Isambard Kingdom Brunel. In her, it was as if Queen Victoria and Florence Nightingale had formed partnership, with some contribution from Bertie Wooster's Aunt Agatha. Bulky, red-faced, grey-haired, in black, rustling skirts, she is always stamping forward, resolutely intolerant, manifestly invulnerable, preferring pronounce-ments to debate, wholly unhampered by finesse. 'I am disgusted with you, I am still more disgusted with your parents,' she blasted Maurice Carr before the assembled school, for attending, on a weekend holiday, the Regent Cinema — H.B. Warner in *Sorrell and Son* — at the risk of infecting us all with disease.

Under that brisk, all-purpose eye, one thought twice about losing one's wicket, and, thinking twice, more easily did so. Her 'possibly but not probably' delivered an unfavourable verdict on the universe itself. 'I do not approve of comedians,' followed an inappropriate entertainer at the annual Cricket Supper, singing about small girls at work in 'Constantinosefull', and we shuddered at inexplicit enormities. 'He indulged in skulduggery,' she said of Clarence Hatry, jailed for fraud, and we nervously fingered our skulls. Her 'Martha!' as she summoned her aide, Miss Pitcher, 'Piché', her 'French!' as she addressed young Miss French, were short cuts to the ends of the earth, like Mrs Proudie's martial 'Bishop!'. Her 'Not Out', delivered without impartiality from the cricket pavilion some three hundred yards from the wicket would have lost nothing beside such stentorians at Peter the Hermit, John of Leyden, Danton, Lloyd George, and the Chatterbox. When I read, years afterwards, of Victoria barking, 'I do not like Bishops,' I at once recalled Gertie. 'You must,' she asserted on occasions, 'pull yourself together,' and this indication of having been scattered far and wide I found alarming, yet challenging.

She was grimly caustic during the 1929 General Election when Tony Tottenham announced his support for Ramsay Mac's Labour party. 'Ah! You believe in hard work! I shall remember.' She remembered much, most of it austere but with some glint of drama. At the start of the Great War she received a little parcel from parents in India. It contained a small pistol with which to shoot their two boys when the Germans landed. I imagined an address, short but unambiguous. 'Next Wednesday's half-holiday has been cancelled. A pork pie found in the Senior Dormitory has been confiscated and despatched to appropriate quarters. Tomorrow will not rain. Last Sunday's church collection was threepence short, a disgraceful occurrence, of which I am heartily ashamed, having been under the impression that I was dealing with sons of gentlemen. The match against Claremont will not now take place, for reasons that reflect no discredit, at least, on Marlborough House. That, for the moment, is all. Ah no. I was forgetting. I wish to see Blake Major and Blake Minor in the cellar. At once. For a few moments only.'

Gertie could be powerfully unforgiving or unexpectedly magnanimous, and I now believe she had a marked sense, not of fun, nor wit, but of rather simple humour, often ironic when speaking of parents, with whom she drove a hard bargain. She was as inescapable as her mentor and associate, God, and, on evidence, more active. In private, she may have been diffident, if scarcely cringing; not so in public. Her wide, determined advance on all fronts . . . Wodehouse's 'stately procession of one' . . . cut swathes through complaint, complacency, conceit. 'My father owns a Daimler,' one boy proudly carolled. Miss White's 'Why?' was curt, devastating, unanswerable. 'Slack by name and slack by nature,' she periodically thrust at Harry Repton Slack. Nietzsche's remark that power makes people stupid she effortlessly refuted. The power was fixed and unshakable: pupil power, converse between rulers and ruled, would have wilted under her blue stare. No relativist, she ruled with Manichean simplicity. Whether one was saved or damned, a team-leader or a comedian, might be a matter of choice, not one's own choice, but one in the spirit of Karl Lueger, Christian Social Party Mayor of Berlin, an influence on the young Hitler: 'I decide who is a Jew.' Delegation of authority was unimaginable. When novice parents asked for the Headmaster, they found only Gertie, frowning at them from the hearthrug on which woven cockatoos gazed up in alarm. Assistant masters rated only slightly above comedians, Hatry and the senior Carrs. Arthur Harrison recollected the glass pane in the staff room door, so that she could see 'that those young men were not up to mischief'.

Masters were forbidden a latch key, their clothes suggested penury, and I was to discover that the school had ignoble pay-rating in the archives of scholastic agencies. A very frightening mask would have had to be worn, to test on her Arthur's dictum in 1968: 'When parents ask me what they should look for in choosing a preparatory school, I always tell them that there is really only one question they need ask the Headmaster: "What do you pay your staff?" Or, what is much the same thing: "How long have your staff been with you?" If you are satisfied on that point, then send your boy there.'

On Sunday evenings we packed her drawing-room for hymns, for which she thumped the piano with a technique once ascribed to the Empress Eugénie, 'who would go to the piano, and there followed a certain amount of noise.' These gatherings had wistful poetry: fading lights, even the bullies' faces tamed and absorbed, the tramp of feet during 'Onward, Christian Soldiers'. The tunes, the words, suggested and withdrew glimpses of 'another, greater, wilder country', enlustring the dying Sunday, repelling Black Monday:

> All glory, laud and honour
> To thee, Redeemer King.'

'Glory' was golden, 'laud', deep bronze, 'honour' crumpled white with thin green tinge, 'Redeemer' was vague but impressive, and 'King' was king. The Green Hill without a city wall was perplexing. 'From Greenland's Icy Mountains' carried me instantly to the Snow Queen's realm, Northern Lights flashing against the ice stuck in Kay's heart, as I sometimes fear it has stuck in mine. 'There is a Fountain Filled with Blood' had lugubrious gusto. There was danger in requesting 'Glorious things of Thee are spoken', for Haydn's majestic tune was that of the Imperial Austrian Anthem, forbidden during the war; 'very properly', Gertie said, and she retained patriotic reservations. Unscrupulously, I goaded my friend Byng to beg for 'Hymn 10, 555', which he was discouraged from repeating.

Afterwards, under her green reading-lamp, she read us *The Talisman*. In the darkened, fire-lit room glimmered oriental vases, a huge polished tortoise shell, rows of books, Gussie Coates' cello, the portrait of an Old Boy, hands resting on a sword hilt, dank pits beneath eyes going red and mad as the fire glowed deeper and the world contracted. The outlandish splendours of Saladin, Templar, Monserat moved me, through what William Empson has called 'the echoes and recesses of words'.

A porcelain hen on a sideboard I held responsible for Gertie's never having married. Alternatively, she ate her suitors. More probably, she was always too busy. Had she ever been young? Did she ever undress? I thought of her in 1960, when encountering a line of Sartre's: 'Forty years later, turning the pages of a family album, Anne-Marie realized that she had been beautiful.'

Like an idol, she collected more legends than anecdotes. She could prise out talent, if not always approving of it. She may have been something, not of a comedian but of an unconscious artist, capable of more than Edith's drawings of Graeco-Romans, more gentlemanly than masculine. Consciously, she drove us towards conformist success: the Scholarship board, the Eleven, silver cups gleaming at the end of life's hard avenues, Sports Day in italics.

I think she liked me. My parents were now living in Persia — my stepfather was now 'in oil' (like a sardine) and, perhaps believing me more miserable, resentful, abandoned than I actually was, she gave me unexpected presents: a large box of chocolates, *The Children's Newspaper* — moralistic, uplifting, unreadable — a gigantic pot of marmalade, to be shared with other boys, who did not like it. I wonder now if these gifts were added to the termly bills.

3

I was never taught by Gertie and never knew what she taught. She should have held master-classes (I used to assume this meant continuous seduction of women). Unaccountably, she procured me an English prize during my first term, choosing it with acumen.

Publishers then produced admirable children's miscellanies — annuals, collections of story and verse, history, general knowledge, articles, pictures, hors d'oeuvres anticipating splendid meals ahead. The stories I read eagerly. Boys harpooned, were cut off by the tide, discovered gold, died young, were kidnapped by slavers and press-gangs but made good; they scored a century on first appearance, were bound to a pillar watching a slow flame crumble the cords of a basket containing snakes, they explored jungle, desert, mountain, discovered 'kopje', 'kraal', 'assegai', stopped runaway horses, became heroes at Rorke's Drift and Ilundi. *Riding Lights*, culled from Masefield and lesser writers, were as evocative as *Northern Lights*, and were awaiting me in the pages of Conrad and H.M. Tomlinson. My prize was Nelson's Annual, 1928, and yet again building beliefs upon error, unaware of publishers, I identified the book with the great admiral himself. I have it before me as I write, and see pieces by Belloc, Dickens, Buchan, Newbolt, Quiller-Couch; appreciations of Bach, Handel, Holman Hunt, Watts, Burne-Jones, Chopin; Barham's 'The Jackdaw of Rheims' and the tale of Aucassin and Nicolette (excluding the account of Nicolette raising her smock to revive a dying pilgrim), the retelling of *The Bohemian Girl* and summaries of Wagner's operas.

Tannhäuser stirred me, for reasons unconnected with music. Indeed, I did not realize that opera was mainly concerned with music and did not know Ed Bishop's remark that opera is when a guy gets stabbed and, instead of bleeding, he sings. The paraphrase of *Tannhäuser* begins: 'When the gods and goddesses fled from Olympus before the advance of Christianity, Venus, retiring to the North, established her court beneath the hill of Hörselberg in Thuringia.' Here was the germ of much of my own work: the theme of conflicts and overlappings; the lingering of once bright beliefs, in the form of superstition.

Clutching my prize, dodging Gertie's blue, slightly bulging eyes, I sensed that the world was in hands ruthless but secure. It was not that Miss White would ever drop a catch, but that not even Ramsay Mac at his worst would dare to bowl.

4

At first I was chiefly taught French and History by rattling, energetic Piché, weatherbeaten, pebble-dashed, with a French accent like that of an orchestra tuning up and reverence for *Little Arthur's History of England* — Matilda fleeing through the snow, the Princes clutching each other in the Tower, the

Houses of York and Lancaster, so different from any house I had yet known. Small abacuses were still used, and I remember no library. In oral lessons we continually moved up and down the table in accordance with our success or failure. Ultimate triumph was rewarded with a chair next to Piché, a perilous office for, when out of temper, she tended to slap the boys nearest her, inevitably those with the most, or else the least, marks. Her favourite punishment was ordering the delinquent to stand on a chair. This I enjoyed, for it gave me a view into the house at the end of the garden, in which a woman called Miss Herring was invariably, seemingly unalterably, seated at a table, munching.

Piché had an aptitude for disconcerting observations. 'A's father,' she told us gratuitously, 'is not quite the gentleman,' and we glared contemptuously at A. Explaining 'shoddy', export of some northern town, she pointed unerringly at B's coat. Her classes were not for the oversensitive; that boys were boys she accepted but scarcely applauded.

More immediately sympathetic was genial, intelligent Tom Paton, still teaching in 1975, with his tales of Homeric cricketers — Hobbs, Sutcliffe, K.S. Duleepsinhji; and Hilda French, at Marlborough House from 1925 to 1962, retiring only to care for her mother. But dates, the courtesan Harriet Willson reflected, make stories dry and ladies nervous; I can only say that Hilda's personality teaches me to this day. She could humanize a stoat, a pickaxe, find colour in colourlessness and transmit it to the blind. With her, history and language became a continuous process: I felt that Black Death might erupt within seconds and that Latin verbs had singular, perhaps disreputable pasts. Her stories of Grinling Gibbons, Louis Napoleon's escape from Ham, Joan in the fire, peopled the world's deserts. With no university degree or educational diploma, backed by no union, she exemplifies the fact, distasteful to politicians and theorists, that teaching is not science but art and personality: like poetry, like friendship, it can be stimulated and encouraged, but cannot be invented by precise legislation and sententious theses. I must already have been sensing that matters of importance cannot often be directly taught, though endlessly implied by a tone of voice, the loan of a book, even by silence. When instructed how to write by reviewers in bad prose, I remember this.

5

Something of the old Dame's School lingered like must. The most regular punishment was deprivation of cake and jam at tea, consequential at the end of a Viking day, hard won against odds. Jam could be the only gleam in a shrouded winter sojourn, to lose it was to lose hope. Three times I forfeited it for an entire month: for being sick after diphtheria, for having my watch stolen, for commenting severely on a master, Mr Shegog. A month! Landmark on Death's high road. A city could be ringed and sacked in a month, America could be reached in less. Like King Henry Fine Scholar I resolved never to smile again: I would remain proud, aloof and unforgiving.

All food was treasure, even if too often buried treasure. Belief in God was apt to depend on the outcome of prayers for breakfast fishcakes instead of porridge. Lunches must have remained unaltered since 1874, named through generations, with distressing glamour: White Baby, Worms, House on Fire, Hardbaked Tombstone, Dead Man's Leg, Old Hundreds, Cat's Illness, Shape, and Stuff. As for Shape, the poet Edward FitzGerald once called it 'Congealed Bridesmaid'. They were the week's true calendar, they controlled our souls, challenged our bodies, created a norm from which the shabbiest railway hotel can soar superior.

Leisure was suspect, a form of loitering with intent, and for this I was often grateful. Whenever we were unleashed, gangs swiftly emerged. Between evening prep and bed, light and dark, Ormuzd and Ahriman, they collected in cellars and staged such savage rituals as The Murder of Becket, with talk of knitting-needles leaving no trace of wounds, of execution by catapults, of some victim pinned to the wall by dividers driven through his hand. There was kicking and pummelling. 'You're going to get laid out,' someone would say, and I awaited the summons with hideous fears.

Games were a branch of work. Walks through Hove parks

36

or to the playing field were in strict crocodile, in which friendships and hatreds settled, matured, fizzed, sometimes exploded. On such a walk I met George Rothery, still a close friend. I had glimpses of the sea, the familiar beggars, and nuns, black and spectral. A phrase came to me, 'straight as the parting in a nun's hair', which I used incessantly, until it was demolished by Byng's revelation that nuns were bald through having been struck by lightning.

Academic hours were long, ending with two hours' prep, the last quarter enlivened by Mr Shegog's illicitly reading us *Bulldog Drummond* or *The Adventures of Sherlock Holmes*. I liked Mr Shegog. His name hinted at nameless atrocities. He was small, ugly, and with manic tempers, but he was friendly and I suspect as vulnerable as his pupils. He probably had *a touch of the tar*. Those torrents of hysterical fury — 'He's waxy' — hoisted the storm cone, at which we crept for cover and emerged awed, breathless, but curiously unscathed, ultimately becoming immune. Wodehouse's line, in *The Little Nugget*, set in a prep school, reminds me of Mr Shegog: 'They heard Mr Glossop bellowing at an amused class.'

Slates were still used, the sound of slate pencil suggestive of music currently being conceived, notably Webern's. Also copybooks. We would copy beautifully calligraphed maxims such as 'All is Not Gold that Glisters', to improve both our morals and script. That what *should* happen frequently does *not* is proved by my present personality and handwriting. To later generations, Kipling's Gods of the Copybook Headings, must seem incomprehensible in their origins:

In the Carboniferous Epoch we were promised abundance
   for all,
By robbing selected Peter to pay for collective Paul;
But though we had plenty of money, there was nothing our
   money could buy,
And the Gods of the Copybook Headings said: *If you don't
work you die.*

Imagination, independence, initiative, though discouraged, nevertheless survived, and could be conditions for survival.

The Murder of Becket did not foster comradeship with those larger than oneself, but though conformist and diffident, I clung, without quite knowing it, to my private secrets. Departure from Southsea, apparently for ever, meant temptation to abandon old heroes, cherished insights, in this roaring pen where darkness had teeth, and day a threatening eye. The sky, cold grin of early morning, an implacable row of ludicrous sums — 'If A runs 100 miles an hour' — a plateful of dirty porridge or congealing mutton fat jabbed the very soul with despairing prongs. Life, however, is a matter of renewals, the transformation of setbacks to assets; and this I was learning for ever. A sudden smile from a maid, an unexpected nod from a bully, were spectacular gains in a campaign perhaps already lost.

6

Education, H.G. Wells asserted, is the building up of the imagination, and the school's puritanism did not drastically inhibit this; indeed, puritanism can derive, sometimes too fiercely, from a dramatic interpretation of life. We were not, as Maurice Richardson over at Claremont came to believe, little victims, little beasts, little fascists, though undoubtedly we had the values (though also the purpose) of a line regiment. My friends who have survived, George Rothery, Byng Maddick, Stanley Pigott, Peter and Michael Self, have carved themselves positions fiercely independent of the ruthless, vindictive and intolerant. On Sundays, in dark blue suits, stiff collars, bowler hats, we marched to the cavernous church, Piché with smelling salts for emergencies, though they could cause more of these than they cured. Drilled into piety, we filled an isolated side-chapel beneath a marble slab cut with names of Old Boys dead in South Africa, France, Belgium, Gallipoli and Jutland. Those in the front pew were forbidden to wear hair oil, for the Vicar, Canon Meyrick — *Canon* was strange, for his voice was low — enjoyed patting heads as he passed. Enticing phrases were bleated, chanted, or intoned: *Suffered under Pontius Pilate* — did Pontius Pilate actually sit on him? — *Descended into Hell* — but how? — *The Throne of the Heavenly Grace*, to which we were told to accompany the priest, but where was it? *Is not such love worth more than all the gold watches of Johannesburg?* Surely not.

I saw Jesus as an impetuous and scornful team leader, dismaying the winners, torturing the losers. I became certain that I was a Pharisee, with no very viable future. In compensation there filtered through me my first poem, of which I was extravagantly proud: 'Squelching through the Gulch — Mombassa.'

I also wrote a History of England, in two pages.

In class, we had to learn verses by heart. Quiet riches could be filched, as it were, behind backs. *'Curfew shall not ring tonight'*: a girl straps herself to a vast bell so that it will not signal her lover's execution by Oliver Cromwell. Also:

> His sword was in its sheath,
>   His fingers held the pen,
> When Kempenfelt went down
>   With twice four hundred men.

While writing this in 1984, I have discovered more of Admiral Kempenfelt, whose flagship, the *Royal George*, suddenly sank on payday, off Portsmouth in 1782, drowning most of the complement.* Perhaps I had sailed over them all on trips to the Isle of Wight. He was an authority on signals and a minor poet, his most celebrated work apparently, 'Burst, Ye Emerald Gates'.

Beauty at Hove had to be prised out of harsh conditions, earned like good marks, much of it recognized only years later, in an air-raid shelter, on a burning street, amongst stacked casualties, and now the more deeply remembered. A bright bird on a gaunt tree, lights and pathways on the sea, Michael Harmsworth's straight drives, the pastel-tints of the hotels melting into each other in summer radiance, as, a few years

*David Ingram survived, to write well of her, and Masefield reveals that salvaged wood was used as binding for a reprint of his naval history. Masefield adds that the authorities were 'very coy about raising her. They feared that too much dishonesty might come to light'.

later, Alan Ross saw them, in his poem, 'Cricket at Brighton':

At night the Front like coloured barley-sugar; but now
Soft blue, all soda, the air goes flat over flower-beds,
Blue railings and beaches. Below, half-painted boats, bow
Up, settle in sand, names like Moss-Rose and Dolphin
Drying in a breeze that flicks at the ribs of the tide.
The chalk coastline folds up its wings of Beachy Head
And Worthing, fluttering white over water like brides.
Regency squares, the Pavilion, oysters and mussels and gin,
Piers like wading confectionery, esplanades of striped tulip.

Beauty too of the bare, rippling line of the Downs, seen
from George Rothery's home at Henfield, where on superb
Sundays I could periodically shelter, exploring gardens,
gobbling strawberries, playing in friendly households. One of
our companions was Denton Welch, of whom I remember
nothing. Once we saw, wrecked on the shore near Rotting-
dean, a large Italian ship, *Nimbo*; could it have been an 'East
Indiaman'? That shipwrecks still occurred was a link with
Steerforth, Jim Hawkins, Jack Easy.

Further allures derived from stamps with outlandish names:
Russian Post Offices in Bokhara, British Field Posts in
Matabeleland, Orange Free State, Grand Duchy of Luxemburg, until Robin MacCunn forced me to swap my collection
for an old sock.

7

Boys, declared Dr Arnold, don't like poetry. He was wrong,
though, in my day, few admitted and others may not have
realized that they enjoyed it. I was stirred almost to the
maudlin by:

Pipes of the misty lowlands,
Voice of the glens and hills.

and bemused by the self-sacrifice of public officials:

> On the low hills to westward
> the Consul fixed his eye.

There was still the rival history littered with the demonic and spectral. Implored to help the starving poor, Bishop Hatto merrily invited them to his barn, locked the door and burned them. In revenge, battalions of rats gathered: they devoured his picture on the wall, then his shrewdly hoarded corn.

> 'I will go to my castle on the Rhine,' quoth he,
> ''tis the safest place in Germany.'

He was wrong. The cat sits screaming on his pillow, crazed with fear, for the rats will swim the deepest river, penetrate the thickest wall.

> They have whetted their teeth against the stones,
>   And now they pick the Bishop's bones:
> They gnawed the flesh from every limb,
>   For they were sent to do judgement on him.

Germany never failed to present such tales. Whatever the theology, here was a flash from a lurid sky. As I crouched among Latin exercises, French grammar, splendid unknowns still quickened my secret thoughts: Admiral Sir Cloudesley Shovel, General Sir Bindon Blood joining hands with GBS, Sir Ralph the Rover, Keats' Meg Merrilies, who ''stead of supper would gaze full hard against the moon.' A disagreeable alternative, I considered.

Adults still provoked uncanny thoughts. There was Miss Wedgewood, who taught while sitting rigid against the wall, convincing Byng and myself that she had no back. She punished with the long, thick, rounded ruler, Black Peter, but her worst infliction would have been to swing round and confront us with that atrocious void, dug, perhaps, by English rats.

Byng seemed the most sophisticated of my friends. He had seen at least the outside of Sherry's, the Brighton nightclub — 'nightclub' suggested the occult and conspiratorial as 'Road

House' would, later – disparaged Ronald Colman's perform-
ance in *Down River* and could repeat verses from popular
concert parties:

> It is my daughter's wedding day,
> A thousand pounds I'll give away.
> On second thoughts, which are the best,
> I'll put it back in the old oak chest.

Myths throve in dormitories, the night world, wolf's territory,
hangman's land. A few terms, a few years ago, once upon a
time, a Tony Dorman had died of ghosts. The Ripper was here
too, stalking beneath the Pier. Shoes must be left at unusual
angles, to see if they moved in the night, and sometimes they
did. Death, it was known, was sleep, but life usually returned
in the morning, though for Tony Dorman it did not. Foreign
magnificoes were up to no good. The Kaiser had personally
sliced off Belgian boys' hands, so that they would never fight
against Germany, 'in Brussels, in the market place', Dick
Laws said with authority. The Pope piled away dead wives in
an airing-room cupboard. The *Titanic* sank: 'The officers stood
there shooting them. Babies were chucked out first, of course.
Only every tenth man was allowed to be saved, to keep things
going. Some dressed up as ladies.'

We disputed whether German bodies were different. I
thought of the German on the beach, concealing some
monstrous blemish. There was no doubt that the Great War
had not wholly ended. Zeppelins still loaded the sky, the Irish
were primed to loot our homes. A story persisted of a Soviet at
Shoreham. At the 1929 General Election, we heard far-away
gunshots. 'The Reds,' Byng stilled us.

Nightly we coveted each other's stamps, cigarette cards,
matchboxes, dreamed of Sir Henry Seagrave, 'the fastest man
on earth', on land and water, killed on Lake Windermere in
1930, and prayed for Edward, Prince of Wales, still in white
and gold, who would usher in the great holiday.

Books had occult habits. No secular book must be placed on
a Bible, lest thunder occur. Breathlessly, we piled *French
without Tears*, *Kennedy's Latin Primer*, *Havet's French Grammar*,

Gradatus, *Little Arthur's History* on top of Roddy Carr-Gomm's Bible and, inexorably, within hours July storms rocked the town, lightning ripped the sky, the moon moaned, thunder cracked and banged, and I thought of the ships sinking, all the captains rigidly at attention on the bridge.

Belief still grew from cross-purposes. It was known that failure to stand at attention for the National Anthem entailed instant blindness. I acquired fantasies that I confided to none and only Stanley Pigott might have understood. Baal, who Byng, on irresolute evidence, unexpectedly announced was 'stony broke', read daily prayers in tones deep but slurred, so that sometimes I seemed to hear 'Love of God', sometimes 'Lower God'. Were there then two Gods? One splendidly enthroned, the other crouching in shadows, wistful, needing a humble burnt offering, a roasted baby, a 'mess of pottage'? The notion fascinated me, and it developed.

We had a craze for writing for free samples and for answering advertisements from those who promised to cure you of pimples, warts, hairs, baldness and to increase your height by five feet, and we vied with each other for the largest postbag. In a travel brochure I read of 'the tomb of Zeus in Crete'. So gods could die! Surely not; after Jesus they became bogies. But Nelson's Annual confirmed it: 'Walhalla is in flames, and with its destruction go the old gods whose ill-gotten power yields before the might of human love.' This fostered my abiding interest in mythology, the collapse of old rituals and the arrival of new, and most of my books have an inner theme, that the collapse is only partial and the new never as new as it assumes: that empires come and go, gadgets emerge and become obsolete, but that the mind remains virtually untouched, in old age resuming the obsessions, myths and perplexities of childhood.

Meanwhile, ill-gotten power appealed to me, and I speculated about the plots, strategems, crimes, with which Gertie must have ousted Baal, a Lower God. Incessant references, on formal occasions, to the overwhelming powers of love were vigorously at odds with life as I was experiencing it.

A new boy has become myth incarnate. Ivor Cousins, in many
of my novels, as a character, atmosphere, bad smell, is rooted
in the dead centre of my imagination. He is not unique. My
friend David Wade builds his disturbing play *Summer of Thirty
Nine* round just such a figure and in a similar setting, a boy
who 'had pulled back a little curtain in the heart and shown
us, grinning, the old Lord of the Flies himself . . . powerful
by being unbelievable.'

Ivor Cousins arrived in mid-term, in 1929 – unprecedented
behaviour. He was small, thin, with pale, neat eyes on a face
sallow, as if washed too often, pinched, a though dried too
long. Outwardly negligible, he had a flair for purposeful,
effective mediocrity. A bully who never lifted a hand, never
showed anger or dismay, he forced the largest of us to tell
stories, turn cartwheels, bring him small savouries of dried
sausage, cold bacon, toothpaste on biscuit. We deferred,
transfixed, enchanted, but by what? I still ask myself, and
from my question, my problem, emerges a plot, character,
theme. Ostensibly by no more than a curious pressure of eye,
unblinking and intense, a certain oldness at the mouth, a
spare, controlled chilliness of demeanour and unusual tidiness
of dress, over-mature in our hobbledehoy impulsive society,
which rendered him akin to Carlyle's 'sea-green Incorruptible',
with a flake of Somerset Maugham's 'Mr Know-all'.

I listened, even Byng, now displaced, listened with
deepening refinement of awe. Ivor Cousins knew that George
V had a wife in Malta and did not share a bed with Queen
Mary, partly because of her wooden leg. To get a laugh from
an adult, you had only to utter, very loudly, what else than
GBS! Here he was wrong, for the uneasy but gullible Bruce
Ross was persuaded to test it on Miss White and, looking
grim, she deigned no answer. Cousins was forerunner of 'The
Others'. In after years, returning from summer holidays
abroad, The Others were to tell me about Edward VIII and
Mrs Simpson long before the newspapers blared it through the
land: they knew who had slept with Mussolini the night before

last. They knew that FDR was class enemy number one, Charles de Gaulle a fascist, Albert Schweitzer lacked progressive social awareness, Florence Nightingale expressed individualism at its most flagrant, and that Redeemer Nkrumah proved that, in Ghana, freed from white shackles, his regime would show compassion, honesty and efficiency hitherto unique. My fear today is that, to my pupils, I myself was one of The Others.

But Ivor Cousins. May the devil, I prayed, drink out of his eye. Occasionally he addressed me, not friendly, without visible hostility, almost as though talking to himself, with his expressive lack of expression. Drily, flatly assertive, he swiftly quenched my nascent self-belief based on skills at soccer and cricket, games he was too contemptuous to play. He had 'a heart', Hilda French said. Well, so had the rest of us, even, I suspected, Gertie. 'Death,' he told me, in a dark corner of the changing room, 'is never easy. Not easy at all. They like to fill up your holes before you're quite done.' He was baleful Chorus to our puny tragedies. What I found so perplexing was that, despite his hitherto unimaginable ranges of knowledge, his classroom marks and answers were so unexceptional. Could Tom Paton, Mr Shegog, even Hilda, conceivably be jealous?

I hear his voice still, softly pattering over us in the night-bound dormitory. 'They were put in carts and dragged through the streets. Your head fell in one go. Kids got born with thin red circles round their necks.' I listened with horrid attention. All hangings were supervised by King George in person, who then gave himself another medal, and this could undeniably explain the glitter of his uniforms. He was perturbing about circumcision. Either it displayed fatal disease, or revealed one's parents' social position. He declined to say more, and indeed to question him about anything exposed one to ridicule more potent by being expressed by no more than a small shrug, a twitch of the lower lip, a stare of subtle imcomprehension. His own physical condition I never saw. Perhaps, possession of 'a heart' prevented him bathing: perhaps . . . I shook aside further speculations, fearful of where they might lead.

Though Christian names were taboo, we all obsequiously

called him Ivor, acting out some natural human propensity to form hierarchies and courts. Unchallenged, for I remember none of the staff or bigger boys appearing to notice him, without physical strength or explicit threats, merely by that coldness of eye and lip and menacing sibilants, by unnatural, or, at least, exceptional tidiness, he reduced the Murder of Becket to a silly charade, sneered at the school's football triumphs, manipulated us into making humiliating confessions and behaving spitefully: for him we tore up a popular boy's stamp collection, a new boy's cigarette cards, stamped on a casket of butterflies. For him we threw away the screws of some cherished Meccano set, to him we rushed to tell 'the latest', to offer the glossiest conker, the most luscious sweet. Still aware of him, in 1972 I wrote a booklet on the capricious nature of power and laughter, the latter so often 'political', cruel and malevolent, revolving around despots grotesquely unfunny. The jokes, like the appearance of Stalin, Hitler, Mussolini, aroused not mirth but a sense of the uncanny. In 1980, I read of a French deputy, convinced that Robespierre was looking at him, reflecting in terror, 'He'll be imagining I was thinking about something.' Comic, in an unpleasant way. Laying down the book, I saw Ivor, in smart peruke, dandified coat, with quiet, deadly suggestions.

He vanished, as he had come, in the middle of the next term and, in keeping with his thin aura, I can find no one who remembers him, or cares to admit it. George, Byng, Stanley, Hilda . . . they profess utter ignorance, with a hint that I am professionally romancing, though my blood and dreams insist that I am not. For me, he grows with the years. History can hinge on the almost stealthy breath of some midget, seated behind a curtain, recoiling from light, but signing a warrant, drafting a proscription, arranging ruin. He dominates talents superior to his own, cows committees, paralyses assemblies, is feared by foreign nations, until suddenly the curtain shrivels, the light bursts through, and someone, hitherto a nonentity, in a solitary instant of grandeur, utters a quiet word, on which the great dictator has nothing to say and is removed as a public nuisance, so easily that generations hence will puzzle over his secret. A remark of Rebecca West comes in handy, and need not be restricted to only one country: 'Whether imperialism or communism is in Moscow, it sits behind locked doors and baulks at shadows.'

From Ivor Cousins I derived a lifelong fascination with moral authority, the powers of charm and dandyism, of fraudulent gurus, saints, orators and spellbinders. 'The dandy,' said Baudelaire, 'is an unemployed Hercules.'

9

Plato has asserted that all knowledge is recollection, and the more I read the more I seem to recognize what I had wordlessly known. The Past was always Now. Words were piling up, weapons against The Others. 'Goitre', suffered by one of the cooks, 'Parliamentarianism', suffered by all of us, 'Private Ward', seemingly a device to rid the world of the unwanted.

> No more History, no more French
> No more sitting on the old school bench,
> No more spiders in my bath
> Trying hard to make me laugh,
> No more earwigs in my tea
> Making googly eyes at me,
> No more Latin, no more Greek,
> No more canes to make me squeak.

Actually, I remember no canes, their existence was perhaps mythical and losing no power for that. An actual cane in Gertie's hand would have been as irrelevant as a handbag, a yo-yo, a gob-stopper. She needed nothing more than a glance and a tone of voice.

I was almost ten, and, recovering from Ivor, had regained some of the assurance necessary for the naval officer, doubtless the Admiral, I was destined to become. Then revolution overtook us. By 1930, Don Bradman's year, changes were due at Marlborough House, perhaps overdue. Tom Bullick's son, Chris, was already on the staff and without warning, harrowing a grey underworld day like a baroque sun-god, in

47

hugely squared blue and silver plus-fours, strode in Robert Arthur Harrison, his former Haileybury colleague, an Anglo-Irish charmer and iconoclast. With these two young men and Rudolf the Dalmation, the school was removed to Hawkhurst, once a smugglers' mart, now a quiet village in Kentish fields, where, in 1985, it remains still.

10

Miss Herring continued to munch. Miss White retired to a small villa, Yelverton, in Shirley Drive, Hove, accompanied by Piché, who gave me, from her own library, Dickens' full-blooded and sensational *A Child's History of England* which she must often have seen me surreptitiously reading. Racy, intolerant and inaccurate, in which James I figures as 'His Sowship', it was also memorable. I would read with what Dickens himself called 'the attractions of repulsion':

'I pray you have a care and do not use me as awkwardly as you used my Lord Russell.'
The executioner, made nervous by this, and trembling, struck once and merely gashed him in the neck.

My eye was being moulded for, and by, the bizarre and the incongruous. Outside Hove Public Baths, a clergyman, as if smitten by the invisible, abruptly fell off his bicycle, but stilled our howl of laughter, savagely rounding on us from the gutter: 'May Christ blind you!' When, years later, Rudolf Nassauer handed me his novel *The Hooligan*, one passage instantaneously evoked that long-gone scene at Hove: the angry priest, the twirling wheels, frightened boys, Mr Shegog's embarrassed, yellowish face.

I believe that Christ was simply one such bird, an eagle soaring through the air with a snake folded about its body, as some philosopher has put it. He was a Man of judgement, one who could tell good from evil. And He Himself was evil too, you know. Did you know that? I have read somewhere

48

about Christ when He was a young man and He was walking through the streets of Nazareth. He came to a corner of the street and some boys came running towards that same corner from the opposite direction, and they ran into Him. One of them stepped on His toes, and He was furious . . . He raised Himself up, pointed and stared at the two little boys – not to bless them, but to curse them. And they fell down dead in the street.

Here was a link with wronged gods, kindly stepfathers becoming giants, kings changing to wolves, hospitable Dr Golder tormenting the children.

I enjoyed then, as I do now, nuggets of unprofitable information. During those lengthy preps and dangerous nights, I would repeatedly read the scores of remote cricket matches, count words beginning with D, examine antique maps of forgotten realms: Kingdom of Rum, Lands of the Visconti, Khanate of the Golden Horde, Dome of Mohammed Abtin, seen as if through rose and silver tissue. Almost wholly outside the school curriculum, like most children I was finding my private way, my vital education, my personality, unconsciously knowing that ultimately I must rely on myself alone. In this spirit of personal enquiry, my friend Oswell Blakeston's tiny *Some Essential Information* gives me unalloyed delight, telling me that Disraeli read aloud the Reform Bill, to the sea; at Tynemouth, Dickens was soaked by a wave while looking at a ship under a rainbow; when Richard Hamilton left Kellie Castle the servants smiled, he gave them nothing but tickled their outstretched hands; James IV paid courtiers to let him extract their teeth; rats obeyed the words of the Dowager Countess of Eglington at the dinner table; at Glenluce Abbey, a monkey forged the Abbot's signature; in one vault at Castle Urquhart is hidden treasure, in another, the plague. Heard the latest?

Three

Single children are always intensely self-absorbed. But also they can't quite imagine that anyone else might ever actually need them.

John Fowles

Small have continual plodders ever won
Save base authority from others' books.
Shakespeare

Take for yourself what you can, and don't be ruled by others; to belong to oneself – the whole savour of life lies in that.

Turgenev

Graves are the mountain tops of a lovely, distant land.
(attributed to) *The Koran*

1

My parents remained 'out East'. No Kipling or Saki abandoned in a house of desolation, I spent holidays, from 1929 to 1931, with Dr Laidlaw and his wife Maud, and their children, in Uffculme, Devon, where some of my mind still lives. A noted naturalist, working an extensive and impoverished practice, Frank Laidlaw did not grant favours from the loftiness of superior skills but gave and shared freely. All people were his fellows, his friends: he put much into life and life returned him much. Without recognizing its author, he, more wholeheartedly than many political zealots, would have accepted 'From each according to his ability, to each according to his needs'. Often too poor to pay his modest bills, villagers would bring a cabbage, a cake, eggs, 'hoping the Doctor will understand'. Eager to show them his latest plants, moths, butterflies, Frank understood as thoroughly as any professional saint, and more humbly, more genially than most. He and Maud possessed the no-nonsense goodness of simplicity within the dedicated, disciplined Scottish medical tradition.

Accompanying him in his old blue Singer between ancient villages, I too began, tentatively, to appreciate the by-ways of Man and nature, observing congenital idiots, perhaps incest's fruit, breeding above Smithincott; gathering a smattering of gipsy lore; listening to gnarled survivors from the last century; exploring Mr Hicks' dahlias glowing deep in sunlit rain, the lilies staring from Miss Marker's pale, green water garden, the medlars on Miss Mitchell's tree, the wet, brilliant daffodils in a Craddock meadow — I was about to write 'field', but this lacks the richness of 'meadow', a distinction I would not then have recognized. Jovial Miss Mills regretted the casualness of the 1931 overthrow of the Spanish Monarchy. 'I like my revolutions to have a bit of gore.' From lamp-lit cottages, unhurried confidences, the folklore of old feuds, injustices, tithes, beliefs, rural tragedies — this man's maimed arm, that girl's club foot — I could, however dimly, sense the raw life surging or rotting beneath 'history' and 'the news'.

Society has made sensational attempts to induce virtue by legislation, planning, threats and punishment. In *The Day's Burden*, T.M. Kettle writes:

The State is the name by which we call the great human conspiracy against hunger and cold, against loneliness and ignorance; the State is the foster-mother and warden of the arts, of love, of comradeship, of all that redeems from despair that strange adventure which we call human life.

Hitherto, my own experience of the arts, love, comradeship has been fostered not by the State but by works of genius, singular individuals, and by that Devon household and countryside. I cannot forget the sour fact that 'minister' once meant 'helper', and 'lord' was 'giver of bread', and that, despite Dr Kettle's eloquence, both have degenerated to 'boss'. The debt owed to the State by Chekhov, Corot, Dickens, Cézanne, Tolstoy, Kafka, Stravinsky is negligible. 'Local Authorities', 'Tribunal', 'Government Department' scarcely imply impulse, initiative, movement; modern socialism, modern statecraft, grant, but do not share. There is a Yugoslav joke: 'Under Capitalism, man is exploited by man. Under Socialism, the reverse.' I appreciate Eldridge Cleaver's remark, that gadflies are needed to gad, not to govern.

Dr Laidlaw would not have realized that he exercised an absolute authority over me, not that of superior strength but of friendly attention, unfailing sympathy, a certain humour of glance and smile, an instinctive tact, and unobtrusive zest for life. He never gave me an order, at most a gentle suggestion; punishment was inconceivable. A slightly apologetic reference to a robbed orchard, a broken microscope, villagers' complaints of uncouth behaviour, was sufficient, and I would mete out my own punishment. He did not, as adults so often did, condemn me for 'sulking'. This word, I later considered, perhaps over-complacently, is often applied by those with too little imagination to those with too much. Frank's own imagination and curiosity took on all comers, with Maud behind him to see that he did not give too much and receive too little.

2

In Devon I enjoyed real freedom, absorbing it with the coloured fields and the soft West Country rains, the expeditions to Dartmoor and Culmstock Beacon, the cricket, tennis, treasure hunts. Within all of it I was reserved, happy in myself. A bicycle secured me full independence within minutes, the roads opening to field, hill, river. The very sheep glowed in echo of the red soil, as if within call of the Red Town. The Culm allegedly flowed over Roman tin. I contemplated crossing the Severn into Gloucestershire, corking up the source of the Thames, which I imagined as flowing out of a tiny hillside crack, then tramping the dried bed through bewildered riverside villages.

I rode towards stark, slightly sinister Blackborough, to Black Down, Norton Fitzwarren, White Sheet Hill, Clyst St Mary, Shepton Beauchamp, Ottery St Mary, Hemyock, Wootton Fitzpaine. They vied with Orinoco, Nijni-Novgorod, Vladivostok, Omsk, Tomsk, Kicking Horse Pass, extravagant flourishes on the broad, curved globe. Whitechurch Canonicorum, Beer, Widecombe in the Moor, Charlton Mackerell, 'Farm of the Free Peasants', Lyme Regis, where doomed youngsters flocked to join Monmouth on a bright summer day; Shepton Mallet, where he held sad council.

Such names had their secrets: Stockleigh Pomeroy, 'Pomeroy's Manor of Stock Wood'; Holcombe Rogus, 'Deep Valley of Rogus' Manor'; Hackpen Hill, opposite our house, 'Snake-head'. All shimmered with old families, tales, occasions, buried yet exhumable. Sedgemoor, Kentisbeare, 'Centel's Grove' which, like Uffculme, had a vicar named Chalk with six children, though they were not related. Our young Chalks were Rosamund, Elizabeth, Brenda, Pauline, Eleanor, Henry. My friends. A missionary, an actress, a don . . . but the trail has gone cold. Do any remember me? Did they exist?

Girls still remained (and remained for too long) fancy dress creatures, from a world I made scant effort to imagine. Sometimes, even in the secure Devonshire haven, I missed George Rothery, fair haired, heroic, somehow protective, as he still is. Ivor was unthinkable in these gardens, on these roads. His cold eye would have withered butterflies and birds.

The Laidlaws had planted so many flowers that the air was wavy with butterflies, which lit the mind. Lost airs, lost colours. China Marks, Adonis Blues, Orange Tips, Purple Emperors, Red Admirals, Camberwell Beauties, Fritillaries, Red Brimstones, Peacocks, Painted Ladies, Commas, Holly Blues, Brown Arguses, Green Hairstreaks, Dingy Slippers, Grizzles Slippers, Duke of Burgundies, Green Veined Whites, Clouded Yellows: what forgotten genius had named them, tapping a popular imagination still unimpaired by mass schooling. They winked in all hues above zinnia and tansy, delphinium, lavender, marigold and much that I cannot name, and between plump hedges rife with the black and crimson, speckled, deep green, the mauve and the yellow. I would like to have known two flowers long remembered by John Masefield in 'Grace before Ploughing': Jack-go-to-Bed-at-noon, which closes its eyes at Midday, and the blue Sinner's Rise, or, What Sinners Get.

Beneath the formal calendar listed in Charles Letts' pocket diaries — interminable Sundays after Trinity, Septuagesima, the misleading Refreshment Sunday, Maundy, the Circumcision, Armistice Day, Ash Wednesday, Partridge Shooting Begins — lay an older, more enticing year — All Fool's Day, All Souls' Day, Midsummer Day, Lammas Tide, May Day, Guy Fawkes Night, Hallowe'en, Shrove Tuesday, Oak Apple Day, suggesting merriment, fireworks, ghosts, fairs, unusual lights and distant movements, bawdy scufflings, the agonized hiss of an effigy toppling into the fire, a decorated cornstook and the last square of uncut grain quivering with scared life, 'the spirit of the field', the rabbits, mice, voles, snakes, crouching from scythes.

3

Books suggested that there were no bores, save perhaps Mycroft Holmes and those in *Little Women*. In a tent behind the tennis court, amongst tall grass, flamboyant dandelions, Queen Anne's Lace, Old Man's Baccy, and within tempting reach of Mr Bryce's luxuriant apples, I lay reading whatever came to hand. Every room had haphazard collections of books.

People occasionally, with a bored look, question me about 'influences' and I sometimes drop the big, rotund names, Tolstoy, Mann, Dostoevsky, Dickens, Proust, quite untruthfully. Ultimately, of course, we influence ourselves, though early readings helped set my imagination on course almost irrespective of particular authors. I read whatever I found.

Writers, I understood, tended to have names substantiating the glamour of their trade. Rafael Sabatini, H. de Vere Stacpoole, E. Temple Thurston, E. Arnot Robertson, E.

Phillips Oppenheim, Sapper, Saki, Crosby Garstin, Sax Rohmer, Warwick Deeping, W. Somerset Maugham, George A. Birmingham, E. Everett Green, F. Tennyson Jesse, Ernest Thompson Seton, Talbot Baines Reed, Harrison Ainsworth, L. du Gard Peach, S. Gorley Putt. Storm Jameson I naturally visualized perpetually sailing for a rockbound coast on a wild sea (and indeed I was to learn that her father was a Yorkshire seacaptain). Soon I was planning to write my own novel, which did not reach much further than my adopted name, E. Mountstuart Temple.

Engrossed, I lie in the summer grass, cool from swimming, hot from tennis or cycling, and, wide-eyed, resume Angela Brazil's *Storm in a Tea Cup*, Talbot Baines Reed's *The Fifth Form at St Dominic's*, with its no-goods prone to Billiards, Bookmakers, Bullying, with a further vice implied when the School Captain asks a small boy 'Will you be my flower?' Then Hugh Walpole's *Jeremy*, E. Nesbit's *Five Children and It*, Richard Jeffries' magical *Bevis*, Buchan's *The Three Hostages*, which I still read once a year, curtains drawn, telephone unhooked; the fireside, the whisky, the old delight. I read, too, Rider Haggard's *She*, eleven times filmed, transformed to opera, to ballet, praised by Jung, hailed by a Freudian as a beautiful allegory of yearnings to return to the womb. From a sentence in Haggard's *Nada the Lily* grew Kipling's *Jungle Books*, and, for Graham Greene, Haggard was 'perhaps the greatest of all who enchanted us when we were young'; Greene cherished the witch Gagool as 'a permanent part of the imagination'. I found the concept of *The Secret Garden* more compelling than the story, but was riveted by scenes from Carlyle's helter-skelter, tumultuous *The French Revolution*, all howls, glitter, mobs and capital letters, and Ivor raising his tiny lorgnette and a towering figure standing sombre in a cart. *Danton, no weakness.*

Rain patters on my tent, as the twenties end, falls over the grass, penetrating the secrets of the earth where boy kings, grenadiers, King Solomon's treasures lie buried, and from which at dawn the White Horse defends the valley against Hengist. Heroes are at my elbow: Dick Hannay, Sir Percy Blakeney, the first of so many unruffled figures, who, in deadly crisis would, smothering a yawn, flick away an imaginary speck of dust from a perfectly contrived sleeve; Alan Quartermaine, Umslopagaas, Sexton Blake, The Count of the Saxon Shore, Vernon-Smith, Prentice Hal.

At night I am in my small room; owls cry from Hackpen, foxes prowl the orchards for Mr Bryce's chickens, Frank is summoned through winter mists to attend delivery or death in some distant hamlet, and, like a moth grubbing through golden tissue, I read on and on through my line of books, understanding perhaps a quarter of any page and the further enticed because of it. Imagination depends on ignorance, perhaps not total ignorance, but on prolonged and spirited gaps between question and answer, the sense of wonders still waiting, dimly-lit comprehension, the glamour of the over-heard, the whispered, the unspoken and masked.

> Men all in fire walk up and down the streets,
> And yesterday the bird of night did sit,
> Even at noon-day, upon the market place,
> Hooting and shrieking. . .

I remember the blue giant akimbo in the garden, the werewolf nuzzling my slippers, then return to *Vice Versa*, *A Room without a Door*, *Lorna Doone*, with Lorna and Jan and Carver living only down the road. *Out for King Monmouth*, and, fatally, the men of Kentisbeare had done just that. Conan Doyle's *Micah Clarke* and, less famous but better, John Masefield's *The Duke's Messenger* marvellously evoked that fateful adventure. I learn that fingernails must never be cut, that giants will one day destroy the world, riding the boat Nalhfar, made from the bones of the dead.

> The sons of Mimir tremble, the tree in the world's
>   centre is in flames,
> Heimdall, horn aloft, loudly calls the alarm;
> Odin consults the head of Mimir.
> Then the ash grown from Yggdrasil,
> That ancient tree, shudders: the Jotun breaks his
>   chains:

The shades quiver upon paths to the lower world,
Until the ardour of Surtur has consumed the tree
   utterly.
Hrym advances from the East. . .

Who were these people? I might never know, but a prophecy
seemed intended, believable enough, and so it remains.
   Such nights were rich with implication.

'*Matilda Briggs* was not the name of a young woman,
Watson,' said Holmes in a reminiscent voice. 'It was a ship
which is associated with the giant rat of Sumatra, a story for
which the world is not yet prepared.'

The world should get itself ready.

4

New words were sprouting like the mushrooms beyond the
orchard. 'Brigantine', 'Bargee', 'Cheapjack', 'Myrmidon',
which I connected, not altogether foolishly, with nakedness,
still very rare, and, more mysterious, 'Thimblerigger'. I had
seen, on Miss Howe's finger, 'a silver palace without a floor'
and 'Rigger' was some sort of ship in Captain Marryat and
Ballantyne, but the connection was empty, imagination folded
inexpert wings and was still. Then, only last week, I met the
word again, an old friend, in a story concerning John
Galsworthy, by Ford Madox Ford. I read how Joseph Conrad
first met Galsworthy: both were young, and Galsworthy was
then the first to read a Conrad manuscript, 'on a ship, in the
starlight, running down off the coast of Africa'.
   The countryside remains an endless trove of story, allusion,
poignancy. An iron wheel still smashes the mill water where a
boy had drowned, and I still wonder whether he was pushed.
A ghost lurks at crossroads. At small country fairs, the witch
muttered in the tent; ruined boxers, veins broken purple on
beef-red faces and smashed noses, fought all comers for
sixpence; for a penny, mounds of crockery could be toppled

with wooden balls, never quite as heavy as they looked, and, in the freaks' booth, a blind child with both ears on one side of his head, stopped my heart.

At Western Zoyland were sad relics of Sedgemoor. John Jones and Alfred Elfing were paid 10s 6d for cleaning the church after the wounded had been dragged away for the rope or the slave plantations. In a radio discussion about reincarnation, in 1976, I heard an elderly Essex man, Edward Ryall, remember his own death in the 1685 battle, having joined Monmouth without enthusiasm. He mentioned details of long-extinct church decoration, at home and abroad, and of the fight itself, his instant of death within the din and the cold clammy mists. A labourer's son, of scanty education, he still felt remorse for his wife, mistress, children, and that unnecessary departure for nothing.

Carved on the Stoke Gabriel Church were the Gabriel Hounds, dogs of hell, and the Dark Hunter himself, Woden of the Wild Hunt. A ride to Aylesbeare revealed a manorial beam inscribed 'The Man that useth much swearing shall be tainted with iniquity and the Plague of God shall never depart from his house.' A tomb at Portlesmouth was inscribed:

> By poison stung he was cut off
> And brought to his death at last,
> It was by his apprentice girl
> On whom there's sentence passed.
>   All you who read fair warning take
>   For she was burnt to a stake

Beneath the organ at Peterhavy, 'Land along the dark river dedicated to Peter', we found a monument to the five young Evelegh daughters:

> They breath'd awhile and look't ye world about,
> And like newly lighted candles soon went out.

Gravestones made laconic comments on the transient and worldly. Ralegh, grave and pointed, observes:

Our graves that hide us from the searching sun
Are like the drawn curtains when the play is done.

In adult life I was to prove slightly more than an antiquarian, considerably less than a historian; any capacity for detached analysis swiftly muffled by pleasure in the incidental and personal. I was long dismayed by this impulsiveness, until German and Russian dogma and impersonality began reducing human beings to statistics, then ashes.

5

'Without curiosity there can be no literature.' I would stare at churches, opening myself to their secrets and stories. At Uffculme's screen, the longest in Britain, and the forbidding, painted Stuart heads secluded behind it; at Kentisbeare, a galleon carved on a capital. I was to bicycle along many roads, reading churches like a book, largely illegible from time and weather, but with stories abbreviated into being more stimulating than perhaps they really were, stories implied, rumoured, embellished. Near Coventry is buried John Parkes, 'of mild disposition, a gladiator by profession, who, having fought 350 battles in the principle parts of Europe. . .'

My eighteenth-century ancestors lived at Bisham Abbey, now a sports training centre, which possessed a memorial to two children, 'by a local and not very credible tradition the off-spring of Queen Elizabeth'. One of my favourite epitaphs is at Ewelme, in Latin and English, a portion of which goes:

'Charlie was born 24th Jan 1859; died of Typhus fever; and he learned to speak French in four months fluently; he possessed a noble mind, and loved truthfulness: indeed his father ever abominating guile, taught him sincerity. He had intended, God willing, when he had finished his education in France, that he should enter universities in Germany and Italy; and then, if he pleased, should take a degree in an English university; but alas his father's hopes have been suddenly blasted: the affliction is as appalling as any ever recorded. By universal Law Death is decreed; but the time may be stayed by the intercessory prayer of parents; but here that was wanting.'

Charlie was 'snatched out of this life when born not quite ten years'. Nervertheless, 'Charlie is not dead; the darling is now gone to school where he will learn forever goodness.'

An Ashbourne memorial is in English, Latin, French and Italian: 'I was not in safety, neither had I rest, and the trouble came.' To Penelope, only child of Sir Brooke and Lady Susannah Boothby. 'Born April 11th, 1785: died March 13th, 1791. She was in form and intellect most exquisite. The unfortunate parents ventured their all on this frail Bark and the wreck was total.' David Roberton lies at Cross Kirk. 'He was a peaceably quiet man and to all appearance a sincere Christian. His death was very much regretted, which was caused by the stupidity of Lawrence Tulloch of Clotherton, who sold him nitrate instead of Epsom Salts.'

Taillis an! To the Coppice! Tally Ho! Landscapes were strewn with words that in my lifetime have dwindled, some vanishing, like the small trains that puffed through the fields between halts, where the station master was also the gardener, his platform brimming with pansies, nasturtiums, giant moon daisies. A vocabulary has collapsed with many of the handicrafts that produced it: 'turner', 'tranter', 'chapman', 'cooper', 'fletcher', 'lapidary', 'hurdle-maker', 'higgler' . . . 'quoin', 'chancel', 'ogee', 'transept' . . . 'matlock' . . . 'fent man', 'fuller', 'reddle man', 'pargeter', 'knapper'. The opening pages of John Fowles' novel, *Daniel Martin*, recalling the West Country in the decade I knew so well, has many such words. Will my step-grandson at once identify 'combe', 'barton', 'leats', 'tinhays', 'knoll', 'wing-canon'; distinguish between 'copse', 'thicket', 'covert', 'grove', 'spinney', 'dell', 'glade', 'hurst', 'holt', 'dene', 'copice'? A poem I much loved, W.S. Blunt's 'The Old Squire' contains 'mense', 'lags', 'gills' and I must confess to forgetting their meanings as I have 'post-and-pan' and even 'tie-beam'.

The Laidlaws worked at Uffculme until the end of the Second World War. Being addressed as 'Doc' by lively

American soldiers slightly ruffled Frank's geniality. They retired to Woodham Mortimer, Essex, then to Foxearth, Suffolk, but their Devon holiday in very old age was a famous progress, people appearing from all sides to greet them, most of whom Frank had helped into the world, repaired in their youth, and whose parents he had comforted at the end.

Four

To some, engines, meccano, scientific experiment:
To some, stamps, flowers, the anatomy of insects:
To some, twisting elbows, torturing, sending to Coventry:
To some, soldiers, battles and miniature howitzers:
To some, football
     in the sadness of an autumn afternoon.

Alan Ross

That song wants a woman to sing it. A woman who could reach out for that last high note and teach it to take a joke. The whole refrain is working up to that. You need Tetrazzini or someone who would just pick that note off the roof and hold it, till the janitor came round to lock up the building for the night.

P.G. Wodehouse

Whoever is endowed with skill alone is a fool, and the imagination that attempts to dispense with skill is nothing more than insane.

Baudelaire

1

Focus of a literature comic or glum, of notorious myths and obscene legends, the British prep school has long been a political and educational butt, remembered with loathing by the intellectual classes — Orwell at St Cyprians, Timothy Pember's Dorset hell governed so wilfully by Old WC, the grim viciousness of the private school in Hugh Walpole's *Fortitude* – Maurice Richardson, Philip Toynbee, Jeremy Potter and so many more.

Each school had its touting prospectus. 'Baths and Religion. Boxing and Riding on request. Hampers strictly forbidden. Home Farm, Matron but no Pets. Fully qualified Staff including one Graduate. Extras, plenty.'

In 1939, a teacher myself, I was entertained by the HMI report on a Watford school: 'The main staircase, in constant use by all pupils, is in a highly dangerous condition, but fortunately the Headmaster is not without hope that this can be remedied in the not too distant future.'

It is common to seek revenge upon one's youth by condemning its oppressors, but this I cannot do. From eight to eighteen I was at boarding school, but my occasional private tears were balanced by fits of immoderate laughter. There was darkness and insensitivity, tolerance, encouragement, a number of good jokes.

2

Hove had been Roundhead: stern, toiling, somewhat self-righteous, in the spirit of Field Marshal Montgomery's favourite hymn:

> Father, hear the prayers we offer,
>   Not for ease our life to be,
> But for strength, that we may ever
>   Live our lives courageously.

New Lodge, Hawkhurst, was Cavalier. The house itself had Augustan graciousness yet was not over-symmetrical, for many additions made a rambling pattern of roofs and angles hinting at secret stairways to attics harbouring creatures of benign but erratic disposition. The Adamesque hall, panelled here, moulded there, glowed with roses, with delphiniums, in fine porcelain, then with deep, heavy chrysanthemums in ochred pots. Outside were woods, gardens bulging with rhododendrons, azaleas and, occasionally, cows. Breathlessly, that September of 1930, we swapped rumours: a wolf in the Dell, treasure, or a buried ship, under the waterlilies. The long, oaken Gallery had Franz Marc blue horses. *Blue.* My stolid mind had to unfreeze a little further. Blue. Yet, in Shakespeare, stones had been known to speak; in old tales, trees had ears, rivers had voices.

Cézannes, van Goghs, Gauguins, began opening windows into the adventurous and possibly accessible. I seldom considered them, any more than I did the air I breathed, but, in my way, I breathed them too.

The school, damaged by 'slump' and the gyrations of Ramsay Mac, was now smaller, but George, Stanley, Byng were there, together with Wilfred Bristow, reticent, always reading wireless magazines and tinkering with arcane gadgets, and whom I rated, though privately, the handsomest and remotest being alive, an avatar, though gentler, of John Armitage. From him I craved no more than a smile, a Christmas card, at best a walk on the Downs during an outing. An old address surfaces as I write: Charles Wilfred Symons Bristow, Eothen, North Road, Hythe, Kent, England, Europe, The World, The Universe. Wilfred disappeared, flying, during the war, itself still barely conceivable; although pale, red-haired Michael Bassett announced that he personally had a very high opinion of Adolf Hitler, who knew what was what.

We had abundant light. Oaks, elms, limes, a scarlet kite flying above the Dell, lilies white and gold on green and silver ponds — I enjoyed the resonant, lingering depths of *pond* — the rich summer sky and russet airs of autumn, the rhododendrons flushing red, mauve, crimson above wide lawns, a grey stone bench among yellow roses. I accepted them as the casual privileges, not of money but of life, becoming most fully aware of them only in harsher years.

From classroom windows, Time was charted by birdsong and colour. The chestnut flame thickened then sank, old walls reddened then dwindled to sodden browns and blacks, re-emerging flamboyantly orange when the kingfisher flew and the sun tutored the young leaves. Once I saw, or thought I saw, the fleeting, headlong scarlets of a hunt seen through mist.

Chris and Arthur were then bachelors, though I was to attend their weddings. Mary Bullick I never knew, but 'Muffet' Harrison, now in her eighties yet a vigorous Suffolk archaeologist, became a cherished friend, exemplifying Camus' definition of charm: a way of getting the answer 'yes' without having made a definite request. Chris was serious, less mercurial than Arthur, a reminder that he was of the family of Flash, Baal, Gertie. He subsequently turned to the Oxford Group and became a grammar-school headmaster elsewhere, doubtless having to shed Frank Buchman's 1936 credo of, 'I thank God for a man like Adolf Hitler who built a front line of defence against the anti-Christ of Communism.' I suspect that Arthur's religious beliefs were, at very best, nominal. Arthur was teasing, ribald, unpredictable, with ill-concealed loathing for Miss White which was amply reciprocated: 'How can anyone trust that man Harrison?'

They had to transmute that undeviating Roundhead pursuit of success into more generous concepts of excellence. Empires, republics, soviets alike crash, through lack of generosity. Implied, rather than stated, was these young men's concern for — it is hard to define and I doubt whether they ever tried — not quite religion, not exactly art or science, never wholly materialistic commonsense, though all were present. Style, panache, friendliness ousted exhortation, dogma, platitude, threat, a style displayed by only one Prime Minister since Lloyd George and today deader than usual. Education seemed intelligent preparation not for high incomes but the holidays. Rewards and punishments were receding. 'I always felt,' Arthur was to reflect, 'that if you couldn't run a school without deterrents and bribes, you were a pretty poor schoolmaster.'

He seemed gigantic, in those squared, glistening tweeds. His irreverence towards rival headmasters, Mr Hartebeest, Mr Nuthatch; his humours, his presence, gave access to new freedoms. 'Arthur Harrison,' a Roundhead voice told me severely, two decades later, 'did not always set a very good example.' I have never ceased to be grateful.

65

He had less breezy moments. Once in a Scripture lesson his large blue eyes went unexpectedly reflective as he read aloud: 'And Isaac went out to meditate in the field at the eventide.'

He spoke of 'meditate' as the most beautiful word in the Bible, playing on it as on a cello, drawing out lingering aspects of repose, quietude, reflection; with Jacob, at the end of a flawed life, made beautiful in the ebbing day. I myself thought far more suggestive was: 'And he bought a parcel of a field, where he had spread his tent, at the hand of the children of Hamor.' I envisaged Hamor's children piping applause as Jacob cut the string, uncrumpled the parcel and saw damp rich earth falling on the harsh desert.

Arthur was always slightly more or less than he appeared. Unlike Chris, he had pronounced and not always consistent likes and dislikes amongst the boys; he could be strangely insensitive, unexpectedly cold, and he enjoyed ridiculing incipient conceit among 'the Swells', arousing hurt feelings, resentment, a little fear. Once I resolved never to speak to him again; he knew my feelings, and next day his sudden mischievous grin restored relations, which endured until his death in 1980. I myself had an occasional habit, which perplexed rather than worried me, of deliberately offending my favourite teacher of the moment, then treasuring my grievance and wrath at his mild retribution. Often, my rudeness was unnoticed, or, more irritatingly, understood and overlooked.

Teaching in the fifties at a self-styled progressive school, I felt that its claims of freedom were scarcely an advance on Chris and Arthur, who would be roundly condemned today as anachronistic exploiters. Small classes geared to intellectual ability and emotional stamina, amusing teachers, ample leisure, agreeable discussion: these were the methods of the Bhaers in *Jo's Boys* from a century before. Kindness, abjuration of absolute judgements, practical concern for delinquents; the opposite of those of Dickens' Mrs Pipchin, whose system was not to encourage a child's mind to develop and expand like a flower, but to open it by force, like an oyster. 'The aim of Education,' wrote Herbert Read, 'is to discover the child's psychological type, and allow each life its natural line of development, its natural form of integration.'

Chris, Arthur and Hilda would have been more laconic, but their practice concurred. Lessons were chatty, could take place among the roses, in a punt or be cancelled for an expedition to the Downs, Camber Sands, a great garden or to an Eastbourne concert conducted by Julius Harrison.

It is when teachers are not formally teaching that they can be most effective. Arthur and F.I.W. Stewart, once his pupil at Haileybury and now Mr Shegog's successor, might spontaneously transform an idle moment with a yodelling duet, a banjo song, a record of 'The Last Round-up' or Robeson singing 'Lindy Lou'.

We had much music and, though I had inherited little of my mother's aptitude and none of her talent, I found that a song, a tune, striking very swiftly, like the smell of cut grass on a city street, induced me to confide secrets and enthusiasms to unlikely companions.

Chris Bullick lent me books. Homer, Kipling, Arnold Bennett, Conrad. The last I very imperfectly understood, my own recollections of the sea addressed me more directly than Conrad himself, giving tone to the grey spaces of the Solent, already so distant. But his tales gave intimations of strictness, dedication, adventures never very obvious and sometimes dull, without humour; but somehow inducing a pledge from me to continue.

Do things for the fun of it, Chris said, on a serious occasion. We did not need Freud and Huizinga to instruct us that play was a wise teacher. I could also watch the sky gleam with harbours and mountains, lagoons and streams glistening in the wake of gods.

My education, then, derived from encouragement from those I respected and indeed loved. Ian Stewart, smoothly conformist – the right clubs and blazers – elegant in dress and at games, casually witty, at whose own school I was later to teach. He died young, mysteriously deranged, naked in a cold Sussex wood, his clothes delicately hung on a sodden branch. I see him crossing a lawn, testing a bat, informative about dance bands, Charlie Kunz at Casani's, Ambrose at the Embassy, Harry Roy at the Mayfair; driving through Kent in his long, open, pillar-box red Lancia, standing under a rainbow-hued golfing umbrella, returning from shooting, coolly swinging the rabbit loyally provided beforehand by his slim red-haired wife, Sylvia.

I still walk and hold my head in ways modelled on this inwardly cursed stylist whose easy friendship suggested that one day, very far away, I might find a voice, write a true sentence. I was also awed by the Lancia, the smart friends at the Savoy, his familiarity with Ambrose, his appearances for the MCC and the Free Foresters, his references to the Kit-Kat; a man of the thirties, on a narrow circuit to which I in part belong. The thirties, somewhat corresponding to Dryden's view of the Restoration era: 'a very merry, dancing, drinking, laughing, quaffing and unthinking time', quite soon smashed to bits from the sky, when J.B. Priestley, after the destruction of the Café de Paris, saw the rich laid out in Coventry Street, covered with sawdust, like broken dolls.

In contrast to Ian was J.T.C. Pember, today a painter, whose *Not me, Sir* is one of the best school novels. Playing cricket in grey shorts, bowling lobs (once with an orange) in good-humoured riposte to Ian's glossy flannels and wristy glides, Tim grinned ironically at those like myself for whom Test Matches were state occasions. I remember a headmaster who always during these games changed into whites and an MCC blazer. Astringent to 'swells' and 'topdogs', sympathetic to the less successful, Tim knew well that scholarship boards can be profitably faked, that a first-class examinee can be a first-class scoundrel, an athletic eminence the accident of brawn or guile.

Representatives of the old order were not quite extinct. We made trips to Flash and Baal in their Downland vicarage, and Miss White occasionally appeared, Arthur taking wing to the Royal Oak Hotel. She seemed unexpectedly frail, an earth-goddess with powers at last diminished through change of territory, and blue horses. Yet something of spirit lingered, capable of eruption. In 1942, I wrote, rather too grandly, to tell her that I had published my first novel. As always, she replied by return: 'I saw the volume you mentioned, in Combridge's Bookshop. I did not receive a copy, nor did I purchase one. It is, I allow, your first book, but the literary style you affect promises that it may also be your last.'

3

Quotidian melodrama had vanished. No green, moonlit, circular window glared down at me like God, dusks were emptied of the Kaiser and the Ripper, dormitories cleared of the Titanic and Tony Dorman. Cellars clattered not with the Murder of Becket but with Wonderbar, a nightclub where Byng distilled nasty lemonade from powder, in collapsible tin mugs, and in the hushed tones of a Mystery hierophant, Blunt ma. introduced a new word, 'bugger', with a recommendation to be sparing of its use. 'The maids like it,' Byng pronounced, slightly upstaged.

Inwardly, in myself, little had changed. Old fears and obsessions merely found new symbols, fortified by the books clutched before the great peat and log Gallery fire, while I chewed toffee and awaited my turn for billiards or table tennis. The books had beguiling openings, instantaneously trapping me: Watson meeting Holmes, *A Study in Scarlet*; the aborted hanging, *Quentin Durward*; Mazarin in Richelieu's chair, *Twenty Years After*; scared children crouching on the Southsea beach, *The Light that Failed*; the desert fortress in the Sahara guarded by corpses holding rifles, in *Beau Geste*; Dick Hannay finding Scudder skewered to the floor, and, at the start of *Greenmantle*: 'I had just finished breakfast and was filling my pipe when I got Bullivant's telegram,' as enticing as Holmes' 'the game's afoot', advising Watson to look out his service revolver or select his heaviest stick.

I was still unable to unfreeze the literal, distinguish symbols, and I was dogged by reverence for the biblical truth of books, however confusing or contradictory. Dumas' account of the execution of Charles I was printed, therefore it was true. These books assumed values that I took for granted, until revoked by Auschwitz, Katyn, Vorduka; that suffering entails redemption, that decency and justice will win on the last page. Singleness of character and motive, neat divisions between pleasure and pain, the reality of appearances — these were assumed, and not yet revoked for me. 'The web of our life is of a mingled yarn, good and ill together: our virtues would be proud if our faults whipped them not and our crimes would despair if they were not cherished by our virtues,' Shakespeare, in his casual way, hands to a First Lord.

Coloured deep red on world maps, the British Empire, on evidence of Old Boys, masters, and text books, was civilizing, merciful, invigorating, disciplined; fed, irrigated, researched, mapped and taught by conscientious adventurers of unshakable morale and small incomes, seen historically in the Lawrences of the Punjab — 'Settle the country,' Henry Lawrence ordered, 'make the people happy, and take care there are no rows' — in the all-purpose Richard Strachey; and fictionally in Kipling's Strickland, Edgar Wallace's Sanders, with periodic interventions by Allan Quartermaine and Sandy Arbuthnot.

War was justified, especially if the foe was weakly armed, and, preferably, coloured. Beautiful women asserted themselves through romantic bitchiness (which left men very stricken or very bored), through espionage, leading to sudden death in exotic circumstances, or through hunting: 'Gad, George, she keeps her seat like a man, damme, she does.' They were not expected to observe codes of decency propounded in club, mess, common room, for a world still of absolute values, the residue of Christianity, masculine Manicheanism and the either/or commandments of the French Revolution: (' "Oh, I am no hero, my friend," smiled de Beaujolais, "but it seemed the right thing to do",' writes P.C. Wren in *Beau Geste*.)

New names drifted through me, then got stuck. Tel-el-Kebir, Abou Klea, Omdurman, Isandhlwana, Osman Digna, the Mahdi, Cetawayo, Mtesa of Uganda.

I constantly reread Mason's *The Four Feathers*. Though relapsing into stock values, it begins by challenging the mess values, as a pack of Crimean veterans celebrate a Crimean anniversary. First-class fighting men, Mason comments, but second-class soldiers, cruel and unimaginative. Dining with them for the first time is their host's child, Harry. 'He will, of course, enter the Service.' That *of course* must have savaged many thousands of lives. Under relentless military portraits and the war-bitten faces of veteran diners, watched by the sympathetic Lieutenant Sutch, Harry listens to paralysing war stories. Lord Willoughby, 'one of the best names in Europe', ostracized even by Piccadilly whores for cowardice before Sebastopol; a military surgeon terrified of Pathan bullets cutting his own femoral artery.

Harry's expression becomes alarming:

> The look was a too familiar one to Lieutenant Sutch . . . and one in particular rose before his mind. An advancing square at Inkermann and a tall big soldier rushing from the line in the eagerness of his attack and then stopping as though he suddenly understood that he was alone, and had to meet alone the charge of a mounted Cossack. Sutch remembered very clearly the fatal wavering glance which the big soldier had thrown backwards towards his companions – a glance accompanied by a queer, sickly smile. He remembered too with equal vividness its consequences. For though the soldier carried a loaded musket and a bayonet locked to the muzzle, he had without an effort of self-defence received the Cossack's lance – thrust in his throat.

I also remembered this, when learning from the American writer S.L.A. Marshall that in the Second World War, US military psychiatrists reported that the most common cause of individual battle failure was not fear of being killed, but fear of killing and of failure. Lawrence Lipton has claimed that in Korea, in one American battle unit under study, only a minority, even in mortal danger, actually used its weapons.

Meanwhile, aged eleven, I remained destined, *of course*, for the Navy, with growing misgivings and seemingly without appeal; though without knowing it, in Arthur Harrison, I already possessed my Lieutenant Sutch.

Incidentally, I have now learnt from Ms Jacqueline Rose that, certainly until 1974, all writing for children, particularly *Peter Pan*, was an adult conspiracy, for 'often perverse and mostly dishonest ends . . . the ongoing sexual and political mystification of the child.'

4

I am to this day a literary enthusiast, never having developed genuine critical insights, and I was once surprised to read in *The Listener* that I had written a structuralist novel. Earlier, I had felt pride swiftly followed by misgivings, when I read Julia Strachey's opinion, in the *New Statesman*, that I was a cubist novelist. Reading Leavis, Edmund Wilson, listening to Michael Hamburger, Philip Toynbee, Erich Heller, V.S. Pritchett, I have been humiliated by what I have failed to observe or enlarge. This amateurishness did not smother my feeling for words, and unperturbed by ambition, I stumbled on Malory, perhaps on recommendation from Tim Pember, perhaps from Stanley Pigott, whose fastidious prose, wicket-keeping and grave erudition made him seem an unofficial member of the staff. The stories bored me but the words enthralled. I wanted to declaim them to vast hushed audiences:

> Now we leave these knights and speak we of Sir Launcelot du Lake that lieth under the Apple Tree sleeping. Even about the noon there came by four queens of great estate; and, for the heat should not annoy them, there rode four knights about them, and bare a cloth of green silk on four spears betwixt them and the sun, and the queens rode by on four white mules. Thus, as they rode, they heard by them a great horse grimly neigh, then were they ware of a sleeping knight that lay all armed under an apple tree; anon as these queens looked on his face, they knew it was Sir Launcelot. Then they began to strive for that knight, every each one said they would have him for their love.

Probably there was now implanted a germ that eventually became my 1978 novel *Lancelot*, though with heroes and heroines far from Malory.

Unsystematic schoolboy reading continued to vindicate my fantasies, which, inaccurate in details, were seldom totally wrong. I was being initiated into secrets that might not assist me in the process of becoming an Admiral but, like the ruined, bemedalled soldiers, like Ivor and the Lower God, and certain tunes, confirmed my sense of the world. 'Hilaire Belloc' seemed the most vital as well as the most beautiful of names, and indeed its mingled grace and pugnacity exactly expresses the literary personality behind it.

I nodded in happy complicity at Sapper's master criminal, Carl Peterson, as he addressed his beautiful 'mistress', a word not actually mentioned, but beginning to gather an allure still imprecise, though Byng said that Chris and Arthur kept their mistresses 'under cover' in a hut at Lamberhurst. I did not venture to ask Stanley to confirm this. Even Byng, even perhaps Ivor, could have learnt something from Peterson. 'Take Drakshoff. That man controls three of the principal governments of Europe. The general public doesn't know it, the governments themselves won't admit it, but it's true. As you know, my dear, that little job I carried out for him in Germany averted a second revolution. He didn't want one at the time so he called me in. And it cost him in all five million pounds. What was that to him? A mere fleabite. A bagatelle.'

Unknown to me, the German millionaire Thyssen was soon to say about Adolf Hitler: 'We've hired him.' The same fatuous miscalculation that Thiers made about Louis Napoleon in 1849: 'We'll give the Prince plenty of women and lead him by the nose.' A mistake that put Thiers out of office for over twenty years.

Lord Lytton's *Rienzi* gave spectacular tableaux of applauding but dangerous Italian street-mobs, roaring promises from the passionate, vast but emptying ideals of brotherhood, ending with the lynching of the despotic Tribune whose ravings, whose theatre, continued too long. Lytton's *The Last Days of Pompeii*, in which the doomed town plays and loves and argues under the shadow of Vesuvius, and early Christianity struggles against a paganism still gleaming but with the brightness of a failing candle, regularly absorbed me. At some public school, a master, when suspecting a boy of insufficient reading, would demand:

'Hey, do you know how babies are born?'
'Well, Sir . . . Well, not exactly.'
'Ah! Then you'll be interested in reading this.'

He would hand over Lytton's sexually innocuous but lengthy melodrama, a strategy usually successful. In this context Wilfrid Blunt quotes a Haileybury master — who later taught me — C.W. Adams, or 'Bill A'; defending Wilfrid from the charge of corrupting boys by lending them art books, he remarked 'I think that if a boy has the patience to read through a book of six hundred pages, he deserves to find a bit of dirt at the end of it.'

Elsewhere, a class might be manipulated into greater interest in classics:

'Do any of you know the point of learning Latin?'
'Actually, Sir . . . No.'
'Well, in a very short time you'll all be getting interested in girls. . .'

The billiard balls clink, rain murmurs against the window, oak floor and panels glimmer, logs crackle, split, turn white, dogs wander in and out, and I sit engrossed with Carl Peterson, Dominic Medina, Dick, Sandy and the Bulldog. Yet, I repeat, the fictions were not lies: life, at its cosiest, remains charged with unlit explosives. Arthur was still headmaster when another Italian Tribune finished hanging upside down in a hooting square in 1945; and even in 1934 the brown-shirted Lower God was screaming in Berlin: 'We all suffer from the disease of mixed, contaminated blood. How can we purify ourselves and make atonement? The eternal life bestowed by the Grail is for the really pure and noble alone.' He was to add: 'It will seem, to the future, like a fairytale.'

Sometimes I desisted from a book, obstructed not by

boredom but excitement. *Don Quixote* so thrilled me that to this day I have never believed that it could sustain its beginning and have never read further.

> In a certain village in La Mancha, which I do not wish to name, there lived not long ago a gentleman — one of those who always have a lance in the rack, and ancient shield and a greyhound for coursing. His habitual diet was a stew, more beef than mutton, of hash most nights, boiled bones on Saturdays, lentils on Fridays, and a young pigeon as a Sunday treat, and on this he spent three-quarters of his income.

Certain sentences, like tunes, retained special powers, like distant hills, Gosport, or of proud ones who never turned their heads. Very slowly, I was acquiring what Rilke calls relationships instead of possessions. Ripples started interlocking, at: 'And so they buried Hector, tamer of horses' and 'There is a pleasure in the pathless woods' and

> Lars Porsena of Clusium
>   By the Nine Gods he swore
> That the great house of Tarquin
>   Should suffer wrong no more.

Faintly, I could sense that, somehow, nine gods were perfect: eleven or fourteen would spoil it.

Reading poetry in Tim Pember's English class I was groping between the vague glamour and the fitful precision of words:

> It was an Abyssinian maid,
> And on her dulcimer she play'd,
> Singing of Mount Abora.

I could not have explained but must have known, wordlessly, that this was superior to:

> It was a Hottentot maid
> And on her banjo she played,

75

Singing of Laurel and Hardy.

Wodehouse must have been the first author from whom I consciously recognized an essence particular to him alone, a flavour which continued independent of the story and, for me, really was the story, a flavour in which a single misplaced or ill-chosen word would wreck the effect: 'He missed short puts because of the uproar of the butterflies in the adjoining meadows' and '"I thought you had retired from business," said Mrs Laura Smith Maplebury, with a sniff that cracked a coffee cup' and 'She was standing scrutinizing the sofa, and heaving gently, like a Welsh rarebit about to come to the height of its fever.'

I have read a suggestion that Wodehouse's Psmith, that enigmatic, all-conquering, non-violent Dandy, may have owed something to Easton, from *The Dash to Khartoum* by G. A. Henty, whose stocky volumes occupied an entire shelf of most school libraries. Of Wodehouse, Somerset Maugham observed to Eddie Marsh that he was entertaining without being interesting, the reverse of *Crime and Punishment*.

A time would come when I would forgo sententious plots, for the poem written in class by a Cambridgeshire boy:

> Hodur, the blind god, roams about the halls,
> For that god he never knows when darkness falls.

For an unknown child's: 'Winter is when the trees are made of wood.' And for Oliver Twist seeing the upright coffins at night, like ghosts with their hands in their pockets.

Five centuries before Beckett and Pinter, the anonymous ballads made breathcatching use of allusion and implication, silence and gaps, the force of the barely mentioned (implicit in George Barker's remark that the unicorn does not exist because it has better things to do), which Ezra Pound has called the sound of the nightingale too far off to be heard:

> Beside Branxton is a brook; breathless they lie
> Gaping against the moon; their ghosts went away.

I ventured into territories of wild beauty and stark clan tradition: love threatened by blood-feud, primitive and steadfast notions of honour, the dark seducer and cruel husband, the knife, the cold season, the dark wind and worse.

'O, whaten a mountain is yon,' she said,
  'all so dreary wi' frost and snow?'
'O yon is the mountain of hell,' he cried,
  'Where you and I will go.'

6

My foremost ambitions however were to bowl very fast for England, and win a nod from Wilfred Bristow, while, not wholly smothered by leaf and rose, vague but harsh noises drifted in from the *Daily Sketch*, *Morning Post*, the *Illustrated London News*, and, in Chris's study, we examined the huge, illustrated volumes of the *Times History of the War*, in which the Southsea beggars were seen younger, complete, scrambling 'over the top' with bayonets ashine, tilting their aircraft over Amiens, over Lille, and occasionally standing tied to a post, blindfolded, sometimes in a gas-mask like the head of an aborted elephant.

We had only half-heard awareness of the League of Nations, the arrest of Gandhi, Russian famine and second Five Year Plan, the Disarmament Conferences, the Indian Round Table Conference, less romantic than it sounded, the Means Test, not comparable to the high dramas at Lord's and Headingley, the British departure from the Gold Standard — inevitably I imagined a flag of 15 carat gold, abandoned upright on a desolate shore — the ending of Free Trade. Neville Chamberlain, later so reviled, was apparently an outstanding Minister of Health, a founder of the Welfare State, but I had yet to hear of him. British engineers were paraded in Moscow for a 'Show Trial', a new and unamiable word, soon to become common, 'Apartheid' was first heard in 1929. 'Depression', in England, 'The Slump', were increasingly heard, at their loudest between 1929 and 1931, when the European banking crisis spread to

America, toppling fortunes and trebling unemployment. Vaguely I was hearing of FDR, and Hindenburg beat Hitler in the German presidential election.

More instructive for me than newspapers and talk were newsreels seen in holiday cinemas, showing Japanese strutting into Manchuria, our fleet in mutiny at Invergordon, hunger marchers tramping south, bearing a million signatures against the Means Test. Shipyards, pits, factories were a soundless wilderness. Dollars were leaving Europe, threats, uniforms and sudden death were multiplying, and had an echo at Hawkhurst in unpaid bills and abrupt disappearances. In many homes, forced cheeriness, ambiguous grins, jokes about a lack of 'tin' revived.

> No more money in the bank,
> No cute baby we can spank,
> What's to do about it?
> Let's turn out the lights and go to sleep.

Inset are two tiny period memories. Outside a railway station, ignored and unwanted amongst gleaming motor taxis, was an old cabby with shabby carriage and despondent horse, hunched in wind and rain, as if frozen. In distress, I chose him for my petty journey: he awoke, glared, swore vilely and raised his whip.

Once, when going alone beyond the school gates to the dentist, I was pelted and chased by ragged children, infuriated by privileged caps and blazers, reminding me again of the grimmer existences beyond my own, from which, in *Gold Diggers of 1933*, Joan Blondell was singing, or miming, 'Remember your Forgotten Man' against a background of shuffling, discarded war-heroes and victims of 'slump', 'depression', 'crisis', whose children now wanted to trample me.

A year or so later, Stephen Spender's poem struck home for me with direct impact:

> My parents kept me from children who were
> rough

And who threw words like stones and who
    wore torn clothes.
Their thighs showed through rags. They ran in
    the street
And climbed cliffs and stripped by the country
    streams.

I feared more than tigers their muscles like
    iron
And their jerking hands and their knees tight
    on my arms.
I feared the salt coarse pointing of those boys
Who copied my lisp behind me on the road.

They were lithe, they sprang out behind
    hedges
Like dogs to bark at our world. They threw
    mud
And I looked another way, pretending to
    smile.
I longed to forgive them, yet they never
    smiled.

7

Heard the latest? News swiftly became history which, like gods, made me feel at home in the world. Occasionally, history came very close, in our last term at Hawkhurst, one evening, commotion filled the sky and we rushed to see a technological masterpiece. The huge silvery airship, R101, Britain's counter to the German *Graf Zeppelin*, was flying over us towards India, the Air Minister on board, and Ramsay Mac's Cabinet preened for the rewards of this inaugural flight. Some of us were to confess, shamefacedly, that, in muddled spite, from a cancer in the common mind, from some inchoate rebellion, we had wished it ill-fortune.

Our elders had already achieved it. I can see George Rothery rushing next morning into the Gallery, fair hair ashine, blue eyes strong: 'The R101 has crashed.'

Political pressures, against expert advice and professional misgivings, notably the captain's, had demanded a premature flight that ended in flame and mass-death on the Beauvais hillside. Eight survived from fifty-four, then two of those died. Within hours, the homes of the widows, it was said, were being robbed, and later the dead commander Irwin allegedly communicated, through Eileen Garrett, non-scientific spiritualist medium, complicated technical evidence responsible for the disaster. The Prince of Wales, his brother the future George VI, Ramsay Mac, attended the State memorial service, together with the Empire leaders of the Imperial Conference, whom the flight was designed to impress. The remains of the airship were auctioned and the airship industry collapsed overnight.

History, yes, but one's memory can deceive. For fifty years I was convinced that, with all others in the rose-lit garden, I had seen the long, dully throbbing silver tube, very slightly head-down, somewhat too low, moving along the blue July sky of 1932, in a network of sunshine; and I wrote for this page an elaborate visual elegy. Yet, checking, I discovered the date was actually October 1930, in rainy, stormy weather conditions, so that we must have seen it at night, possibly never seen it.

8

1933. I was thirteen. Arthur drove me to London, we lunched at the RAC and there, methodical, slow, alone in the swimming bath, was who else but pale, ancient, spindle-shanked GBS, with an indifferent attendant ready to collect him should he start to dissolve.

That afternoon I had been interviewed for admission to the Royal Naval College, Dartmouth, at last meeting the Admirals. I feared I had done too well — some question about coloured shirts allowed me to speak some fluent nonsense about Mussolini, which seemed to provoke admiring smiles. I passed glumly to the medical inspection and triumphed absolutely. Utterly substandard eyesight, my appearance on the bridge would have ruined the Fleet within seconds: also muffled hints of elements of worse. A kindly doctor, holding a cloth as if to staunch my tears, explained that I could never enter the Army, let alone the Navy. I dutifully assumed a tragic mask, but said nothing to Arthur. Later he gravely informed me that I would never reach Dartmouth; he was sympathetic, he was grave, he was wise: he gave me another immense conspiratorial wink and said nothing more.

I left Hawkhurst in the summer of 1934, with sadness. My worldly simplicity had not been markedly impaired. Chris and Arthur had explained sex in friendly fashion, but leaving me stranded between incredulity and horror, with a resolution to avoid public lavatories. Arthur had unexpectedly mentioned Edward VII. Romantic friendships, or hope of them, troubled me, but vitiated boredom. I still had no Best Friend; George, Wilfred, Stanley, Byng, all had gone. A temporary pupil Jean Jacquier, shot to bits in the coming war, obsessed me: he was French, dark-haired, violet-eyed, and for a few thrilling Sundays we explored woods, dammed streams, shared meringues; but I was stammering, possessive, nervous, and he soon abandoned me for a boy called Cronk.

I had been happy amongst intelligent and good-natured people. Certainly, to rejoice in personal happiness defended by social privilege is dubious; to prefer good nature to good social arrangements is amateurish. I acknowledge that I had been granted minor elitism, in a society resounding with passionate complaints, but feel no great guilt, save in having disappointed a number of well-wishers.

A reasonable man does not object to equality, though he may reasonably dislike standardization. *Equality* is an ideal which, rather arrogantly, I neglect. I will never be as handsome as Paul Newman, as gifted as Thomas Mann, as intelligent as Isaiah Berlin, and would be embarrassed to be treated as if I were. My schools prepared me for these glum truths which I have accepted with equanimity, though without self-satisfaction, and left me proof against eloquent zealots.

I had my private estate, distillation of the real and

imaginary: Gosport, the Red Town, La Mancha, Troy, Tyburn, the Somme, Broadway with its melody . . . from where strode heroes and villains from whom it seemed unlikely I would ever escape. Most important of all, that apprehension of the powers of words. Longfellow's verse, simple, perhaps trite, yielded a lasting invitation to reflect and even build a little for myself:

> Once the Emperor Charles of Spain
> > with his swarthy, grave commanders,
> I forget in what campaign,
> Long besieged in mud and rain
> > some old frontier town of Flanders.

Five

It is difficult to speak adequately, or justly, of London. It is not a pleasant place; it is not agreeable or easy, or exempt from reproach. It is only magnificent.

Henry James

One's first impression is of a heavy city, a place of aching heads. The very name London has tonnage in it. The two syllables are two thumps of the steam hammer, the slow clump-clump of a policeman's feet, the cannoning of shunting engines, or the sound of coal thundering down the holes in the pavements of Victorian terraces.

V.S. Pritchett

Look at his window, Watson, see how the figures loom up, are dimly seen, and then blend once more into the cloud-bank. The thief and the murderer can roam London on such a day as the tiger does the jungle, unseen until he pounces, and then evident only to his victim.

Arthur Conan Doyle

1

For me, the thirties are tennis players in long white trousers, village cricket at Chalfont St Giles, Eton Wick, Bray, blazers and straw hats on crowded beaches at Brighton, Southsea, Torquay, the saxophones and muted trumpets of West End dance bands and the trumpet blues of Gershwin's 'An American in Paris', which I want played at my funeral, several times; two shilling, yellow-jacketed Hodder and Stoughton thrillers; coupled names – Clapham and Dwyer, Hobbs and Sutcliffe, Hendren and Hearne, Laurel and Hardy, Astaire and Rogers, Layton and Johnson; bandstands, with very slender conductors always playing Jerome Kern, and the songs of Gertie Miller and Gracie Fields; and a humour more fanciful, less malicious than today. 'This afternoon he asked me to be his wife, and I turned him down like a bedspread.'

My mother had returned from Persia. She was small, elegant, affectionate, easily weakened by a hard luck plea she simultaneously knew was fraudulent. A vivid amateur actress, she was musical, having trained in Germany as a concert pianist, yet without sustained interest in music: like myself, entangled in tunes, she published at least one composition, a tango. She was well-read rather than bookish, collected with fine taste oriental carpets and antique furniture. Writing this, I see a Cromwellian table, Tudor chest, Queen Anne candle-sticks, William and Mary mirror-table. She carved gardens out of desert and scrub, arranged flowers superbly. Imaginative and resourceful, she gardened and entertained long into old age, rode, played tennis, squash, golf. Politically conservative, she admired each Tory premier in turn, save one, probably feeling that women had small place in Parliament and none in Downing Street; a bias doubtless reinforced by a stint as secretary to a socialist junior minister, Edith Summerskill, whose wartime claim that butter was indistinguishable from margarine irritated a lean and suffering nation.

Born in Cairo in 1895, my mother's many sojourns in the Middle East made her assume than a handclap, a nod, a gesture, would always produce instant service and indeed entitled her to it. I myself, in riposte, was an arrogant and boring socialist, and, with the huge Labour victory in 1945, was convinced that human nature had changed, pronouncedly for the better. She had period handicaps of extravagant royalism, mechanical anti-semitism, snobbery, together with undeviating courage. For nearly three years she drove an ambulance in all seasons and perils, in wartime East London. Her letter, following the most savage onslaught of the Blitz, through which she drove unerringly for thirty-six hours, ignored this, but was enthusiastic about a pear tree she had acquired for her balcony. Almost daily, I still pass a clump of iris in a Hampstead garden, which she planted in 1938.

I have had malignant failures with human beings, mysterious to myself, seen as coldness by others; most notably with my mother, explained only partially by her absences and my boarding schools, and forcing me to ponder the limits of free will. Repeatedly, returning from school, Oxford, various homes, I would resolve to be warm, easy, responsive, yet infrequently found it possible. She made friends easily, particularly with the young, more easily and lastingly than I do, yet we failed each other. Some gaunt block obstructed us, stuck there by myself, for, against all odds, she remained charming, excitable, thrilled by some petty success of my own or the survival of some plant or bird, always hopeful, infinitely generous without the material means to back her intentions, until her sudden death in 1982, a grim Christmas twenty-four hours in which, alone with her, I still found myself wracked by my hateful silence and impatience. She had resisted the hospital with a vehemence that revealed that even she recognized that leaving her home meant, at last, the end. She was nearing ninety, yet still eager for a life she had never quite achieved. When the ambulance at last arrived, hours late, and I stood, inadequate and ashamed, she begged me to write to thank Jean and Arthur Galsworthy for their Christmas present. She died that night, leaving me to reflect that, for me, in much pain there is much retribution.

It had been an outrageous waste of spirit. Her true memorial is not her son, but her garden. My curiosity, elsewhere unsleeping, died in her presence. I would like to have questioned her about her memories: the dancing bears, the Great War, pre-1914 Germany, old country houses and gardens, and my own father, obscurely dying before my birth, and of whose appearance, talents, disposition and interests I know nothing.

Essentially, I suppose, she had from the start threatened my independence and knew too many aspects of myself that I rejected, feared, despised. Independence has created the best of my life, and has been the excuse for the nastiest.

Labour had collapsed in 1931, during the Bankers' Crisis. Britain was slowly emerging from slump under a coalition still headed by Ramsay Mac. Philip Guedalla wrote that MacDonald became his own successor and so saved England from himself. Oswald Mosley had left the Labour party, frustrated by its indifference to his sensible plans for re-employment and the rehabilitation of depressed areas, and founded the New Party in 1931, supported by John Strachey, Harold Nicolson, C.E.M. Joad, Osbert Sitwell, though these deserted when the New Party was reorganized as the British Union of Fascists, apparently with financial support from Mussolini.

I remember fragments of sight and sound: bowler hats, Homburg hats, trilbies, pork-pie hats, boaters, spats, Oxford Bags, co-respondent shoes, plus fours, Eddie Marsh's monocle; 'Amy, Wonderful Amy' in a flimsy, patched-up plane flying to Australia over shark seas, desolate mountains, heavy jungles; Lady Houston's millionaire yacht with 'Wake up, England' sparkling between masts; Astaire's top hat and cane, tunes of heady brilliance, 'Varsity Drag', 'Blue Moon', Cole Porter's:

> You're the Top, . . .
> You're Mussolini, You're Mrs Sweeney,
> You're Camembert. . .
> You're Mahatma Gandhi. . .
> You're Napoleon Brandy. . .
> You're the Top. . .

Eddie Cantor's huge dark eyes rolling as he sang 'Makin' Whoopee'.

T.S. Eliot had recently mentioned to Virginia University that 'reasons of race and culture combine to make any large numbers of free-thinking Jews undesirable', though of Jews I knew only that Ivor Cousins had said that, enviably, they lived in unparalleled luxury.

Papers still featured the undiminished Prince of Wales, and

GBS; also T.E. Lawrence, Oswald Mosley, Greta Garbo, Harold Larwood the Notts Express, Epstein, Edgar Wallace, Alex James of the Arsenal, Dixie Dean of Spurs, Mussolini, and the Chatterbox hailing Ramsay Mac as the Boneless Wonder. The *Duce*, once the timid schoolmaster, was now giving new lessons: 'In that hard and metallic word "struggle" lay the whole programme of Fascism as I dreamed of it, as I wanted it, as I created it.'

3

During school holidays in 1933 and 1934, I had to adjust myself to London, which presented beguiling questions, and intriguing nomenclature. Houses were ranged in Roads, Streets, Crescents, Closes, Mews, Greens, Bridges, Commons, Alleys, Rides, Hills, Parks, Malls, Rows, Wharfs, Paths, Terraces, Rises, Walks, Squares, Drives, Avenues, Lanes, Ways, Gardens, Precincts, Villas, Gates, Yards, Passages, each with its story, origin, sometimes the hint of a lost countryside, estate, cricket oval, custom.

Hampstead suited me. Not quite country, not absolutely town, it still offers a particular sense of roots and oddity, undeterred since its few huts and hundred pigs listed in Domesday Book. Its historian, F.L.M. Thompson, describes how the wild Heath and steep hill helped keep it a small frontier community; Defoe noted that the steepness 'did check the Humour of the Town'. Mineral waters, remembered in Flask Walk, Well Road, and probably spurious, helped make a fashionable Hanoverian spa but very soon 'its nearness to London brings so many loose women in vampt-up clothes to catch the City apprentices, that modest company are ashamed to appear here.' The writer John MacKay, added that Hampstead was 'overstocked with Jews and sharpers.' The lordly but disreputable Kit-Kat Club, which included some of my own forbears, met at the Upper Flask. Defoe observed 'more gallantry than modesty' about Hampstead Wells, as can still be seen. Despite latter-day artistic pretensions, Hampstead was long famed for trade, law, finance. In 1874 the *Pall*

Mall Gazette rated it 'half-civilized', due partly to lack of a resident nobility. Professor Thompson found that in 1901 it was the least servanted area in London in all but butlers.

Fourteen years old, less healthy than I appeared, I was soon trudging and sauntering, and, like Virginia Woolf, wondering what went on behind faces, quickly learning that history can seep through street and yard, canal and tunnel, as thickly as in field, wood, on hills and by rivers. Pilgrims' Lane, Constable Close, Leigh Hunt Cottage, Romney House, Keats Grove, Rowland Hill Street, Windmill House, Admiral's Walk. Thurlow Road commemorated an outstanding Cromwellian civil servant, long underestimated. Fleet Road stretched above the River Fleet which, in Dr Johnson's day, was stuffed with dead pigs, dead babies. In woods near the Bull and Bush was a ruined house with an upstairs padded room for a youngish man, during periods of mental breakdown, William Pitt. Crown Lodge, close to us, had allegedly belonged to Lucy Walters, Monmouth's mother. The local pub was named after Richard Steele. An alley sheltered the Chapel of the Sacred Moose, an Indian chief who arrived in James I's day and had remained, in one manifestation or another, ever since, advising adepts.

A rural flavour survived the coming of the Metropolitan and St John's Wood Railway. As happens too often to support glib social prognostications, bad motives sometimes induced useful results; excellent intentions caused blight. Civic meanness preserved the Heath, not as a trim park but as natural wilderness. A fifteen-acre farm adjoined the High Street in my grandmother's childhood, and, nearly a century later, I saw a fox's litter some three hundred yards from Hampstead Tube Station. Traditional dislike of planners preserved open spaces and architectural variety, some of it deplorable. Fitzjohn's Avenue, with its turrets and aura of East Indian nabobs, was hailed as London's equivalent of Louis Napoleon's boulevards, though no more convincingly than Mr T. Dan Smith's plan, in the early sixties, to transform Newcastle into the English Venice, with motor-roads instead of canals.

Daylight held green trees, glittering shops, tennis courts, security, but further down the hill with its pillared, commanding mansions, were darker areas: Kentish Town, Camden Town, Mornington Crescent, Chalk Farm. Here lurked the children who were rough, and those of their fathers who had survived to cheer Haig's death. Old men could still remember tales of such children being rounded up by industrial contractors and Poor Law commissioners, and deported to northern slave-hells and the colonies. The Victorian, Dr Lankaster, had asserted that in 1866, sixteen thousand women murdered their babies. In London alone, thirty-seven million articles were pawned in 1870, and I could see plenty of golden balls hanging in these shabby streets and rookeries. Scraps of sadness or infamy, like hints of human sacrifice lurking within the charming fairytale, or the ever-bleeding head buried beneath magnificent Rome.

Safe frontiers wavered as dusk hovered, thickened. Greedy for the adventures I simultaneously feared, I would move away from the lights and step cautiously into barbarism. The North London Railway arches were the visible frontiers, though no defence against the coalmen, railway workers, Irish unemployed, the drunks on area steps, doubtless the 'plug uglies' of whom I had read, with nothing to recommend them.

From pubs were growled songs at odds with the dainty melodies of Coward, Gershwin, Kern, Cole Porter:

> So it's up the rope I go, up I go,
> So it's up the rope I go, yes I go,
> And those bastards down below
> Will yell 'Sam, we told you so,
> Yes, we told you so.'
> God damn their eyes.

This municipal fastness had long traditions of violence: from the navvies hacking out railway and canal, from Irish immigrants assailed by Scots and English, from the General Strike, when a local communist MP was jailed for sedition. Now a man stood with a tray of matches, *blind*, yet he cursed my grey suit and school tie, a handless giant watched me from behind a broken pillar and I remembered Ivor's tale that behind a jeweller's window was always a small guillotine: you

89

smash the glass, grope, and then. . .

For a lonely boy, life seemed dramatic without being sensational. There were no absolute strangers or opposites: everyone was a Sandy Arbuthnot liable to remove his mask at any moment, an unknown person suddenly giving me money, a Regal-Zonophone record, a copy of *Bevis*. We were all spies in undisclosed minor campaigns with the banal and horrible inextricably entwined. That locked door concealed a scaffold; a bright hoarding disguised a charnal house.

I wandered, explored, feeling myself a Dr David Livingstone in an Africa alternately dark and light. Along the canal, not yet a public footpath but accessible, were ancient wharves, warehouses, silent factories, within earshot of the smokey, bumping railway that had eliminated old meadows, drastically spliced the hamlets, greens, homes, and supposedly attenuated the class divisions. More stories could be found. Macclesfield Bridge was 'the Blow up', where, 1874, a barge loaded with gunpowder exploded, killing all hands. Barges glided past, as Masefield had seen them as a boy in Hereford, painted with traditional fancies: roses, jewels, candles, blowsy nymphs, Britannia like a lapsed angel, a Venetian Moor, castles; the brass shining, portholes allowing glimpses of tiny homes within.

I had long to wait before encountering David Thompson's revelations of the cost to the Gaelic navvies who cut water-beds, laid tracks. Usually homeless, swindled by greedy employers, reckless, killed and maimed at work, often thick with smallpox, feared by householders, they had their generous heroes, legends, rites. For marriage, the couple jumped over a broomstick, then were bedded by the guests. In *In Camden Town* David Thompson quotes an early nineteenth-century Paddington missionary journal which observed 'that coachmen, guards, hackney-coachmen, chaise-drivers, porters, waiters, ostlers, boots, sailors, boaters and wharfingers became an easy prey to Jews, crimps, publicans and harlots'. Ostlers too had an evil reputation.

Beyond the dark arches, dangers were small, personal, furtive. I had not yet seen racial and political furies, the East End hoots, stones, blood during Mosley's Fascist marches, though in 1931 some thirty-five towns suffered brutality in clashes between police and unemployed. In these streets were not the hunger-marchers, but some deadly, pitted women, 'I'll give you a good time, dearie,' while scowling, listless youths straggled outside pubs with names apparently strayed from some sinister common: The Gypsy Queen, The Mother Shipton, The Mother Red Cap. Here, Bulldog Drummond hunted the Black gang, Sandy passed by, dyed and bearded, shabby men at dirty windows reported to Mr Drakshoff. The contrast between high, light, genteel Hampstead, and this brooding, messy greyness eventually became a novel, *The Dark Arches*, which I dispatched importantly to the literary agents A.P. Watt, who returned it the same week, accompanied by 'Stamps for Postage would oblige'.

I did not know it, but Dickens had briefly schooled and lived in Camden Town, Marx in Maitland Park, Engels in Regent's Park Road; further up the hill were, or had been, the Muirs, Galsworthy, H.G. Wells, D.H. Lawrence, Masefield, Yeats, Gerald du Maurier, Gracie Fields, Conrad Veidt. In a dingy bookshop opposite the Playhouse Cinema, where I saw Judy Garland's first film, a tall, thin, abrupt man tried unsuccessfully to sell me *Trader Horn in Madagascar* when I wanted Wodehouse's *A Damsel in Distress*. He was, one day, to send me the first book I ever reviewed, outside school, and, to my astonishment, paid me £1: George Orwell.

4

I explored the old Antrim Grove public library. Ill-lit, hushed, it had subfusc glamour, like a temple of some never quite named underworld deity. All books were bound in identical black which seemed to render *The Bab Ballads, The Invisible Man, The Garden of Allah, The Constant Nymph, What Katy Did* separate volumes of the same book. I therefore chose at random: to read was more important than mere titles. I bored through single shelves of books, on this principle, often bewildered, fatigued, sometimes engrossed or startled: Wodehouse, Walpole, Lew Wallace, Edgar Wallace, Wells,

Wasserman, Werfel, P.F. Warner, Alice Werner, William Watson, Weyman, Mrs Humphrey Ward. Perhaps fortunately, Virginia Woolf was absent.

Gods still troubled me, arousing loyalty to naked, impossible forms glimmering in woods, above fountains, heroes radiant or sulky, heroines trim and vindictive – the Great Goddess has aspects of terror. I desired voyages through purple seas towards vine-clad, panther-infested shores where oracles spoke all tongues save my own. Gods remained more remarkable than God or Jesus though conceivably less real. Cursing a blameless fig tree, swearing at Pharisees and lawyers, 'getting baity' with Peter, Jesus was unattractive but plausible. Gods were, and were not, like Best Friends.

A title at Antrim Grove appealed to me, a reminder of the Lower God: *The Death of the Gods*, by Dmitri Merezhkowsky, today long vanished from British libraries. Much of it I could not understand, but again this meant romantic mystery, fruitful gaps. The story was that of the Roman Emperor, Julian the Apostate, and his lost campaign against Christianity, to restore the Olympians. Here was Nelson's Annual rewritten for adults. Reading, I hated the spiteful Christians, unloving and unwashed, as they smashed the silver statue of Diana, in fury at that beauty, that nakedness! 'This forty years I have never washed, that I might not see my nakedness, nor fall into temptation. And yet coming into cities, straight one perceives these accursed gods without a rag on them. How long must we endure these devilish temptations?' I was at one with Julian as he watched the goddess melt in the fire, the drops of silver rotting on her face as if in a death-sweat, and the lips still keeping their invincible smile.

This book underlay much of my adolescent writing, and I still have a story 'After Merezhkowsky', printed in my school literary magazine. I felt Julian's failure contributed to the elimination of healthy Mediterranean light, a superficial attitude largely derived from a misunderstanding of the 'Dark Ages'. I was a novice, puzzled by too much of life, perhaps by too much life, and certainly fascinated by failure.

Newsreels were still the great teachers for those post-war times, and I was starting to see wider perspectives. Many European monarchies had vanished for ever in blood and confusion, officers hiding their ribbons and burying their epaulettes from peoples deceived by too much gold braid. Much of the confusion remained, many knives were out in Central Europe. In the old Court Cinema, today a filling-station, with its fourpenny seats and ushers regularly squirting us with disinfectants, and at the similar Kentish Town Gaisford, I had seen the Stavisky riots in Paris 1933, the Reichstag in flames, SA hooligans burning books and musical scores on the streets – Thomas and Heinrich Mann, Heine, Mendelssohn, Offenbach – and, deep in Manchuria, Japanese beheading Chinese: the officer raised his gloved hand, the sword fell, the head leapt, to be caught by a sort of scrum-half. I saw Alexander of Yugoslavia assassinated at Marseilles in 1934, dying in an open car; FDR flashing smiles like banknotes; the riven corpse of Dillinger, in 1934, the American Public Enemy Number One. I was to see revolutions, civil wars, stampeding crowds, Ministers of the Interior fleeing to the interior. In these my favourite cinemas the dirtiness of the screen, outspread like a lodger's sheet, made all actors blotched, all actresses half-caste, blending into me dark whorls of grime. There were, of course, other delights. 'Delicious debauchery' murmured Charles Laughton, as Nero, watching Claudette Colbert bathe in milk in *The Sign of the Cross*.

All this put my imagination at the mercy of the grandiose, sensational and bizarre, in which smaller but vital clues to existence were easily overlooked. A look exchanged between frozen-heads at dinner, a master's over-casual remark, a man warming his hands at an empty grate, might take years to convey to me some inner significance, teaching the truth of Flaubert's belief that the theatre is not an art but a secret. Dr Johnson's observation that Charles XII was extraordinary without being great would have been a useful brake on a vulgarity always threatening my make-up.

Murderers concerned me, in such books as *Famous Trials*, and *Twelve Monstrous Criminals*, which began with Nero. Neal Cream, Dr Crippen, Major Armstrong slowly poisoning a tiresome wife. Arthur Seddon, frantically making the masonic sign to the judge, vain, chatty Alfred Arthur Rouse who burnt an unknown man in a car in 1930 and departing, doomed himself by wishing a passer-by goodnight, unable to restrain his salesman's charm. I remember my shudder of excitement at the *Daily Express*'s headline: 'Rouse's Last Desperate Fight for Life' and I now oppose capital punishment not for the effect it has upon the killer, but for what it did to me and probably almost all children.

These murderers were civilian counter-heroes, perhaps antidotes to the clear-eyed, clean-limbed stalwarts of *Chums* and the *Boys' Own Paper*. At the last they were often presented with some wistful pathos, allowing, of course, for the prevalence of ghost-writers. Another salesman, George Joseph Smith, thought it best to insure his brides before drowning them in a bath and playing hymns over their corpses on a portable organ. From the condemned cell he addressed his lover, Miss Pegler, in terms — his own or another's — which, common enough, seemed designed to make himself the injured party:

Dear Love, Your pure heart and conscience free from stain helps me to believe that, whilst memory holds a seat within your sacred brow you will remember me. You are the last person in the world to whom I shall write . . . I could write volumes of pathos prompted by the cruel position wherein I am now placed. But I have too much respect for your feelings to do so . . . Don't be alone on the last day, when I shall have left this weary ark behind, where perjury, malice, spite, vindictiveness, prejudice, and all other earthly ills will have done their best, and can harm me no more . . . I truly believe and feel that my sincere prayers have been answered . . . I shall have an extraordinary peace, perfect peace. May an old age, serene and bright, and as lovely as a Lapland night, lead thee to thy grave.

94

6

Beloved places in Devon, Hants, Kent, Sussex, Bucks — and an old walled quince-tree garden in Chalfont St Giles — were never obliterated by the stony London of the mid-thirties, but were etherealized into a mental Hesperides to which I could sail without the formalities of travel. I at least had green, empty Primrose Hill, elegant Regent's Park and, above all, the Heath. The kingfisher still flashed over Kenwood Lake; foxes, owls, woodpeckers, a mighty parliament of rooks, dwelled in the woods, outside which sheep still munched and wandered. In Golders Hill Park a peacock merged with the herbaceous beds, then suddenly awoke, as if the flowers had decided to move elsewhere. Riders were sunlit against hillside and cloud, kites swung, as they still do, above Parliament Hill, their tails scribbling ghosts, snakes, spectres, on the blue and white air. The green dome of a Highgate church enticed me, like distant Gosport, floating through mists, through sunshine, never quite near enough to reach.

The Heath has never lacked dangers — in the sixties a youth was found crucified — but it was only from canal and arch that I knew fear. On the Heath in 1935, nannies gossiped beneath trees, as they had done at Southsea, and children formed their transient loves and conspiracies. Once a young man, bald, slightly painted, murmured, 'Will you show me yours?' but assuming he was a painter, I smiled and said that I had left mine at home.

Neo-Classical art with its woods, pools, nakedness, notably from Tiepolo and Titian, did little more than make me yearn to get raped. More powerful were Madame Tussaud's Horrors, with a man seated on a spike which protruded through his stomach. The Tower was even better, though the shape of the executioner's axe puzzled me, and the block seemed too small, reminding me of Lady Jane Grey blindfolded and on her knees, fumbling, murmuring, 'Where is it, where is it?' Onlookers were astonished that so small a body gushed so much blood. In the Armoury, more moving than the shining, decorated cannon and engraved swords were two scythe-blades tied to

95

poles, from Sedgemoor.

I would sit in prim teashops over crumpets and honey, where sedate trios played 'Lover Come Back to Me', 'I Give My Heart', themes from 'Rhapsody in Blue', and, rashly, 'Tiger Rag'; less appealing was Violet Laurence Hope's 'Pale Hands I Love', elsewhere bellowed by Clara Butt, crooned by Rudolph Valentino. Violet Hope was wife to General Nicholson who crossed Indian rivers on backs of crocodiles and on his death she allowed herself two months to settle her literary affairs, then swallowed poison.

The arcane language of pub signs opened up a past simultaneously colourful and faded: Red Lion of Gaunt, Wheatsheaf of Exeter, White Horse of Arundel, White Swan of Cleves. Inset on pavements were round wrought-iron coal-hole covers, each with number, lettering, often embellished with foliage, scrolls and other traditional motifs. My dour and literal mind was gratified by realizing that Lombards had inhabited Lombard Street, fens had covered Fenchurch Street, Romans had built walls at London Wall and Covent Garden had once been a convent garden.

Promoted to long trousers, preparing for my first term in a new school, certain that the world had eyes for me alone, I ventured into cavernous side-streets with small, crammed shops for fishermen, pigeon fanciers, collectors of parrots, tortoises, marmosets, hamsters, the white mice so often featured in Edwardian school stories, snakes – my friend Marion Elmes would teach with a grass snake at her wrist; male, she said, with disputable authority. I loved the friendly, miscellaneous stores with their windows stuffed with packets of flower seeds – promising hollyhocks poking the sky, marigolds firing the world, pansies like sad, expensive tigers – and foreign stamps, biscuits, Mazawattee Tea, round silvery tins of Gibbs' Dentifrice ('Protect those Ivory Castles'); Fox's Glacier Mints, vast Gobstoppers, Carter's Little Liver Pills, Codliver Oil and Malt, marbles, all stripes and depths; royal photographs, old cigarette cards, 'Craven A' cigarettes, rows of books to be borrowed at tuppence a week, written by Zane Gray, Denise Robins, Mrs Henry de la Pasteur, Ethel M. Dell, Gene Stratton Porter. More titles patter back: *Freckles, Lord*

Tony's Wife, Paddy the Next Best Thing, The Girl of the Limberlost, The Secret of the Everglades, The King of the Speedway ('where others faltered, Harverson smashed through'), *The Keeper of the Bees, Rebecca of Sunnybrook Farm*. I loved the Fruit Bon Bons in their bright, pictorial wrappings: one very early memory is of my mother at a high window tossing them down at me on a daisy-covered lawn, and they seemed culled from an enchanted garden. I could buy, and sometimes did, *Peg's Paper* and *Tit Bits* and learn that someone had dribbled a hard-boiled egg from Bodmin to Morecombe with his nose; and fourpenny Sexton Blake paperbacks: *The Lincoln's Inn Murder*, all mists and looming, walking oblongs, and Blake leaving a lighted cigarette on a darkened window ledge to trick the killer into thinking he was still standing there, and a powerful story in which cocaine was heaped in a cage of thin glass. You had only to break the pane and reach over, avoiding, of course, the coiled watchful viper.

There were wig-makers, picture framers, taxidermists, hatters, dyers, dolls' hospitals, vets — one now replaced by 'canine psychologist' — grubby postcards advertising palmists, clairvoyants, crystalgazers and 'Edith'. Street stalls sold clothes, whelks, shrimps, sponges, cracked gramophone records of Paul Whiteman, Caruso, John McCormick. Lamplighter and Muffin Man had apparently disappeared but not cat's meat men, organ-grinders, gipsies, dutch-auctioneers, harpists, contortionists, men tearing telephone directories apart crossways, eel-skinners, knife-sharpeners, flower-vendors like Maggie in Hampstead High Street, giving change according to the appearance of the customer.

The dead don't die, wrote D.H. Lawrence, they look on and help. They were always near: Nelson on his column; Richard I outside Parliament, which, had it existed in his day, he would surely have closed; Dr Johnson in Fleet Steet; Charles I in Whitehall, pursued by Lionel Johnson's poem:

> Alone he rides, alone.
> The fair and fatal King:
> Dark night is all alone,
> That strange and solemn thing.

Despite the long trousers, I was not sufficiently venture-some to search for Wapping Old Stairs where hanged pirates had dried in the sun and Jeffreys had tried to hide during the Revolution. It was said, though by Ivor, that Guy's Hospital had his gallstone, the size of a cricket ball; and that he had perpetually to drink cider to keep it afloat. *Tit Bits* encouraged me to believe that a rich baroness, friend of Dickens, haunted a Covent Garden bank. A small cross at St James' Palace Yard marked 'the leprous virgin' buried beneath.

All is movement. The dead slip in and out of life. The very Heath changes complexion with the Bank Holiday fairs, the clashing roundabouts and helter-skelter, yards of candyfloss, the dodgems, raucous music, the board with pound notes outspread and the blunted darts with which to claim them, the cod and whitebait fried, perhaps, in the Fat Lady's sweat, the wooden café where the owner licks the knife before cutting the bread, her taciturnity suggesting that she had once licked it too fiercely. Night has naked lamps and gas-flares through which the wild horses rise and fall, children look sharp and old, sudden violence erupts, a scream behind a tent submerges us in the old, brutal London, older than the Ripper, older than Fred Manning at judgement: 'He moaned, I never liked him well. And I battered his head with a ripping chisel.' Voices are abroad, as if from the marsh and river locked beneath London's grandeur, the underground hells where naked Victorian 'Toshers' in sewer and tunnel, lantern-lit catacombs, prodded for coins, iron, bones of mammoth and tiger, black mud seeking their throats and the stench turning solid.

Hot lines through chinks of Time reached back to the roaring beggar-ghettoes which acknowledged no Tudor writ, where Westminster and Lambeth dared not intrude. The London of gibbet, mauled bears swaying on hot coals, maimed acrobats, child pimps and whores, the prize-fighters slamming each other bare-knuckled through seventy rounds. Boys and girls were trained as whores in Flash Houses, some of which are still standing. To impersonate a Chelsea pensioner or to consort with a gipsy had legally entailed the gallows. I could imagine well enough the ballad cries, trade cries, huzzas, threats — to the lord in his carriage, the felon in his cart — the yells of 'Wilkes and Liberty', the outlaws in their impregnable rookeries, Fagin in his kitchen, in Newgate: 'what right have they to butcher me?'. The swarming rag-and-boners, mountebanks, body-snatchers, vile landlords and their diseased tenants clinging to a rope, at which they slept upright, for the charge of an extra penny. A rival civilization, not dead, as riot and protest regularly demonstrate, and which may outlive us. In 1979 I read of Miss Corling, a housemother jailed at eighteen for poisoning three partially blind children. 'I was,' she explained, 'fed up.'

7

I am still continuing those early explorings, delighting in names and allusions. A Celtic god, Bel, remembered in Billingsgate, the smoothfield, used for jousting, and, as Smithfield, for burnings and boilings of religious dissidents, thinkers and nuisances; the churches – St Mildred Poultry, St Michael-at-Plea, St Andrew by the Wardrobe (I was early perplexed by Edward II's addiction to ruling 'through the wardrobe': did it have secret holes?) St Andrew Undershaft, St Michael Crooked Lane, St Nicholas Flee Shambles, St Mary Axe, St Anne-in-the-Willows, St Nicholas all Forlorn; St Katherine Cree held annual service for the rescue from a lion of Lord Mayor John Gregor; Southwark Cathedral, with its recumbent *gisante*, starkly emaciated beneath its trappings, was to instance Whitman's 'Hell under the skull-bones; Death under the breast-bone'. A link with Hilda French was St Paul's, Covent Garden, 'the handsomest barn in London', where lay Grinling Gibbons, hero of one of her stories. 'Kensal Green' attracted me, from Chesterton's poem, inappropriate to my then station, praising national singularity expressed by excess of ale.

> For there is good news yet to hear and fine things to be seen,
> Before we go to Paradise by way of Kensal Green.

Here was an epitaph to Mr Punch's biographer and Dickens'

illustrator, George Cruikshank, who would have displeased Chesterton by being 'For thirty years a Total Abstainer and Ardent Pioneer by Pencil, Wood and Pen of Universal Abstinence from Intoxicating Drinks.' More grimly incised is St Sepulchre's where the bellman tolled for the last night of the condemned. I read that they would hear an admonitory sermon, seated with their coffins beside them. Who could have devised so macabre a ritual, who given the order? Dickens mentioned that in Newgate Chapel a portion of the burial service was 'on some dreadful occasions' performed over the quick and not upon the dead. A gentleman, with perhaps more charity, or wealth, than imagination, had left fifty pounds for the regular recitation of:

> All you that in the condemned cell do lie
> Prepare you, for tomorrow you shall die.
> Watch all, and pray,
> The hour is drawing near,
> That you before the Almighty must appear.
>
> Examine well yourselves: in time repent,
> That you may not to eternal flames be sent.

Always I was breathing in more than could at first be recognized: the useless, the unforgettable, the unmentionable.

Six

The true educator gives you access to something in yourself which is quite incapable of being educated. He does not shape it for you but helps you unchain it.

Nietzsche

The best schools in the world are the English Public Schools, and they are dreadful.

Talleyrand

At school, friendship is a passion. It entrances the being, all loves of after-life can never bring its rapture. . .
What tenderness and what devotion, what insane sensitiveness, and what frantic sensibility, what earthquakes of the heart and whirlwinds of the soul are confined in that simple phrase, a schoolboy's friendship.

Disraeli

'Then he's a first-class, six-cylindered, copper-bottomed highbrow. A gentlemanly Communist. An intellectual who doesn't forget to shave. The patron of every new fad in painting and sculpture and writing. Mighty condescending about all that ordinary chaps like you and me like, but liable to enthuse about monstrosities, provided that they're brand-new and for preference foreign. I should think it was a genuine taste, for he has that kind of rootless, marginal mind. He backs his fancy too. For years he has kept the — going' (Macgillivray mentioned a peevishly superior weekly journal), 'and he imports at his own expense all kinds of exponents of the *dernier cri*. His line is that he despises capitalism, as he despises all orthodoxies, but that as long as the beastly thing lasts, he will try to make his bit out of it, and spend the proceeds in hastening its end.'

John Buchan

1

I enjoy a paragraph in Evelyn Waugh's *Scott-King's Modern Europe*:

Granchester is not the most illustrious of English public schools, but it is, or, as Scott-King would maintain, was, entirely respectable; it numbers a dozen or so famous men among its old boys, who, in general, declare without apology: 'I was at Granchester' – unlike the sons of lesser places, who are apt to say: 'as a matter of fact I was at a place called ——. You see, at the time my father. . .'

Public schools are denounced for Dr Arnold's preference for character over brains, so at odds with French and German educationalists. This puzzles me, when I remember those PhDs of Gestapo officials at Treblinka, Belsen, Auschwitz; and the high IQs of most of those condemned at Nuremburg. The twentieth century is strewn with millions of dead, despatched by those of high intelligence and low, scarcely visible, character.

They are also accused of promoting conformity, though anecdotes trotted out since the eighteenth century derive largely from the eccentric, the singular, the half-mad, together with a cool and snobbish rudeness like that of the Etonian, Beau Brummell, with his opinion, to the footman, of his host's champagne: 'Some more of that cider'.

Though engendering considerable fantasy, even myth, these places were undeniably philistine and perhaps still are, though I can imagine chapel and quad now vibrating with pot-parties and indeed vibrators; rugger fields transformed to allotments; headmasters reading *Lolita* to bored classes; study orgies of goat's milk, nut-cutlets and endive, and thin voices singing Gaelic.

The long national decline has been blamed squarely on a privileged governing class. In a symposium on Public Schools, Lord Vaizey erupted: 'The patronizing effortless air of Wykhamists who, more than any other group, have brought this country to its knees by their foolish advice and politics . . . has probably been responsible for more ill-feeling between classes than any body since the Russian aristocracy.' In the same book, *The World of the Public School*, Dr Anthony Storr coldly recalls conformist patterns, lack of privacy, undemocratic hierarchies, yet rejects much conventional patter about mother-fixated homosexuals and queries some rather glib salesmanship of co-education.

My own teachers displayed and fostered sexual reticence, discouraged emotional candour, emphatically between different age groups, and I have wondered how many of their charges enjoyed exciting marriages or sexual experiment. Though my own marriage to a sensitive and intelligent girl with a delightful and humorous daughter failed, entirely through myself, I am reluctant to unload the blame on to my schools. If Freud has validity, the damage was done long before school entry. I probably enjoy sex as much as my non-public school coevals, but am more interested in Augustus' achievements than in the irresponsibility of Antony and Cleopatra; I can imagine dedicating myself to a major breakthrough in art, politics, science, social conditions or sport, but scarcely in sex.

The schools have also been praised, often for the wrong reasons. I learn from Paul Johnson that the Duke of Wellington's claim that Waterloo was won on the playing fields of Eton originated when the college lacked any such fields, and emerged from a garbled version of a French translation of 'I really believe that I owe my spirit of enterprise to the tricks I used to play in the garden.'

They can also be attacked by outsiders who fail to distinguish between what should happen, yet frequently does not. Ted Morgan's biography, describing Winston Churchill at Harrow, mentions 'the humiliation and inculcation of servility that derived from fagging'. His example is ill-judged. Beaten by his fag-master, a future bishop, Churchill remarked cheerfully, 'I shall be a greater man than you.' For myself, fagging brought a virtually unearned income of cakes, cribs, hard cash.

2

Haileybury College is in green, loosely-wooded Hertfordshire above the quiet River Lea with such anglers' pubs as The Fish and Eels, and alongside a reputed Roman road and the Domesday village of Hertford Heath, in the ancient manor of Hailey – 'Two villeins with two bordars have there half a plough-land. There are three cottars and one slave. One plough-land of meadow, pasture for the cattle, woods for 50 pigs, from the weir 50 eels.'

Hertfordshire had been firmly Puritan during the Civil War, and this I could trace on *exeats*, cycling between churches. Mr Humiliation Scratcher had lived at Ware, Mr Mephibosheth Lamprey at Datchworth, and, a little further on, Mr Lamentation Caudle.

The College originally served the East India Company, in which my ancestors had some part, more concerned with the Bengali loot than with military heroism. After the Mutiny and the political extinction of John Company, the College was reconstituted as a Public School, though retaining Indian links. In my day the most valued Old Boy was Field Marshal Lord Allenby. Excluded was Erskine Childers, of *The Riddle of the Sands*, for the solecism of suffering execution during the Irish 'troubles', and the most underrated was 'Major Attlee', then Leader of the Opposition.

Clement Attlee had learnt socialism while serving the Haileybury Mission, a working boys' club in Stepney, where he was later Mayor. Ironically, he, more than any other individual, worked to end the British Raj. The contempt thrown on him at Haileybury in the thirties rallied me to his side. He seemed to me a good man – a do-gooder, as a later period would put it, usually with a sneering intimation that a do-harmer is preferable; the same voice that rates badly-made art above well-made. Haileybury was not alone in its judgement. Kenneth Harris's biography gives telling instances. 'A little mouse,' asserted the socialist, Hugh Dalton. 'A miserable little man': Lord Beaverbrook. 'A small man': Field Marshal Lord Wavell. 'A cowardly cur': Neville Chamberlain. George Orwell wrote, 'Attlee reminds me of nothing so much as a recently dead fish, before it has had time to stiffen.' Before the 1945 General Election, Harold Laski, Labour Chairman, told him: 'You are a grave handicap to our hopes.' Having routed Winston Churchill with one of the most effective broadcasts of the age, Attlee had to suffer Herbert Morrison's complaint, 'We cannot have this man as our leader.' Some years later, Aneurin Bevan declared, 'Attlee never did anything.'

'A modest little man with a great deal to be modest about,' his chief opponent thought, but Attlee was a veteran of Gallipoli where he must have heard disappointing comments on the mighty Winston himself. He possessed what I so much admire and perhaps admire too much: staying power. Of himself, he wrote:

> Few thought he was even a starter,
> There were many who thought themselves smarter,
> But he ended PM,
> CH and OM,
> An earl and a Knight of the Garter.

Physical mediocrity belied his toughness. In Flanders he threatened to shoot an officer for cowardice. As socialist Premier, he used troops during a dock strike. He decided to make Britain an Atomic Power, without reference to the people, to Parliament or most of the Cabinet.

Years later, his sustained opinion of Russia as cruel and incompetent had weight with me, with the moral that third-rate politicians with first-rate ideas can be a public nuisance, and that cruelty does not cease to be cruelty because it succeeds in building a drain. During my schooldays, the virtues of the German *autobahn* and the Russian Metro and

White Sea Canal were incessantly trumpeted, but the incidence of slave labour was underplayed. Similarly, in their vast book on Russia, the socialist Webbs virtually ignored the secret police and capital punishment.

Though I rather too grandly called myself socialist — muddled sympathies with beggars, hunger-marchers, unemployed, were entangled with youthful hostility to conventional authority and my mother's prejudices — I had little comprehension of its meaning, and now I have less. Louis Napoleon, Adolf Hitler, Lenin, Rosa Luxemburg, Stalin, Trotsky, Marx, Bukharin, Castro, GBS, Wells, Molotov, Beria, Mao, Harold Wilson, Attlee . . . called themselves socialists, but few had much in common and fewer would have liked each other. Attlee, by not claiming too much, clarified, for me, much more. He, like a Lincoln, Jefferson, Jaurès, was more truly and wisely revolutionary than the ranting bigots who, like unimaginative schoolmasters, reach for the cane and reach too often. I am always astonished that European 'progressives' so consistently look for guidance to Robespierre, Napoleon, Marx, Lenin, rather than Cromwell, Jefferson, Jaurès, Luxemburg. Robespierre's belief in 'the Despotism of Liberty', in as much as I can understand it, is foreign to my temperament. A passage from Orwell clinks about in my mind: 'People always say "under socialism", looking forward to being on top, with all the others underneath, being told what is good for them.'

Meditating on this, I read that, after electoral defeat, Anthony Wedgwood Benn declared 'Politics is above personalities.' This seems ludicrous. What separates humans from ants is precisely that the validity of institutions, sects, ideas, depends on the calibre of their staff and thinkers. 'Power,' wrote Alfred the Great, 'be not good unless he be good who holds it.' His knowledge of men and affairs, crisis and decision, is unrivalled by any living parliamentarian.

As for Attlee, I came to compare him with an unlikely figure: Wellington. How so? It is an offshoot of Kenneth Harris' observation that Attlee would have preferred a moral society led by aristocrats, to an immoral society led by collectivists. Attlee's 'We had a fine welcome in Dublin, where I signed a treaty while the family shopped' is akin to

Wellington's postscript to his brother, 'I forget whether I mentioned that I have been made a Duke.' Both men loathed armchair theorists, combined aloofness with the common touch, and as 'Uncle Clem' and 'Mr Duke' were liked by children. Both, sometimes with dry wit, rated Party interests lower than national and international well-being. Both accepted pain stoically, and political set-backs without rancour. The aristocrat would have accepted the unostentatious solicitor's son's dislike of 'appealing to cupidity and stupidity', though Attlee might have jibbed at the Iron Duke's action, told by his biographer Elizabeth Longford, when, triumphant in Paris, he was seen 'picking up some tiny, dirty French child from the boulevards and eating something horrible it offered him'. I learnt from Attlee, Nansen, Jaurès, Chekhov, that agnosticism or atheism, no less than religion, can promote generosity and charity, and that leadership need not always be identified with vanity, thuggery, rhetoric, greedy pressure-groups and the dishing out of honours to palpable crooks. Good government should not be exciting government.

I have again to confess my share in social unfairness. With many of my friends I can associate my youth not with first-hand artistic masterpieces or inspired teaching or access to unusual scholarship, but with glowing gardens, great trees, water and hedges, satisfying buildings. Nothing, of course, was unalloyed. There are always busybodies, sly or hectoring. Since Tudor times, a Nosey Parker has been one of the types most resented.

3

The principal architect of Haileybury was the early eighteenth-century William Wilkins who designed the National Gallery's neo-classical facade and dome, castigated by the *Literary Gazette* as 'half barbarous, half Grecian and half Gothic'; Downing College, Cambridge; University College, London; the Ionic columns of St George's Hospital and, for my college, the Ionic portico, the long frontage styled from the Erechtheum: a white and pale, long-lined facade which speaks directly of the calmness, simplicity and self-assurance of his employers. My art master, Wilfrid Blunt, botanist, biographer, *lieder* singer, painter, curator, a close friend of Arthur and 'Muffet' Harrison, wrote in 'The Haileybury Buildings' in 1936: 'Wilkins gave us a fine and dignified place to live in, we have spent a century trying, very successfully, to spoil it.' Wilkins' successors added red-brick functional nastiness and many ugly details, doubtless to remind us that life is imperfect, hell exists, and even young gentlemen stand condemned before God.

'Wilkins,' Wilfrid continues, was 'a man of sensibility and culture, and he built for gentlemen.' Arriving at Haileybury in September 1934, I myself spent as little time contemplating Wilkins as I did testing myself for marks of a gentleman, but, as at Hawkhurst and Uffculme, I must have absorbed some awareness of spacious freedoms and proportions, contrasts of lawn and stone, column and frieze, tree and river. I did consciously enjoy afternoon lights on the Master's oriental trees and willow ponds, bronze, green, crimson, as the Madrigal Society sang 'Shoot soft, Sweet Dove, for fear you shoot alone', the willow itself derived from a cutting of a tree above Napoleon's grave.

I committed an aesthetic gaffe in admiring the Victorian dome of the Chapel which blatantly outrages Wilkins' pure line. 'I see you have an observatory here,' a visitor remarked. Wilfrid reflects that 'it is sometimes assumed that architectural ugliness is usually the result of economy. This is fallacious. It generally costs quite a lot of money to make a building really ugly, as the Chapel showed.'

4

My Haileybury sojourn began with another medical inspection. 'Come in, my boy,' chuckled Dr Lemprière, 'I've been doctor here twenty-five years. Only twenty-five boys have died.' He poked and prodded, as they had done at the Admiralty, and, once again, I saw a slight frown, some arcane questions, a dissatisfied pause, a shake of the head, but with nothing definite disclosed, save that I was very soon forced in spectacles, on the insistence of a science master, H.G. Roberts, 'Bloody R', who erroneously believed that my resistance to science derived from inability to read his handwriting.

I endured, and indeed survived, the customary rituals — Officers Training Corps, Cold Baths, Runs and Games, which I loved. Cricket and rugger enabled me to leap free of the earth, dive into swift, unreflective elation, and I thoroughly understand the ambition of the unathletic Harold Nicolson to make 99, LBW, against Australia, though I would prefer Hit Wicket.

Life proved not gross but cheerfully hearty. Neville Cardus's *Cricket* was compulsory reading, but so was John Strachey's edition of Marx's *Capital.* My favourite meal, today seldom offered, remains blackened fishcakes, baked beans, crumpets, blackened sausages, bacon, fried potatoes, marrow and ginger jam, cream and jam sponge role, all on the same plate.

Cultural opportunities were offered, not invariably accepted. I remember a Gordon Jacob orchestral premiere, visiting quartets, many visiting theatricals, including a group from the Comédie Française. Plays were regularly acted by ourselves. Also, visits from Charles Williams, speaking on William Blake with cyclonic energy, so that I began to think, rather uneasily, that he was Blake himself. I remember an Old Boy, Robert Speaight, talking on Thomas Becket — he was then starring in *Murder in the Cathedral* — and a talk with Frank Vosper, another Old Boy, who had acted with Conrad Veidt in *Jew Süss*, and later vanished mysteriously at sea. There were visits by St John Ervine, the vivid, even passionate John Allen from the Communist Unity Theatre, the painter Lynton Lamb, Basil Jellicoe (another Old Boy), saintly social worker in the East End, Geoffrey Crowther, editor of the *Economist.* Attlee occasionally appeared for VIth form discussions. Wilfrid Blunt's Arts Society dissolved barriers of rank and age as, under an El Greco and a destination board detached from Waterloo Station, lounging on sumptuous cushions, we listened to Toscanini broadcasts, talks on Braque and Picasso.

I did not display my own hankerings for George Scott-Wood and his Six Swingers, jazzing up Handel, and Nat Gonella hurling his Georgians through 'Momma Won't Allow It'.

Still seeking a Best Friend I had long weeks of controlled euphoria, periodically disrupted by bouts of glumness. These I preferred to rate as poetic despair, comparing myself to Lytton Strachey's Essex: 'The blood ran through his veins in vigorous vitality; he ran and tilted with the sprightliest; and then suddenly health would ebb away from him, and the pale boy would lie for hours in his chamber, obscurely melancholy, with a Virgil in his hand.' This personal assessment would not have been confirmed by my associates, who probably suspected constipation.

The prevailing mid-thirties flavour mingled neo-Victorian values with disrespect. The masters were personalities almost to a man, and all treated me with a forbearance and amiability for which I am still grateful. One, a mathematical near-genius, rumoured to have broken a boy's leg with a kick, liked to be pelted with wastepaper, and had already reserved a seat in any attempt to be made on the moon. Lionel Gough, an aesthete, was yet a mighty rider to hounds, and devotee of Surtees. 'The Moke' was known to have driven his car at speed into his garage and crashed out again through the further end. Mr Joce had allegedly arrested and released Trotsky, in some escapade on the high seas. H.D. Dawes, 'Daddy', 'The Admiral', white-haired, monocled, continually left the class-room to attend to his bulldog: the dog existed; so, we suspected, did the whisky. Daddy apparently, had only been appointed for one term, but decided on his own to stay longer, actually for many years, the authorities not noticing or pretending not to. Revd Johnny Bower pleased me with his dire puns, sermons of impressive dullness, his unstinted kindness. In charge of French lessons, military men either spoke that language well, without understanding the words, or understood the words they failed to pronounce, which provoked curious situations during holidays abroad. A famous cricketer who taught geography held that Greenland was so named from the colour of its people. Another beak mused, 'I was in Moscow myself once. Or was it my brother?' Genial atheists would stumble through Scripture lessons, 'Now, take this fellow Moses . . .'. F.M. Heywood, scholar and athlete, and Lionel Gough, fastidiously cultivated, founded a literary magazine, *Extra*, which first gave me a voice in the world in 1936, for it could be bought at Hatchards in London and Heffer's, in Cambridge. Wilfrid Blunt, six feet four, with 'a crop of unruly hair aptly likened by an impertinent barber to heather', was informal, friendly, a reassuring presence. He, like a music master, R.B. Ferry, allowed boys to use his room, as bolt-hole, arts centre, club, in an atmosphere of Wagner and talk, Post-Impressionists, ikons, African carvings, startling curtains and rugs, oriental prints. One heard of Stravinsky, Kremlin art treasures, Paris, Diaghilev, streets and bridges, Bavarian monarchs, eastern adventurers, Proust, Italian operas and their audiences. His autobiography, *Married to a Single Life*, tells a story about his childhood, the point of which would have escaped me in 1935. Wilfrid, a collector of 'bugs' (butterflies) caused comment by suddenly addressing the Bishop of Winchester: 'I say, Bishop, are you a bugger too?' Friend of Roger Fry, with wide impressionistic ties and a green pullover stitched with a large white rabbit, he had for me the striding dash, ebullient self-confidence, Bohemian flair or genius to which I so greatly aspired, and I am relieved, as I read today, that he too had youthful gaucheness, shyness, streaks of doubt and lack of enterprise, and a worldly ignorance almost in excess of my own. There was Martin Wight, later assistant to Arnold Toynbee, a pacifist, with pictures of Christ and Lenin on his wall, and of whom Professor Elie Kedourie spoke so highly and touchingly in the Fourth Martin Wight Memorial Lecture, delivered at Sussex University in 1978.

My housemaster, Edgar Matthews, shy, subtle, gifted actor and linguist, I fully appreciated only in later life. I am grateful for his inclusion of me in his Shakespeare productions, to experience the masterpieces as working plays rather than classroom exercises. That resonant line, 'Well, well, well' was not to be coveted, but

The Norweyan banners flout the sky

telescoped time and words in a single shock. In contrast, I remember, crossing Quad, a bored voice from someone in the Political Science VI: 'We are only just beginning to adumbrate an approach to the fringe of the problem.'

5

1933—40 cut the most sharply into my imagination, then at its most ignorant and most receptive. The era of Hit and Muss, as the Unity Theatre wits had it, of Gandhi, FDR, Mosley, Mrs Simpson, Franco, and, inevitably, GBS. 'Breadline' was heard, never wholly rebuffed by 'We're in the Money', the exuberant song from my cherished movie, *Gold Diggers of 1933*. Hindsight is unfair, but my retentive memory at least galvanized curiosity, evidence of life, and occasionally rigged the evidence. Even then I kept a notebook, irritating to my friends to this day, but essential to grab the oddities flying past me.

Was it really true that 11,000 workers of the Port of London Authority were known thieves? I treasure a story that Eddie Marsh told Christopher Hassall, that a friend of Princess Marthe Bibesco, carrying her portrait by Picasso, was held up at the Spanish frontier for attempting to smuggle out a map of the fortifications of Madrid. Apparently the famous Jarrow hunger-marchers were given practical support by local Tories, and considerable opposition in Parliament from Labour.

'Heard the latest?' rang through my youth, and I never had: those tales of GBS, the Prince and Miss Penelope Dudley Ward, and the Chatterbox. Now, at the Haileybury Arts Society, the elite subdued me with talk of 'Morgan', 'Auden', 'Betjeman', 'Osbert', and Osbert's butt, 'Mr Muddleton Moral'.

Heard the latest? The century was fascinated by power and debasement. Saki, scarcely a man of blood, once admitted that he had always looked forward to the romance of a European War. It came, and it killed him. Resolute arsonists got applauded by their most probable victims; Hitler observing that those who get beaten up are the first to apply for Party membership. 'Cruelty impresses.' Russian millionaires helped found *Pravda*, hating their country, their class, themselves. Dictators, fishers of men, simultaneously flattered the people and spat on them, like early Hollywood supplying *Anna Karenina* with a happy ending for rural audiences, a sad one for urban. Politically, the Modernists were wilful absurditechts: Ezra Pound, whose verse I much admired, was sneering at 'Mr Jewsevelt', 'Stinkie Roosenstein', 'Franklin Finkelstein Roosevelt', maintaining that 'every human being who is not a hopeless idiotic worm should realize that Fascism is superior in every way to Russian Jewocracy and that capitalism stinks.' He also declared that *Mein Kampf* was 'keenly analysed history' and, from wartime Rome, broadcast that Hitler had taught the Germans manners, and that *Duce* and *Führer* were sustaining the traditions of Jefferson and Adams. He asserted in 1945, that Hitler was 'like Jeanne d'Arc, a saint, a martyr'. Rilke, like Freud, had praised the *Duce*. T.S. Eliot would spell Jew with a small j. The kindly, magnetic, hard-working GBS, whom Chesterton called a tree with its roots in the air, in love with the Caesar of his own play, admired Stalin, Mussolini, and, with some reservations, Hitler, and was by then condemning British parliamentarianism as slavery for nine-tenths of the people and slave-exploitation or parasitic idolatory and snobbery for the rest. Mosley, 'bounder' and 'cad' in one, could be heard yelling that Britain owed free speech to Fascism. 'What luck for rulers,' Hitler continues, 'that people do not think!' He could rest assured of praise from Wyndham Lewis, and the contempt for liberal democracy of W.B. Yeats, though even Hitler might have blinked at the poet's remark, at a London dinner, that 'The First World War did not have much reality'. I would not have risked that on the maimed and broken war-veterans on the Southsea Streets.

Orwell noted Yeats' approval of the century likely to prove 'hierarchical, masculine, harsh, surgical'. He himself, T.R. Fyvel remembers, appeared to have surprisingly little interest in Nazi Germany, and wrote of *Mein Kampf* in 1940, in tones that fascinated me, for in many ways I consider him my most readable and influential teacher:

> I should like to put it on record that I have never been able
> to dislike Hitler. Ever since he came to power — till then,
> like nearly everyone, I had been deceived into thinking that
> he did not matter — I have reflected that I would certainly
> kill him if I could get within reach of him, but that I could
> feel no personal animosity. The fact is that there is
> something deeply appealing about him . . . a pathetic
> dog-like face, the face of a man suffering under intolerable
> wrongs. In a rather more manly way it reproduces the
> expression of innumerable pictures of Christ crucified.

I would like to believe that Lord Halifax, Foreign Secretary,
originally mistook Hitler for a footman and handed him his
hat. More ascertainable is that he found the dictator 'very
sincere', and Goering 'frankly attractive and sincere', comparing him to a head gamekeeper. Arnold Toynbee met Hitler in
1936, and left 'convinced of his sincerity in describing peace in
Europe'. Lord Boothby told Neville Chamberlain that he was
dealing 'with a fanatic and ferocious madman, with a
destructive genius almost without parallel in history' but only
got the reply, 'I'm afraid I don't agree with you. I trust
Hitler.' So may have Richard Strauss, who addressed him as
'the great architect of German society'. Outstandingly good
and cultured people could be, in all good faith, self-
condemned for tolerance and wishful thinking. In her
biography of Wilfrid Israel, Naomi Shepherd quotes Leonard
Montefiore, Joint Chairman of the Anglo-Jewish Joint Foreign
Committee in October 1933, as saying that

> he would not assert that the Nazi movement was only
> composed of hatred and prejudice and all that was evil . . .
> there were certain good elements among the Nazis, a certain
> austerity and readiness for self-sacrifice, a spirit of patriot-
> ism . . . were it not for the anti-semitic plank in the Nazi
> programme there was no doubt that a large proportion of
> young German Jews would be enthusiastic followers of the
> movement.

Goering enjoyed calling himself the Last Man of the Renaissance, but admitted that whenever he had to confront his boss, 'my heart falls into my trousers'.

In Rebecca West's opinion, the Last Man of the Renaissance was not the Reichmarshal but my cousin, Robert Vansittart, Permanent Under-Secretary for Foreign Affairs (1930–1938); of his only encounter with Hitler in 1936, he recorded:

> An aimiably simple, rather shy, rotundly ascetic *bourgeois*, with the fine hair and thin skin that accompany extreme sensitiveness, a man of almost obvious physical integrity, very much in earnest, not humorous, nor alarming, not magnetic, but convinced of a variable mission and able to impress himself so strongly that he impresses himself on those around him, perhaps I should say even on those constantly around him.

King George V emerges rather better than the intellectual know-alls, in his distrust of the dictators as political symptoms, loathing their personal style. He would scarcely have applauded the Nazi salute awarded to his son, George VI, by Hitler's ambassador, 'Herr von Brickendrop'. Meanwhile Sartre and de Beauvoir were ignoring the Fascist leaders. The latter remembered, 'I avoided all problems posed by Hitler's political activities and regarded the rest of the world with an indifferent eye.'

These were my formative years, which makes me flog dead horses so hard that they sit up and talk, very badly, like Pirandello on Italy's heroic bombing and gassing of defenceless Ethiopian villagers. 'The Author of this great feat is also a Poet who knows his trade. He acts in the Theatre of the Centuries both as author and protagonist.' This would have been small beer for the *Duce* who spoke of himself as the most intelligent animal that ever existed on the face of the earth. Hilaire Belloc was more temperate, merely finding him, 'disinterested, and lacking in personal ambition'. The chorus of praise was supplemented by Edison, who called Mussolini 'the greatest genius of the age', by Pope Pius XI, 'a man sent us by God', and by Winston Churchill. Ernest Hemingway, an honourable exception, very early rated him the biggest bluff in Europe and Noel Coward years later was likewise disrespectful, when he saw the new Rienzi, the new Caesar, 'like an over-ripe tomato plum squeezed into a white uniform'.

Here was an era, like all eras, of fake appearances, through which the *Duce* rode high. I was hypnotized by it all, more or less, perhaps not entirely, fooled by the drums, the big parades, 'the stampede of suburbia'.

To me, as I sat in cinemas, watching him belabour huge crowds with wild phrases, operatic gestures, he was an irresistible machine, though a machine made for wonder rather than practical use. That a real man existed within that metallic casing, that the hard, bald head was disfigured by an immense swelling like a potato, I was yet to know, let alone the ineptitude of his rule. When he made his ignoble entry into the war, at the heels of that other dictator before whom he, like Goering, seemed to quail, he neglected to inform his merchant navy, and much of it was promptly interned by the democracies he despised, and despised too long.

Horses, like doornails, are seldom as dead as they seem. Political mountebanks and hooligans abound today as freely as they did in my youth, with much the same appeal, inducing much the same disappointments. Their predecessors inoculated me, leaving me sceptical but not, I believe, wholly cynical.

Two facts have very slightly endeared Mussolini to me. I learnt that in his early years he was a schoolmaster but unable to keep order, quietening his pupils only with a regular bag of sweets. (This would have shocked Gertie!) As dictator, he learned from the films of Laurel and Hardy to discard the bowler hat he had been so unwise to wear. The bag of sweets, the bowler hat, somewhat reconciled him to the real human beings whom he treated so contemptuously, failed so absurdly. I scarcely considered this until a decade later, when the Milanese, having a few days earlier frantically acclaimed his last hopeless oration, were jeering at his carcass hanging upside down in the square and scrawling 'Butcher's Meat at Bargain Prices' over his pictures. After all the trumpets, the bludgeonings, the processions and fiascos, he never strayed so very far from the nervous dole of sweets and the debt he owed to Laurel and Hardy.

I did not, in 1934, know much about the Left, save that I secreted some respect for Stalin. Tolstoy's opinion that the difference between Left and Right was the difference between cat dung and dog dung would not have amused me. Isherwood was judging them by their attitude to homosexuals. To the Nazis they were 'sexual Bolsheviks'; he hoped for better from Russia, but, alas, Stalin in 1934 condemned them as 'Fascist perverts'. (This I would not have known, and would have barely understood if I had. Schoolboy loves we called 'cases' and did not treat too seriously. I had my own strong but muffled feelings, which no single word seemed to fit.)

A colder eye had, six years before, surveyed surging Europe of too many captains and insufficient rudder:

> If democracy is so stupid as to reward us . . . with free fares and parliamentary pay, then that is its own business. We are content to use all legal means to revolutionize the present state of affairs. Mussolini too entered Parliament. Let none imagine that parliamentarianism is our Damascus. We come as enemies! Like the wolf falling upon a herd of sheep, that is how we come!

Thus Josef Goebbels, the Berliner with whom Sir Robert Vansittart 'got on best . . . a limping eloquent slip of a Jacobin'.

First revealed to me by my exciting English teacher, P.H. 'Val' Rogers, W.H. Auden was chipping at the decade in phrases pictorial, kinetic, slightly fairytale.

> Ten thousand of the desperate marching by
> Five feet, six feet, seven feet high:
> Hitler and Mussolini in their wooing poses
> Churchill acknowledging the voter's greeting
> Roosevelt at the microphone, Van der Lubbe laughing
> And our first meeting.

For many, perhaps most of us, the thirties seemed to have

induced moral and political simplicity, surprising in an age that readily gulped down Freud. Exciting opposites, or apparent opposites, forbade neutrality. Decency fought Terror, Efficiency denounced Corruption and Torpor; Left was against Right, though less consistently than I thought, notably in Weimar Germany, where Reds and Blacks could unite in strikes to weaken the Social Democratic Republic. Hitler was on one side, the Versailles Treaty, the Jews, Jesse Owens, were on the other; FDR grappled with 'the Bankers' in his New Deal.

6

A certain pro-German bias was discernible at Haileybury, which I probably exaggerated in my 1952 school novel, *A Verdict of Treason*. We had a German Club: sweet cakes, *lieder* and guitars, solemn Teutonic visitors glad of our parrot denunciations of Versailles. One of them announced that modern psychology was invented by Goering's brother. A lively film, *Marching through Germany with Hitler's Armies*, was shown in Big School. Processions, uniforms, cheap but stirring tunes, had narcotic powers which I have found easier to condemn than to expurgate. A film of the Berlin Olympic Games in 1936 gave most of us thrills somewhat modified by Hitler's reputed snub to the magnificent American black, Jesse Owens, who thoroughly out-ran the vaunted Ayrans.

One master, a Christian Union leader, encouraged us to spend summer holidays at a German Labour Camp, where, he guaranteed, most interesting things were occurring. This was expanded in *Extra* (Christmas number, 1936). These camps, apparently, had

> the happy results of completing the breakdown of snobbery and class-distinction. The disadvantages are equally clear. While fitting the individuals to take their place without question in a highly organized national life, the system gives them no time to think for themselves, and actually discourages any such desire . . . If the ideal is co-operation

and peace, perhaps the price is justified; if it is not, the outcome can only be disaster in an unparalleled scale.

Songs were quoted from the Nuremburg rallies, those vast patterns of sound and movement reproduced visually if not spiritually in the coeval Busby Berkeley Hollywood musicals.

Hitler, Goebbels, seemed vulgar fellows of absurd appearance and suspect intelligence, but behind them were romantic peaks, distant castles, broad, haunted rivers, lonely passes, great forests covering the gingerbread cottage, the wizard's hut, the wolf. 'God, children know something they can't tell, they like Red Riding Hood and the wolf in bed' wrote Djuna Barnes. I find Thomas Mann revealing, writing back in 1925, 'German Fascism is a pagan folk religion, a Wotan cult: it is, to be invidious — and I mean to be invidious — romantic barbarism.' The *Führer* did not disdain the language of scientific romance: 'We all suffer from the disease of mixed, contaminated blood.' The Nazis were fostering a delusive cult of trees, farms, sun, peasants, nakedness which appealed to me and which I attempted to examine more objectively, a few years ago, in *The Death of Robin Hood*. Hitler's belief that 'parliamentary decision by the majority sins against the aristocratic basis of nature,' while perplexing in association with his personal appearance and style, and those of his followers, did not seem a total libel on the antics of French Governments and our own Ministers dithering about unemployment and foreign policy. Many could share Yeats' craving for 'the old exalted life, the old splendour', ignorant of how spurious both had actually been, not least in Ireland.

A letter by the mass-murderer Heinrich Himmler to his Baltic doctor Kersten, which I mentioned in the novel, 1981, makes curious reading:

Nature is so marvellously beautiful and every animal has a right to live. It is just this point of view that I admire so much in our forefathers. They, for instance, formally declared war on rats and mice which were required to cease their depredations and leave a fixed area within a definite time, before a campaign of extermination was begun against them. You will find this respect for animals in all Indo-Germanic people . . . even today Buddhist monks, when they pass through a wood in the evening, carry a bell, to warn any woodland animal, so that no harm will come to them!

Himmler particularly prided himself on his collections of skulls, extracted from Russian prisoners-of-war. He would have been at one with his SS subordinate, Ludwig Ramdohr, at whose trial for torture and killing in 1946, witnesses spoke of his feeling for nature: 'Sometimes as he walked in the country he gave small, queer jumps to avoid crushing a snail or a lizard under his foot.'

In 1936, at sixteen, I was still romantic and muddled, covering my diffidence with pomposity, easily deceived by an unexpected smile, gesture, gift. I could not yet understand that people were not all of a piece. Like Philip Toynbee's Dick Abbeville, I demanded that:

> The good were to be good; the rich grossly opulent;
> thieves were to rob and parsons preach on the spot.

My obsessions with Germany continued for many years and produced a clutch of novels. Not until long after the war did I actually visit the country and I was alarmed but excited to visit towns and landscapes I had described in some detail. The visit answered the questions hitherto catered for by my imagination and I have never since written of Germany.

Visiting Berlin, in 1965, I was alert for signs of traditional militarism and arrogance, and was slightly aggrieved to find German police and officials gratuitously helpful and genial. Then at last I saw what I had hoped to find: swaggering soldiers knocking aside civilians, rampant rudeness, hectoring music, hard faces. Prussian militarism to the life, the Kaiser's god-children, Goering's legacy. Finally I realized that I had wandered far from the British zone, and that these uniformed ruffians were French.

Meanwhile, in the thirties, the Great War was manifestly still occurring under different labels. I once visited, though platonically, the bedroom of a very senior master, R.L. Ashcroft, and was surprised, and slightly disturbed, to see a wall lined with war novels.

I too read war novels, with gruesome curiosity. Philip Gibbs (I was displeased in 1959, to have one of my own novels praised as 'almost as good as Philip Gibbs, not quite at his best), Richard Aldington, C.E. Montague whose *Rough Justice*, written in 1926 from Montague's experiences on the Western Front as Manchester Guardian correspondent, I frequently reread. It begins as a pastoral, rich evening bird song, dew on smooth lawns, old moon above fresh hay, a girl's voice, 'Fun tomorrow Bron'. Then it slides into the casual folly of 1914, the sunlight turns red and lurid as useless offensives smash the young and cripple many beyond endurance and the children's golden hero is shot for desertion. This scene I watched re-enacted on the stage in 1983 in my *Voices from the Great War*, and I was at once sent back to the Haileybury library, spellbound with the sick glamour of a time I had not known but would never forget.

7

Writing evolves from obsessions: my own I could not, through shyness, communicate in talk. My first printed story, in which I was raw enough to allow a major to carry a rifle, appeared in *Extra* in 1935; worthless enough, a rotten step on a rickety ladder, but it briefly assuaged my self-doubts. The half-crown prize was the first money I had ever earned, given me by Barney Keenan, later the literary editor of a Catholic newspaper. Symbolism, allusion, the indirect had not yet modified my stolidity; Emily Dickinson's injunction to 'Tell all the Truth but tell it slant' would have baffled me, though 'A Narrow Fellow In The Grass' would have struck home. With awed perplexity I resisted Val Rogers' impressive exposition of the significance of Forster's description of flies on the ceiling in *A Passage to India*.

Likewise, no Braque, no Picasso, could conceivably surpass the apparent realism of Hogarth, Bruegel, Bosch, and

Watteau. I was intrigued, some forty years later, to buy the *Listener* for an article entitled 'Bosch and Watteau', only to discover that it was a review of my own novel about the French Revolution, in which, although they are not named, the critic Kenneth Graham, perceived these ancient influences.

I could sense, indeed sometimes feel, that life was a dim forest in which among roots and shadows was hidden the golden torch. Here, in a trumpery way, was vision, but I was denied visions, despite my self-styled poem which began: 'I had a vision, a vision of earthly prominence. . .'

'Did you have it?' Gerard Irvine enquired, genuinely curious, but I had to confess that I had not. Gerard, later a confidant of Stevie Smith and a priest with a considerable following, I seem to remember addressing masters as 'lovey' — a line of defence or attack which impressed me.

My verse would begin with some resounding stage thunder:

> Down in a hedge of a bare rough field,
> Far away by the windswept pastures. . .

Followed by a number of thudding lies. I always wanted to share my puny discoveries — and was to become a school-teacher, with an enthusiasm usually overdone — which must have made me a tyrannical bore and zealot of the type I particularly dislike. I had discovered that most of us, Hitler, Beaverbrook, Swinburne, even myself, could get drunk on words.

My politics, whenever present, were still dulled by accepting words at face value, like Dick Abbeville. Communists were presumably almost fulsomely generous. That they could evict and exterminate millions, collaborate with Nazis against the equivalents of Attlee, Morrison, Bevin — ''Erbert, this jam tastes fishy,' the great Bevin complained of the caviare — would have seemed mere newspaper bias. I could not foresee the Hitler–Stalin Pact ('It felt like being among old Party comrades,' Ribbentrop said in Moscow), nor had I heard the British Communist Party secretary, Harry Pollitt, pronounce on the General Strike: 'Do you think we care a damn about the miners? What we're interested in is the road to revolution.'

Marlborough House, Hove, 1930. The author was at school here from 1928-30

The author's mother, and her dog Bruce, in the garden at Kersey

Arthur and Muffet Harrison, in the forties

Haileybury from the air, 1932

The author at eighteen

Wilfrid Israel

The author at thirty

The author's house in
Hampstead

The author at Hampstead

Jacket design for *The Overseer*
1949

Jacket design for *The Friends of
God* 1963

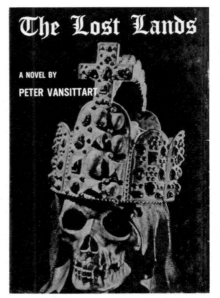

Jacket design for *The Lost Lands* 1964

Philip Toynbee

The author at a party in Northampton, 1984

The author at a party in Northampton, 1984 with fellow (unknown) guest

The Ford, Kersey, Suffolk

I do remember my incredulity at a 1937 newsreel showing the Red Army goosestepping through Moscow. I had always imagined Red troops operating in a disorderly, democratic slouch, as General Krasnov had seen them, quoted in a book by my teacher, Hampden Jackson: 'Pallid, scowling, with shadowy starved faces, narrow-shouldered and clumsy, in long trousers and old boots done up with string, this army in a drab mass rolled along the streets smoking cigarettes.'

Surely revolutionaries were pledged to destroy all else? That a Yugoslav Jew could head a savagely anti-semitic Catholic faction seemed a bundle of contradictions, as much against nature as a wood climbing a hill to attack a king. (In July 1940 I was to be thrilled by the aptness with which the only French Senator to vote against the forced dissolution of the Third Republic turned out to be the great-grandson of Lafayette.) Such shocks, reversing ingrained beliefs and unquestioned idolatories, are of course essential. At Haileybury, reading a book by H.E. Howard, edited by Jackson, I read with incredulity: 'The best governed states were Baden, where serfdom was abolished in 1781, and Saxe-Weimar, where philosophers were collected to produce an enlightened atmosphere. Goethe, that colossal bore, made it sound all very exciting. '*That colossal bore.* I had never encountered such a verdict in serious print and the effect was liberating; for some weeks, in and out of class, I applied it too literally on many sacred cows. Fortunately, I am still susceptible to such shocks. In 1974, I gaped at C.P. Snow's arraignment of W.G. Grace for 'extreme meanness, trickery' – so far, possible, but Snow continued 'and perhaps, oddest of all, physical cowardice', about which, knowing something of very fast bowlers on abnormally rough wickets, I remain sceptical. Soon afterwards, I was surprised by G.R. Elton's assessment of Sir Thomas More, about whom I had too long accepted received opinions. More 'at no time troubled himself about such things as scholarly convictions, chivalrous moderation or even elementary truthfulness' and indeed compared to most previous chancellors, More's religious intolerance and heresy-hunting were outstanding. He burned the heretics, the much abused Wolsey did not.

8

From such period novels as Isherwood's *Lions and Shadows* the history master can be seen as an intellectual base in many public schools. On me, a most powerful influence was exercised by Martin Wight's predecessor, John Hampden Jackson. Stocky, russetty, perceptive, with stylized mannerisms, he was energetic, ironic, pungent.

One boy he was said to abhor so much that their professional relationship dwindled to an unofficial correspondence course. He had already published several books, was an enthusiastic authority on the smaller democracies, particularly Finland and the Baltic States, whose enslavement to Russia since 1940 has been so blandly ignored by the Left, including a powerful advocate of freedom, Sartre. All organic, unambitious communities interested him. 'Surely where socialism went wrong,' he wrote me in 1943, 'was in bowing to the inevitability of the big power units, instead of concentrating on small cooperative units.' This was to have a permanent effect on me. From him I learnt to distrust the Napoleonic, grandiose, declamatory, to desire not total revolution or the perfect society, but better government. Likewise, he shaped my belief in small schools, factories, towns.

Like Orwell, whom he must have known, he loved the English village where, in ancient pubs, he would discuss cricket, long-established though somewhat ludicrous institutions of church and state, country legends and radical politics with whoever might be present — a farmer, Philip Toynbee, General Sir Edmund Ironside, who together with General Sir Bindon Blood had begun military life with some advantage of nomenclature. Frequently he referred to Max Plowman, R.H. Tawney, Eileen Power, J.B.S. Haldane and Middleton Murry, for whom he wrote in *The Adelphi*, published in the Adelphi Community, a small agricultural commune in Essex led by Max Plowman and, after his death, by Murry. I myself suffered a few weeks there in fruitless experiment of organic living. Spade and hoe, stinging nettles and high-mindedness were not for me. Untroubled by class-guilt and mock-modesty, Jackson later joined a more congenial berth as Director of Cambridge Extra-Mural Studies, and served East Anglia well. He became an authority on post-revolutionary French politics, publishing on such figures as Proudhon, Fourier, Clemenceau, and his particular hero, Jaurès.

For *Extra* he secured an article by the Leader of the Opposition, who likewise admired the small northern democracies. Writing on Public Service, Attlee's tone was of a pitch that only later I came not just to value but depend on:

> Naturally I think that when my Party is in power things are better done but the division into good and bad local authorities is not drawn strictly on party lines. There are councils to which my Party has never penetrated in any great numbers which have outstanding records in some branch or other of public service, health, education or amenities. There are, however, a number of councils where the quality of the representatives is very poor; Local Government has been allowed to remain in the hands of narrow-minded persons without vision.

In his civics lessons, Jackson introduced us to Marx, about whom he was informative though caustic. He was always encouraging, treating us as fellow-adults, answering our questions honestly, and giving me books to review for the college magazine. The authors included Aldous Huxley, Chesterton, Galsworthy, Auden, Pound, Samuel Butler, Sacheverell Sitwell and Feuchtwanger, and for all save the last I had to gather basic information from the famous reviewers in the weeklies available in the library. I was fluent, unimaginative, and conscientious. Evelyn Waugh's complaint would not have occurred to me: 'I used to have a rule when I reviewed books as a young man never to give an unfavourable review to a book I hadn't read. I find even this simple rule flagrantly broken now.'

Privately I still stole back to Buchan and Haggard, and would have been depressed by Siegfried Sassoon's finding Haggard's books 'feeble and depressing rubbish'. Pound presented some incidental beauties:

> The dull round towers encroaching on the field,
> The tents tight drawn, horses at tether
> Farther and out of reach, the purple night,
> The crackling of small fires, the bannerets,
> The lazy leopards on the largest banner,
> Stray gleams on hanging mail, an armourer's torch-flame
> Melting on steel.

Through Jackson's commentaries, social conscience and Labour propositions were linking the ragged boys on Hertford Heath and Haileybury House, Stepney, with the pitiful crocks of my childhood. The waste of lives and bodies was inescapable. That a rich, imperial country was so visibly shabby was emphasized by Wells, Priestley and indeed Mosley, and D.H. Lawrence.

Personalities were teaching me more than text books: Jackson, Val Rogers, Wilfrid Blunt, Neville Bewley, all friends in later life. GBS had condemned the school text book, 'a book from which no human being can learn anything: a book which, though you may decipher it, you cannot in any fruitful sense read, though the enforced attempt will make you loathe the sight of a book all the rest of your life'.

The book undeniably had too much to do and, in my teaching days, having to goad pupils through examinations, I tended to agree with Shaw, though as a boy I objected less. 'Set books' at Haileybury included Forster, Jane Austen, Shakespeare, Belloc, Butler, G.M. Trevelyan, Matthew Arnold, Dickens, Coleridge, Chaucer, Neville Cardus, the Golden Treasury and other anthologies which included Spender, Prokosch, MacNeice, Auden, Campbell, Barker, de la Mare, Rex Warner; only Shakespeare's Sonnets I actually rejected.

For some years after leaving school and college I was ashamed of my lack of systematic reading, indeed my addictions to the second-rate. It had seemed a chronicle of misspent time. I had read nothing of Joyce, Eliot, Woolf; I read Tolstoy's *Childhood, Adolescence, Youth* only in hopes, unfulfilled, that the middle word would give a sensual revelation appropriate to my needs. Saki I ignored, crassley mistrusting the name. Mostly, though surrounded by fine libraries, I continued my Antrim Grove habit of selecting books at random, through laziness, and abstruse fears of the new, though explanations are seldom complete. Somehow, I feared rejection by books and, like Dr Watson, mistook the unusual for the mysterious.

I could respond still to the power of an opening paragraph, that of *A Passage to India* ('the Ganges happens not to be holy here'), *Bleak House, Hamlet,* and the first sentence of Balzac's *History of the Thirteen*: 'In Paris under the Empire, thirteen men came together.' Individual words continued to engross. Dylan Thomas said that the most beautiful in the language was 'aerodrome', with its appropriate ascent and descent. The ugliest that I have ever met is 'Bigshottification', to be found in John K. Dickenson's translation of Helmut Heiber's *Goebbels*, which also offers 'Massification of the Individual' and 'Manifestations of optical and acoustical razzmatazz'.

At masters' parties, Arts Society teas, I could meet, if scarcely hold spellbound, dazzling seniors: Gerard Irvine, Gavin Townend, Peter Barton, the last a handsome cricketer who, in *Extra*, coolly supplied an ending for 'Kubla Khan'. A few years ago, Peter wrote to me describing his long days huddled on an Oxford bench in all weathers, apparently doing nothing, feeling nothing, after a decade of sponging letters to Hampden Jackson. He died a few months later.

I yearned for the Peters, the Gavins, the Gerards, to turn their heads, but when they did so I was exposed in dumb foolishness. When I found Talleyrand's remark that man is given speech in order to conceal his thoughts, I eagerly grabbed it as an alibi, though it has never been an impeccable one.

They all appeared glittering, invincible. When I grandly

informed Denis Mack Smith that Greek society had been undermined by the depredation of olive trees by goats, he casually told me who had bred the goats. Such superiority drove me headlong into myself, leaving me the silent bore amid the clink and clatter. I can hear their voices: 'Would you say,' an amused face glances at me, for an instant only, 'that H.G. Wells knows how to write?'

It was like Al Alvarez today, shuddering at the belief that Walter de la Mare was a poet, or like Mrs Patrick Campbell at rehearsal, irritated at the producer's obstinate assumption that *Macbeth* is a tragedy. I kept what I hoped was enigmatic silence, disloyally, for Wells' *History of the World* had opened vistas to me as much poetic as factual:

> It is not until we come to sands that are almost a quarter of a million years old that we find any particle of a sub-human being. But there are plenty of implements, and they are steadily improving in quality. . . They are no longer clumsy Eoliths; they are now shapely instruments made with considerable skill. *And they are much bigger than the similar instruments made by True Men.*

The italics gave a delicious shock, the sensation of lives on the verge, totally new sounds about to emerge.

Meanwhile, I provoked a pained gasp from a friendly master, D.H. Thompson, when I produced Oedipus, as 'Oydiphus' at a reading of *The Ascent of F.6*. I was humiliated by an awed murmur that Val Rogers 'had met Wystan'. Was this enviable, was it shocking? Whatever the truth of this phenomenon, Val too treated us as intelligent insiders, was a humane presence in a world ostensibly easy but which might swiftly turn terrible. He introduced us to Chekhov, he had a surfeit capacity for sheer fun, and a laugh that almost cracked the ceiling.

He read us Auden's topical 'Spain':

> On that arid square, that fragment nipped off from hot
> Africa, soldered so crudely to inventive Europe,
> On that tableland scored by rivers,

Auden's brilliance of detail and vivid, brisk juxtapositions always dazed me:

The horrible nurses itching to boil their children

The hum of the printing presses turning forests into lies

O little restaurant where the lovers eat each other

My dear one is mine as mirrors are lonely

and the crack in the tea-cup opens a lane to the land of the dead

I never spoke to Auden. Once, at a party, to which I had brought a pupil, I saw him but felt insufficiently brave to accost him. Not so Arthur:

'Ah, Auden! Now, what are you up to at the moment?'
'I am writing an opera.'
'So am I. I'll tell you all about it. . .'

Years later on a flight from Vienna, Auden was seated beside me, absorbed in a crossword. In my pocket was a proof-copy of my latest novel, in which I had, as a foreword, printed a poem of his. But I could not disturb him, and said nothing. On landing he suddenly grinned at me, very slightly hesitated, I nodded clumsily, friends at once divided us, and shortly afterwards he was dead.

10

My relish for biography and historical narrative helped separate me from Haileybury writers, who were poets and critics to a man. I felt at home with John Wheeler-Bennet's *Hindenburg, the Wooden Titan*, and its description of the giant wooden effigies of the old military father-figure built in wartime Germany, into which patriotic citizens, paying a

129

mark for war funds, then hammered a nail. I knew nothing of Freud, but saw an image, ponderous, momentous, and tragic.

Duff Cooper's *Talleyrand* engrossed me, and Emil Ludwig's *Napoleon*. Clive Bell's *Civilization*, an early Pelican book, gave small handy phrases: 'Sense of Values', 'Significant Form'. Spender's line about a 'wet-dream dictator' seemed excitingly modern.

Nevertheless, dreaming of cricket and a particular boy, I was spending very little of my reading-time on poetry and serious novels. Wodehouse, Sapper, Buchan, were still the bulk of my stock-in-trade. Snobbishly, I scarcely boasted of this, nor of my addiction to the novels of Ian Hay.

This writer, in private life Major I.H. Beith, scripted for Alfred Hitchcock such films as *Sabotage* and *The Thirty Nine Steps*, and was categorized by Orwell as 'an exponent of the clean-living Englishman tradition at its silliest.' It was Hay who noted the distinction between 'funny Peculiar' and 'funny Ha-ha', in his play *Housemaster*. I discuss him now because the silliness has always been a considerable part of myself, though his language is not mine.

> Muggeridge, I don't know you very intimately, but I know this, that you were always a worm and a bounder . . . when it comes to disturbing our crew, who have to fight the battle of the college on behalf of worms like you and these gentlemen here whose passionate sport is probably billiards – well, that's what I call a bit thick.

Much of it can be mistaken for parody: 'still, he maintained a stiff upper lip and maintained his watch like a man.'

Both are extracts from *A Man's Man* published in 1919. Like all his stories, it is provocatively public-school, and, like Sapper's, more aware of the dead officers in Flanders than of the Amritsar Massacre. Influenced by Kipling, Hay enjoyed referring to 'the Breed', seemed thoughtlessly anti-semitic, sentimental about English manors, and reflected a sunny, pre-Freudian estimate of human nature and education, shared, before 1914, by Shaw, Wells, Russell. 'Most of us have the right stuff concealed in us somewhere'; this optimism is at the root of such novels as *A Man's Man, Pip, a Romance of Youth, A Knight on Wheels, Carrying On* and *The Right Stuff*. In all these books the Knight-errant crusading in a mechanized world recurs, inarticulately dedicated to the Lady, whom he eventually wins, though their sex-play is unimaginable, even self-contradictory. Bad manners, bitchiness, nastiness appear, but no evil: the Mr Drakshoffs and Carl Petersons, but no Streichers, Eichmanns, Himmlers, Berias. Children's scenes are entertaining. In one, two youngsters venture into a restaurant. Flummoxed by the menu, one orders a whitebait. The waiter looks incredulous:

'A whole one?'
'Yes.'

and, in time, the waiter produces it.

A Man's Man is a minor part of the experience of Kipling and Saki, of the middle-class child sent home from India. The hero, Hughie Marrable, would have forgathered easily with Dick Hannay, Archie Roylance, Sir Henry Curtis, Raffles, Drummond. He is seen at Cambridge May Week, 'A strong-limbed, clean-run young man', and the races have period flavour: 'The last boat, remote, unfriended, melancholy, slow, accompanied by a coloured gentleman ringing a dinner-bell and a bespectacled don who trotted alongside chanting "Well rowed, Non-Collegiate Students," creaked dismally past.'

While others reminisced about Wystan, Edith and John, I was secretly curled up in a library corner with a pile of august unreadables grandly concealing *A Man's Man*. Disappointed in love, Marrable globe-trots for nine years, like some Mystery candidate. 'He had mixed cocktails behind a Nevada bar; learnt to fire a revolver without taking it out of his pocket; accompanied a freight-train over the Rockies in the capacity of assistant brakesman — his duties were chiefly confined to standing by with a coupling-pin, to discourage the enterprise of those gentlemen of the road who proposed to travel without tickets; and once, in a Southern State, he had been privileged to be present at the enobling spectacle to which the brightest nation on earth occasionally treats the representatives of an older civilization — the lynching of a negro.'

A Coney Island bar fight to rescue a girl — 'Hallo! The Hound! This must stop!' — gets him shanghaied on to a coffin-ship. Most of the crew desert in mid-Atlantic with an eye on the insurance, but Marrable remains behind for a rigorous but successful odyssey. Back on shore, he assumes wardship of Joan, beautiful, twenty-two, 'utterly spoilt but fundamentally sound'. The journey becomes rougher. 'His wanderings, though they had made him more than ever a master of men, had done little to eradicate his innate attitude of quiet, determined, and occasionally quite undeserved reverence towards women.' Conventions then demanded a cad, here a dubious actor, 'with dark eyes and dangerous eyelids — one felt instinctively that he was a good card-player, and probably objected to cold baths and early rising'. Despite this competition, an accusation of financial malpractice, and the clumsiest marriage proposal still on record, as foolish but briefer than that of Mr Collins, he wins Joan, a long-lost rich uncle appearing on cue.

The sentimentality here is actually no grosser than most pop music, but, part of the large philistine dream, it helps explain how for so many of us, educated for inheritances, proconsular jobs, endowed leisure, the Second World War was a godsend, hauling refulgent cricketers, embryo heroes, superannuated prefects, the swells and the bloods from minor clerkships and decayed commonrooms into the death or glory fields, as the world reverted to the hands of those whom Richard Usborne calls 'Clubland Heroes'.

What sort of dream and how silly? Looking back, I am less ashamed of my joy in such books than I was when young, though I may be discussing them too lengthily. 'Lingering, even with intimate things, is not permitted.' In these adolescent fantasies, violence indeed erupted, but, as in coeval westerns, from valid moral crisis — injustice, blackmail, cruelty to women — always resolved happily and, in a wider perspective, untruthfully. Responsibility is preferred to mere power and crude ambition.

In this land, sex is only the latecomer's interpretation of chivalry which, in its medieval heyday, was a disgusting process of exploitations, idealized only in its decline. P.C. Wren's George Lawrence seemed to me natural and admirable. 'He had taken her refusal like the man he was, and had sought an outlet and an anodyne in work in Central Africa' (*Beau Geste*). In the same novel was the finalized model of a man's man:

A tall, bronzed, lean Englishman, forbidding and grim, who never used two words where one would suffice; his cold grey eye looking through, or over, those who surrounded him; his iron-grey hair and moustache, his iron-firm chin and mouth, suggesting the iron that had entered into his soul and made him the hard, cold, bitter person that he was, lonely, aloof, and self-suffering.

It was seldom, however, that I could accept this as a convincing portrait of myself.

In Hay's *Pip* I responded to the young hero in his first house match taking seven wickets (I think) for no runs, though less readily when he allowed his marriage to depend on a round of golf in which he unselfishly cheats (GBS gibed about Englishmen drinking golf instead of wisdom.)

The luminous Dandy, Percy Blakeney, Aramis, Psmith, reappears in Ian Hay's work, 'the composed, the unruffled fashion which stamps the high-caste Englishman all over the globe'. My friend, Michael Rouse, was something of a dandy at Haileybury, always cool, slightly at odds with the regulations. During the Second World War, he was leading Indian troops through a jungle, carrying only a swagger stick, his men all with rifles. Suddenly a cobra reared up before them. The Sergeant-Major smartly stood aside and saluted. 'The Sahib will now remove the snake!' The Sahib knew less than any of them, but his expression of friendly unconcern faintly tinged with cynical curiosity ousted the intruder. An echo here of Beau Brummell, summoning a footman and handing him a guinea to remain and listen to the remainder of a bishop's tedious anecdote.

133

The Men's Man, 'the Breed', possessed 'pluck', a preference for honesty rather than truth, the open air rather than domesticity, and for sportsmanship. Hughie's coach rows in the rival boat, and even Muggeridge applauds his assailant's triumph. All this is liable to be mocked, not as actually worthless, but as bad taste, like Polonius's saws and Kipling's 'If'. Yet by now I see the men's men, at distant remove, in such a figure as Fridtjof Nansen: Arctic explorer, ski-ing champion, scientist, first Norwegian ambassador to Britain after he had helped arrange the peaceful separation of Norway from Sweden; the humanitarian hailed by Maxim Gorky as the conscience of Europe, whose initiative in 1922 rescued millions of Russians from famine, after the civilized powers had disowned them and the League of Nations rejected them. Founder of the Nansen Passport for the Stateless, he repatriated hundreds of Russians after 1918 and effected a Greek–Turkish population exchange in 1922. He was a one-man League of Nations whose son, a hostage for the Norwegian King during the Second World War, found respect in the Concentration Camps, even from the SS.

James Bond has clobbered the Marrables out of existence, out of memory, yet the men's men, despite elitism founded on unearned incomes and remote schools, were neither ignoble nor unrealistic, though the failure of Asiatic millions to rally to the Empire in its extremity in 1941 scotched their moderate imperialism. Indeed, Buchenwald, Belsen, stamped out any belief that goodness of itself will ultimately win, as it did the pacifist belief that war solves nothing. The ghosts of the Tasmanians have an answer to that.

Only very briefly have I preferred idealists who, unlike Nansen, would not combine ideals with action. I was not tempted to applaud a post-war Archbishop of Canterbury when he reflected on the consequences of renewed atomic warfare: 'The very worst it could do would be to sweep a vast number of people at one moment from this world into the other and more vital world, into which anyhow they must all pass at some time.' I remember a piece of graffiti from the Punic Wars – 'I just want to go home' – and can see that unknown man, and would not wish his descendants swept from *their* homes. Still, I would not insure their lives with pietists, pacifists, anarchists. In my schoolboy reading, I was relieved when, usually around page 40, a Sandy remarks: 'The time has come, I think, for me to take a hand in the game.' Today, there may be a Sandy, there is certainly a field, but I can no longer discern the game.

Sophistication, has not, on evidence, produced a world superior to that of which Hay's mentor, Kipling, wrote:

> If any question why we died,
> Tell them, because our fathers lied.

The old men of the nineteenth century — Lincoln, Gladstone, Disraeli, Louis Napoleon, Alexander II, Franz-Josef, Jaurès, even Bismarck — would have gasped incredulously at twentieth-century genocide, slavery, terrorism, censorship. Today, from Havana to the Far East, more capital punishment exists than under any Romanov or Habsburg.

Camus wrote of the Hungarian rising in 1956, that 'the executions of Nagy and Palmater following promises of safe-conduct is the anti-communist case in a nutshell.' (How dismal, incidentally, is the present corruption of 'comrade', once respectable enough amongst the men's men!) We are back with Macgillivray and his derided 'honour', for, in their headstrong, unreflective, sometimes callous way, the Dicks and Hughies, even the Bulldog, knew from the start what superior intellects took years to discover, or never did, or discovered only to sneer at. They are related, at a coarser level, to Conrad's honour-bound seacaptains and flawed heroes, and Ford Madox Ford's reticent gentlemen. Conrad and Ford might not have called moral qualities 'the right stuff' but would not have shrugged aside the concept. There is seldom too much pluck but what there is can be too often used for the atrocious. 'The human heart,' wrote Conrad, 'is vast enough to contain all the world. It is valiant enough to bear the burden, but where is the courage that would cast it off?' The future world war would produce more: Enzo Sereni deliberately landing his plane at Belsen to join and comfort the gas-queues; Jean Moulin, resistance leader, handed paper on which to betray the names of his associates and scribbling a caricature of the chief SS torturer, Klaus Barbie; Orde Wingate; Douglas Bader; Bishop von Galen denouncing the Nazis from the pulpit of Münster Cathedral, once stormed by the Anabaptists; King Christian of Denmark and his government defying the Nazis on behalf of Danish Jews. Earlier, Lauro de Bosis had drowned, after his amateur but desperate flight over Rome, to drop anti-Fascist leaflets to rouse the king and people from moral and political torpor.

In their brutal way, the Fascist dictators were understanding this better than our leaders, the Baldwins, Chamberlains, Daladiers. Now they were growing gigantic, their voices blasting a world with banners, false suns, their fraudulent simplicities masquerading as an embrace from the marvellous as they bellowed 'you've won' through a million amplifiers. G.K. Chesterton had already said that it takes an age that has nothing to say, to invent the loudspeaker. An age which was to produce the dreadful silence that must have shrouded Magda and Josef Goebbels on a stark day in 1945, when they decided to poison their six children.

11

I must be sounding intolerably priggish and exploiting hindsight beyond the legitimate. Fortunately, antidotes existed. Val Rogers introduced me to the novels of Evelyn Waugh, which so exactly reproduced life as I had known it that I did not at first realize that they were funny. Wodehouse, whom Waugh acknowledged as a master, could be terse with men's men. One of his characters remarks. 'I like a man to be a clean, strong, upstanding Englishman who can look his gnu in the face and put an ounce of lead into it.' Wodehouse, more than Carlyle, more even than Dickens, continued to make me aware that language could matter as much or more than event, indeed, could *be* event. With him, I would not race through pages to discover the ending, for I was beginning at last to understand, as I believe John Wain has put it, the difference between the Ancient Mariner and the old sailor. Wodehouse himself remarked that he made musical comedy without music.

'I said that smoking was dangerous to the health. And it is.'
'It isn't.'
'It is. I can prove it from my own personal experience. I was once a smoker myself, and the vile habit reduced me to a physical wreck. My cheeks sagged, my eyes became bleary, my whole face gaunt and yellow and hideously lined. It was giving up smoking that brought about the change.'
'What change?'

The exiled Kaiser, then still alive, admired Wodehouse, and when offended with his entourage, would read him aloud, in English.

Another of my favourite writers was Hugh Walpole. His schoolboy character, Jeremy, had suffered my own joys and misunderstandings, despairs and affronts, standing foursquare in a world of captious despots, unexpected treats, grossly unfair wraths. I was pleased to see Simon Raven's 1984 reference to *Jeremy at Crale*, as ' a superb account of mental and physical endeavour', though now, 'sunk without a trace'.

At Haileybury I prayed regularly to be able to write a novel almost as profound as the least of Walpole's and to be, like him, published by Macmillan, in thick green cloth with golden lettering. Not for me the cheap bright yellow volumes in which Sapper allowed Hodder & Stoughton to sell him, or the strident productions of Victor Gollancz. My prayer was answered. I am at this instant touching my novel, *The Lost Lands*, green binding, gold lettering, published by Macmillan in 1964 with deplorable results.

Little of Walpole's large and hasty output remains in print. Flattered by his ironic friend Henry James, compared, though not recently, to Balzac — he would have appreciated, but not written, 'their ruined mouths were armed with greedy teeth' — and to Trollope, he was ridiculed as 'Alroy Kerr', the go-getting, mediocre novelist in Somerset Maugham's *Cakes and Ale*. Philip Toynbee told a story, allegedly true, of Harold Nicolson reviewing the novel and, wishing to soothe Walpole, mentioning that Kerr was based on John Drinkwater, not, as vulgar rumour had it, on Hugh Walpole. This at once elicited a telephone call from Maugham: 'Really, Harold, to think that I do not write sufficiently well for you to be able to differentiate between Walpole and Drinkwater. . .' This was followed by another call, from Walpole: 'Really, Harold, to think that, trivial as I am, you could drag me down to the level of Drinkwater. . .' Later, entering his club, the kindly Nicolson was ostentatiously cut by an old friend. John Drinkwater.

Walpole gave a considerable helping hand to the singer Melchior, and early on helped J.B. Priestley, whose superior intellectual curiosity has secured him greater staying power. Walpole's massive historical chronicles, his public school novel, *Mr Perrin and Mr Traill*, are probably still read, and *The Old Ladies* and *Above the Dark Circus* should be. Walpole himself craved for more, always hoping, though vainly, for unstinted admiration from Rebecca West, Katherine Mansfield, Virginia Woolf, as he may have imagined he had had from James and Conrad. He was dismissed by F.R. Leavis as 'an utterly untalented manufacturer of Book Society "Classics"', though I suspect that Graham Greene and Angus Wilson would soften this. His biographer, Rupert Hart-Davis, saw in him a suggestion of Mr Pooter. Incidentally, Priestley mentions that, while staying with Siegfried Wagner, Walpole was despatched on walks with 'a shabby and rather pathetic little man', Adolf Hitler.

His vigorous narrative gift could undeniably be smothered by undisciplined, rapturous description, cosiness, facile symbols. Virginia Woolf wrote of his work: 'True, it's competent enough, spare in the wording — but words without roots, yes, that's it. All a trivial litter of bright objects to be swept up.' But no such criticism deterred me. I read him and reread him. In *Fortitude* he had a text which I mistook for major philosophy, as perhaps, more briefly, did Walpole himself: ' 'Tisn't life that matters! 'Tis the courage you bring to it.' Walpole must have read with suspicion Bertie Wooster's 'In this life it is not aunts that matter but the courage that one brings to them.'

My favourite authors knew each other. Seated next to Wodehouse at some luncheon, Walpole confessed his astonishment that Hilaire Belloc had rated Wodehouse the best living English writer. He may have been consoled when Sean O'Casey gibed at Wodehouse as a 'performing flea'. This the victim amiably adopted as a title for an autobiography.

I think that Walpole spoke to me directly, because, despite a glib romanticism, he had deeply-felt awareness of the darkly malignant coiled within a bright nursery, a Cumberland landscape of blue water and daffodils, a quiet cathedral town, a lighted room above a darkened Piccadilly Circus, always about to lift a deadly, staring head. Ivor Cousins he would have recognized at once, as an enemy. Here, Walpole knew what he was writing about. His *Times* obituary, the nastiest I have ever read, drew protests from T.S. Eliot, Isherwood, Osbert Sitwell and many others.

Walpole, in Russia on Red Cross and Propaganda service during the Great War, witnessed fighting and revolution, and wrote vivid letters home, to his family, to Henry James and to Arnold Bennett, extracts of which I included in my anthology *Voices from the Great War* in 1981, and was delighted when they won surprised praise from critics.

12

I have mentioned by prayer. I have generally found that prayers get answered, but by a power sardonic, ironic, occasionally malign; from a universe derived from a guffaw. A marvellous, long-awaited encounter produces boring twins, the marriage, so eagerly demanded, wilts within seconds; one wins the prize and loses all one's friends; selected against all odds, one drops the catch, or the ball itself is spiked.

In my last two years at Haileybury between 1936 and 1938, I was writing ludicrous reviews for *The Haileyburian*, stories and verse for *Extra*. The latter's standards seemed to me disquieteningly high, even during my own editorship. It printed poems in French, a satire on Anglo-Catholicism, pastiches of Horace, Spencer, Tennyson, Chesterton, the

Sitwells, the Chinese, a translation of Rilke's 'Song of the Love and Death of Cornet Christopher Rilke von Langenau'. Traditional verbiage abounded: 'I long for the streams of Lethe and blest oblivion.' But Gerard Irvine continued to leave me hopelessly becalmed in the sententious and pompous, as he wrote:

> Janus and Gaia
> higher and higher
> sing as they sit in the
> county gaol:
> purple on yellow
> and scarlet the mellow
> notes rise as they follow
> the chromatic scale.

What was the chromatic scale? I was too stiff and self-concerned to risk asking, and Huxley's *Chrome Yellow* gave no help. I could never match Gerard's:

> This is the time of sparks, the Grafin's hour:
> the abbess stumbles down the homelong way
> devouring others' cheeks, the eaglet horde. . .

— which he was to amend slightly, in his volume *Sunset and Evening Star*.

I had no voice of my own, unable to trust my small private visions: Louis Napoleon's agony at Sedan, the Lower God, Danton's last days, 'thinking much of woods and fields', Monmouth, abject after Sedgemoor, taken to London, and seeing printed sheets advertising the sale of 'the late Duke of Monmouth's horses', the giant in the garden, the wolf sniffing my legs, the guillotine behind the jeweller's window, Mombasa and the gulch. The son of 'the False Dmitri', publicly hanged, aged four, haunted me for years. Remarkable experiences, life itself, happened only to others. Gerard knew Betjeman, Michael Rouse knew C.J. Kortright, reputedly the fastest bowler in history. Alan Ross, when very young in India, had seen, above him in his bath, the live monstrous hood of a cobra, of which in a future year he wrote:

> The cobra, all gun metal and slime, but
> with eyes like a poetess,
>   swung itself gently
> Down the hot cough of bath pipes.
> The bearer, as near white as ever
> He was likely to be, ran, clutching his dhoti,
> returning, teeth chattering and betal-stained, armed
> with a stick from the compound; and
> the snake's hood slithered flat, all slack,
> over me like rubber hose.

I can scarcely wish to experience that, but the poem reinforces my view of Alan, as slightly remote, elusive, touched by adventures under alien suns, on exotic shores, remembering what I can never know. Fear I have experienced, like all others, but little evil, and not much horror. During the Blitz I picked up a shoe, with a woman's foot in it; a child, fumbling for his lost legs, whispered before dying, 'Don't tell mum.' But, in a blazing time, these surfaced only a long time afterwards.

I had nothing to pit against Gerard, Gavin, Peter, Denis. I covered page after page but grew no ear for dialogue, could create no characters, only myself squinted at from various angles. A gift for phrases was not harnessed to direct observation, and too often I discarded even this and borrowed the sententious, too often missing the irony with which it might have been originally used. Mistaking eloquence and rhetoric for good writing, I was drunk on adjectives, reckless with adverbs. Fortunately, doggedly, I still asked myself questions. Why did I lack a Best Friend? Was the Empire exceptionally fine or exceptionally criminal? I won a history prize in 1937, Lord Acton's *Lectures on Modern History*. Rather boring and not modern, but one sentence made me pause: 'Hundreds of humble Anabaptists suffered a like fate and nobody minded.' I wanted more. The Anabaptists' fate remained unspecified but was obviously gruesome. Who were they? Why did nobody mind? Because they were humble? What had they done? The claims of fast bowling, the quest for the Best Friend swiftly removed any urgency to discover, yet, intermittently, the sentence rankled. A few years later I read in a Saki story of a boy who was convinced that his favourite hen was an Anabaptist, but this confused me further.

During war, love and absurdity, marriage and travel, deaths of old friends, delight and dismay with new, the Anabaptists hovered in half thoughts, complained in dreams, whispered — like cromlechs and broken roads, old walls, a death-mask, an empty house — 'Tell our story'. I began a small notebook. GBS mentioned them in prefaces, Meyerbeer wrote of them in the grandest of grand operas, Wilde's Dr Chasuble discloses that he had refuted Anabaptism in an unpublished book. Henry VIII seemed to have boiled some, alive; Elizabeth had certainly burned two at Smithfield, who died 'in great horror with roaring and courage'.

I retain that notebook, its untidy shorthand containing sharp or grotesque feelers. A three years' siege of Münster, Luther and the Pope denounced as the two halves of the same bum, polygamy, the dictatorship of the Elect, mass-executions, a crazed court under a young, glittering Messiah, a man on a red-hot throne with a red-hot crown rammed over his head. A terrible voice, 'the fire will fall from heaven and the asp and the dromedary will be about the streets', three cages on a cathedral tower — you can see them yet — and in 1944, the RAF dropping the fire, hitting the zoo, and indeed sending the asp and dromedary into the streets.

Most of my novels began from some barely noticed remark, event, even glance that lingered, and perhaps years hence, pushed up like a mushroom through concrete to become a situation, and perhaps to disclose a theme. In the sixties, I at last wrote my novel, *The Friends of God*, about those Anabaptists; a long, ponderous book, heavy as Hindenburg, myself apparently doing little more than watch my hand move over the paper, as if I were copying words from a blackboard. Its best chapter I can quote in its entirety, for the words are not my own: 'We are in the desert, on a wild heath, under the bare heavens.'

Anabaptism had been a fanaticism which terrorized sixteenth-century Europe, and had some smouldering place in the origins of the Second World War. People were so immobilized by inordinate power displayed by the plausible and charismatic that they gladly offered their throats to be cut for crimes they had not committed. Power had ceased to be a responsibility; it degenerated into appetite, with resounding consequences.

'Was there nothing worse', she said 'than these things? They saw even the Prince-Bishop is ill with it. Dying. He will never forget what we had to see.'

Jacob pulled his white, tangled beard, the heavy bible on his knee. He no longer thought of sin, there had been too much hate. News had also come that the tree, planted where Munzer had died, had blossomed on Christmas Day.

He said gently, 'No, darling . . . no one will ever have to face worse. We were no longer people, they robbed us even of our selves. All of them. For so many years. And of us, why, even a bird lives longer than we do. The thing is, however, where does it lead? Was our King's way the beginning or the end?'

The towering old man waited. Now it was as if he were alone on a plain. His voice, with new indignations, reached out over the wastes as he sat under the filthy chimney-hole and that black-raftered ceiling hung with sacks, straw, onions.

'For us, who's left to say anything else? For you, my daughter, well, there's life, and perhaps forgiveness, somewhere, and peace. This is to say, in the end, in the very end, they, all people, the whole world, will learn what it was we stuck our heads into!'

13

Uncertain, an unfunny clown, I was seeking the Best Friend,

who, in sad fact, throughout life, appears from nowhere in particular, stays awhile, then yawns and drifts away. I wanted, as in school stories, to be loved and followed, like Bevis and his Mark in Richard Jeffries' wonderful idyll, preferably in farmlands, woods and by rivers.

Michael Rouse was an ally against institutional absurdities, but we exchanged not souls but chuckles. Denis Mack Smith was too grand; at sixteen he seemed, like Stanley Pigott before him, an unofficial member of the staff. Alan Ross was too young, a liability almost capital in its reaches, Gerard too senior and esoteric. My quest ended, but with no apparent success. Walpole's Jeremy had watched from afar the aloof, romantic-looking Ridley; I saw, in another house, Graham, in whom John Armitage, Jean Jacquier, Wilfred Bristow flowered into perfections.

For three years I was trapped in the pleasures of grief, misunderstanding, secret conflicts sharp as lovers' nails. Girls I was not to meet until several years later, precipitating many stumbles, false starts, cul-de-sacs, *non sequiturs* and farce. At this period, my thoughts of them were mostly disdainful; I imagined even the beautiful as running with straight legs on the backs of their heels.

My callow emotions had urgency: loyalties were unambiguous and fierce, confusion helter-skeltered. Graham knew something of my feelings, and distrusted them. We met seldom and exchanged no word. I crossed and recrossed the Quad on chance of passing him; for his eye I bowled ever faster, ever wider; in chapel I sang noisily, tunelessly, in an effort to make him turn his head. My shoddy, derivative stories in *Extra* were directed at him, and to him I promised the dedication of my first novel.

Graham was outwardly a philistine man's man, 'the Breed' in person, with no external glamour, walking slightly lop-sided like a bear, saying little, a fine batsman but destined only for the army, and never, as Arthur Harrison would have put it, 'One of the Swells'. He was more akin to me than to Gerard and Denis, let alone George Bradford, a specialist in antiques, who, tipping the college porter five shillings, was informed that only paper was acceptable, on which he withdrew the shillings and substituted a penny stamp. I wept my full when in Cecil Roberts' best-selling *Spears against Us*, a war novel about the fall of the Habsburgs, I found a character with the identical name, bearing, personality. Virginia Woolf, too, exactly reproduces him, as Percival, in *The Waves*. Like Graham, Percival was no poet, but he provoked poety in others. In chapel:

> He sees nothing; he hears nothing. He is remote from us all in a pagan universe. But look — he flicks his hand to the back of this neck. For such gestures one falls hopelessly in love for a life-time. Dalton, Jones, Edger and Bateman flick their hands to the backs of their necks likewise. But they do not succeed.

He did not turn his head, we exchanged no sign, I could only watch and pray, and eventually my prayers were answered, but as ever, in the manner of gods, oracles, and major artists when asked a simple question.

14

Despite my love of churches, graveyards, hymns, I had no reverence for priestcraft, and while possessing a religious temperament, I shied from formal beliefs. The religious phase, obligatory in novels, eluded me, notably a rash of Anglo-Catholicism which prompted some of my associates to address the grave, low-church Headmaster, Canon Bonhote, as 'Father'. They seemed obscurely, perhaps shadily, connected with religion. Some residue of the Lower God occasionally induced me to start the morning with the resolution, 'Today I will believe,' as I might, 'Today I will be vague and sad and interesting,' or 'Today I will look very angry, with veins standing out like knotted cords.' I sat stolidly in the mock Lombard Romanesque chapel beneath medallions of the Evangelists, known locally as the Four Methods of Cribbing, enjoying hearty tunes, the King James' Version's resonant prose, Stanford's *Te Deum*, occasionally startled by a sermon, particularly one that began, 'Imagine your own mother crucified on the cross, and then you will understand something, *something*, of the love of God.'

I was amply structured to believe almost anything without evidence. God might well have made the world but he had scarcely made it very well. Thus he could not risk visibility, and was felt only rarely, when the moon glared and the moth flew.

I enjoyed the Old Testament as I did the Iliad, Odyssey, Heroes of Asgard. There was discrepancy, often welcome, between injunctions wafted from the pulpit and the anecdotes read from the lectern. 'Thus saith the Lord. In the place where dogs licked the blood of Naboth shall dogs lick thy blood;' and 'And Elisha turned back and looked on the little children, and cursed them in the name of the Lord. And there came forth two she-bears out of the wood and tore forty-two of them;' and 'And Samuel hewed Agag in pieces before the Lord in Gigal.' I was glad never having, as far as I knew, encountered the Lord. 'Then Jael, Heber's wife, took a nail of the tent, and a hammer in her hand, and went softly to Sisera, and smote the nail into his temples, and fastened it to the ground, for he was soundly asleep and weary.'

I did regret that nothing was told about the domestic fortunes of Heber. Again, prompted by the Lord, 'Ehud put forth his left hand and took the dagger from the right, and thrust it into the king's belly; and the dirt came out.' A passage I was to recall in the forties when hearing of Pastor Dietriech Bonhoeffer, who after long agonizing with his conscience, decided to assent to the proposed assassination of Adolf Hitler, as compatible with Christianity.

To me at sixteen, Jesus seemed as ambiguous as a comedian, as dexterous as a juggler whose feats were liable to failure, of uncertain temper and considerable inconsistency, explicable, I suppose, in a nature not divine but convincingly human, or through meagre evidence and disputable translation. Once more I heard, 'May Christ blind you!' saw the scared boys in the white, frozen silence, after reading Christ's implacable curse not only on Scribes and Pharisees but the blameless fig tree. 'No man shall eat of thee forever!' Someone later explained that the fig tree symbolized unenlightened Jewry. It may be so. But the nature of Jesus' love, wavering between Good Shepherd and Avenging Judge eluded me. In *Lancelot*, as a precaution against mere physical appeal, I borrowed a legend that Jesus was unusually ugly, swarthy, with eyebrows meeting, perhaps a hunchback.

Vaguely, almost wordlessly, in religion, as in politics, I was seeking less the right answers than the right questions. In the context of 1937, would the Sermon on the Mount provide much more than considerable cannon-fodder? Religion had only poetic appeal. 'Prayers are the daughters of Zeus.' The most powerful rulers, teachers, heroes, saviours, seemed those who had not literally existed. I saw Jesus as akin to Arthur, Robin Hood, Odysseus, Don Quixote, Mr Pickwick, Mr Murdstone, Hamlet, Sherlock Holmes, Cinderella. Yeats put it well, though not, at that period, to me: 'Because these imaginary people are created out of the deepest instinct of Man, to be his measure and his norm, whatever I imagine those mouths speaking may be the nearest I can go to truth.'

Confirmation – 'The following boys will represent the House at Boxing. . .', 'The following boys will attend the OTC Camp. . .', 'The following boys will be Confirmed. . .' – briefly provoked unjustified expectations of instantaneous moral transformation, which a glance at my seniors would have swiftly amended. That Canon Bonhote, 'The Boot', when already ordained, had volunteered for the Machine Gun Corps in the Great War, was impressive, though in the spirit of Heber's wife.

I doubt if I ever credited a creator, but can sometimes envisage some purposeful magnetism existing within consciousness, helping to sustain and enlarge it. I would have welcomed the notion of a God *it* rather than *he*, to be reached as through journeys into deepening spirals of awareness, or unexpectedly glimpsed in some passionate instant, a phenomenon not axiomatically benevolent, but dynamic. Today I am interested in figures in labyrinths, stages of psychic resurrection, moral rebirth, symbolized in myth and fairytale, though in spirit I incline towards Voltaire, when he wrote to Boswell: 'You seem solicitous about that pretty thing called

Soul. . . I do protest you, I know nothing about it; nor whether it is, nor what it is, nor what it shall be. Young scholars and priests know all that perfectly, for my part I am a very ignorant fellow.'

Christianity, I subsequently began to realize, in a fumbling way, has had to adapt itself to the apparent failure of Christ's promise of a speedy Second Coming, thus necessitating interpretations of Kingdom, Love, Afterlife, sometimes sublime and generous sometimes incongruous or cruel.

Chiefly, I desired to live for ever on a bland sunlit cricket field with books and Graham, though the Bible gave scant hopes of this. Today, my friend the Norwegian theologian, the Revd Dr Krister Stendahl, has maintained that human immortality has decreasing place in Christian thought, and that its presence there, unjustified by Bible teachings, largely derives from misunderstanding. 'The end of Life is thus in the mystery of the Will of God and in the coming of the Kingdom. The issue is not what happens to me but what happens to God's fight for His creation.' Immortality may consist of one's own effort towards this fight. Life is ever concerned with rebirths and resurrections, but these are convulsions of understanding, not a physical prolongation in what Aldous Huxley termed a 'harp and shriek' Afterlife.

Unaware of such speculations, I continued my random browsings, learned an ancient belief that none has entered heaven since AD 333, that Jesus was confirmed as a god by majority vote in 335, and that another majority vote generously allowed the existence of God, in the French Revolutionary Convention.

Theology has never interested me, unlike myth and fairytale, particularly after discovering a claim that the poetic yet rather innocuous 'fairytale' was a fourteenth-century corruption of the sterner, more truthful 'fatetale', which continued the original psychic structure of the Quest: the grand resolution, reached through question and answer, degrees of initiation, under-standing, reality; with fate dependent on personal choice, the observances of certain rules, on endurance, with periodic setbacks. Fall and Resurrection. Here, we are simultaneously miners and climbers, and Rilke wrote:

> We are found, through our waxing and waning,
> fitter for use by remaining
> forgers of ultimate ends.

and:

> Yes, for your task is to stamp this provisional, mortal earth
> into ourselves so deeply, so painfully and passionately, that
> its being may rise again, 'invisibly', in us.

Temperamentally, I have never inclined greatly to saints
and gurus, and moreover I have seen sentimentality and
superstition about Isis and Jesus constantly transferred to State
and Leader. I suspect that the words of some unfortunate
awaiting the gallows after the Gordon Riots must have applied
to many of my teachers seated amongst us in Chapel, and to
this day to many thousands in North and South Ireland:
'Damn my eyes, I have no religion, but I have to keep it up for
the good of the cause.'

The sainthood of a Gandhi, a Tolstoy, seems to me the best
method yet known for getting one's own way all the time
without court of appeal. Neither would have passed Cyril
Connolly's test — judge a man's character by the health of his
wife. I prefer the amused, yet practical scepticism of
Talleyrand, who dozed off, over a list of his own faults given
him by some busybody. Learning not to accept reputations on
trust, I was glad of a paragraph from Anatole France,
encountered as I browsed in the library: 'There was in London,
during the age of Queen Elizabeth, a certain Dr Bog, or
Bogus, who achieved great celebrity on account of his treatise
concerning Human Error, which no one had read.'

15

Haileybury was an imperialist school, retaining some traces of
the old East India Company. Imperialism then had more
restricted meanings than it does now, when Russia and
America have given new tints to a world once flamboyant with

the red of the British Empire, stamping ground of 'the Breed'.

Like, I imagine, most British people in the thirties, I was never quite certain of my own feelings about the Empire. It possessed the tawdry attractions of conquest and possession, and the exoticism of 'Katmandu', 'Mandalay', 'Federated Malay States', 'Hong Kong'. Simultaneously, 'Progressive opinion' . . . GBS, Wells, Leonard Woolf, Leonard Barnes, A.L. Morton . . . denounced racialist land acts, 'exploitation', salt tax, hut tax, poll tax, enforced imports, imprisonment of debtors; hookworm, malnutrition, exclusion of Indians from British clubs, which so angered George V, and 'No Dogs, No Chinese, allowed'. 'Why,' Aldous Huxley demanded, 'would the loss of Hong Kong be a mortal blow to Britain's honour while its seizure after a war in which Britain attempted to force the Chinese to buy opium was in no way a stain upon the same honour?' This was neat, persuasive, and I read with horror of Governor Eyre, even Amritsar, a name not pronounced loudly at Haileybury, indeed seemingly a code name for the subterranean and infernal. Apparently Victorian manhunters in Tasmania earned £5 for each dead aboriginal adult, £2 for a child. Through Left Book Club publications I grew familiar with such hallowed enormities as Rhodes' manipulations of King Lobengula, Lugard's hardness to King Mawanga, the melancholy ousting of King Prempeh of the Ashanti, 'a very dignified, self-contained, quiet but powerful person, rather like Lord Baldwin in appearance and manner, but with more reserves of strength and no pipe' (from Leonard Barnes, *Empire or Democracy?*, Gollancz, 1939). For all that, Prempeh was robbed of his sovereignty, and his people of their national totem, the Gold Stool, mistaken by the British in full ignorance of anthropology, ancient symbolism, elementary psychology, for a vulgar throne. I would have had to admit, though unwillingly, the truth uttered some forty years later by Archie Moore, world champion boxer: 'The White Men say all men are equal, and they hate the Black Men for believing it.'

All this could not wholly undermine my inborn incredulity that the bronzed proconsuls and cheery generals who addressed us so pleasantly on Speech Day, men's men to a man, actually had blood on their hands. A Haileybury master, C.E.

Carrington, still a prominent authority on the Empire and author of a standard work on Kipling, had written a history of England, in collaboration with Hampden Jackson, who later published his own book, *England since the Industrial Revolution*, which concluded with a verse he enjoyed repeating:

> The good old rule,
> The simple plan,
> That they should take who have the power
> And they should keep who can.

From these I could balance recorded atrocities with undeniable benefits, though doubtless from disgusting motives and performed with stern impersonality: new towns, quinine, tea, cocoa, rubber, abolition of widow-burning, banditry and the rest. I was not ashamed of my ancestor, Vice-Admiral Edward Vansittart, who suppressed piracy in China between 1852 and 1855. But whatever the truth, the Empire could not be ignored.

Cinemas showed films in which rampantly heroic, conventionally paternalist British presented the thin red line to fuzzy-wuzzy hordes, outwitted silky Khans, tamed tribes, led desperate rescues. In *Sanders of the River*, Paul Robeson intoned magnificently:

> Sandi the Strong, Sandi the Wise,
> Righter of Wrongs, Hater of Lies.

And I remembered John and Henry Lawrence, General Nicholson, Richard Strachey. I admired Haggard's Alan Quartermain, Kipling's Strickland, and do so still, and was pleased with a card from India, sent in 1982, by Alan Ross, who had just discovered that 'R. Vansittart, son of Peter, made 101 here for ICS in 1804.'

I was nevertheless as confused about the Empire as I was about politics and war. I had read Winwood Reade's *The Martyrdom of Man*, one of those squat, brown, sixpenny volumes of the Rationalist Press Association, prominent on railway bookstalls, written by renegade monks, militant atheists, wistful pantheists. I have some still: Renan, T.H. Huxley, Wells, Llewellyn Powys, Voltaire, C.E.M. Joad. Reade gave a history of cruelty without fear or favour, with no evidence of noble savages or ripe, thriving civilizations destroyed by white thugs. Traditional African, Mexican, Asiatic customs, let alone Carthaginian and Celtic, included mass human sacrifice, head hunting, cannibalism, slavery, arbitrary royal killings, burying alive, prolonged torture. Preventable disease, ignorance, priestcraft seemed to balance the European disposition towards slavery, hooded tribunals, industrial mayhem, and the book might still astonish readers today.

In the flux of history, headlines fade fast. An old Indian villager was asked, some years ago, his considered opinion of India since the departure of the British. He confessed that he had noticed no difference, he had not realized that the British had ever come.

The men's men and their gossipy, strutting wives compare well enough with their present-day supplanters. Leonard Woolf, once a district magistrate in Ceylon, would not have tolerated the subsequent murders and evictions inflicted by rich Sinhalese on the Tamil minority. The drift towards one-party states, while consistent with ancient tradition, scarcely sanctifies that tradition. *The Times* (July 1976) quoted an Indian newspaper produced by an illegal cell of Marxists and liberals:

Even the British did not impose such censorship when the country was fighting for its freedom. The British are colonialists, but they were not Fascist dictators, and therefore the struggle against the British could be conducted in more general conditions. Individually, too, the British generally had a conscience, something that Mrs Gandhi was not born with. The British were at least answerable to their people back home, but the new Indian despot is a law unto herself, and has only toadies around her.

That other Amritsar Massacre in June, 1984, provoked me to mixed feelings, some ironical, not all of them admirable.

152

Seven

An Englishman never respects you until you stand up to him. Then he begins to like you. He is afraid of nothing physical, but he is very mortally afraid of his own conscience if you ever appeal to it and show him to be in the wrong. He does not like to be rebuked for wrong-doing at first but he will think it over and it will get hold of him and hurt him till he does something to put it right.

Mahatma Gandhi

With a firm grasp of half-truths, with political short sight,
With a belief we could disarm and at the same time fight,
And that only the Left Wing could ever be right,
And that Moscow, of all places, was the sole source of light,
Just like a young hopeful between the wars.

William Plomer

A man ought to vote with all of himself, as he worships or gets married. The difficulty with English democracy in all elections is that it is simply less than itself. The question is not so much whether only a minority of the electorate votes. The point is that only a minority of the elector votes.

G.K. Chesterton

In the Soviet Union the worker has gained within a few years more freedom than the workers in other countries have gained in a century.

Jurgen Kuczynski

Stalin is no oriental despot. His new Constitution shows it.

153

His readiness to relinquish power shows it. His willingness to lead his people down unfamiliar paths of democracy shows it. The easier course would have been to add to his own power and develop autocratic rule. His genius is revealed in the short, simple sentences which enshrine the Basic Law of the USSR, where in clear, clean language stands the charter of the new rights of man in the Socialist Society. Here is a document which ranks amongst the greatest in all human documents in its love of humanity and its reverence for human dignity. To read this astonishing document, to compare it with its predecessors, to trace the growth and blossoming and fruitage of what began years ago as a young and very tender plant, gives fresh encouragement to every democrat in every land, and invites him afresh to struggle against every opposition, and in face, if need be, of the most brutal oppression, for that new and richer freedom that all the world's great minds looked for and longed for.

Hewlett Johnson, Dean of Canterbury

I do not want Britain to be defeated, nor do I want her to be victorious in a trial of brute strength, whether expressed through the muscle or the brain. I venture to present you with another and braver way, worthy of the bravest soldier. I want you to fight Nazism without arms. You will invite Herr Hitler and Signor Mussolini to take what they want of your beautiful green island. If these gentlemen choose to occupy your homes you will vacate them. If they do not give you a free passage out, you will allow yourself, man, woman, and child, to be slaughtered, but you will refuse to owe allegiance to them.

Mahatma Gandhi

1

Heard the latest? The years 1936, 1937, 1938, were humming with Abyssinian war, Spanish war, Sino-Japanese war. Red Ellen had led the Jarrow hunger-marches to London in 1936. New words erupted: 'stormtrooper', 'liquidate', 'Anschluss', 'Dollfuss', 'purge', 'show trial', 'Sudetenland', uttered in a grotesque theatre under the eyes of the Great War dead. The Prince of Wales indiscreetly confided in the German ambassador and his father reflected to Baldwin, 'After I am dead, the boy will ruin himself in twelve months.'

Soon we would be practising Air Raid Precautions, sand-bagging buildings, awaiting gas-masks, as war threatened over Czechoslovakia and Chamberlain hastened to cross swords, or less, with Hitler.

Uninterested in ideas, I had Gradgrind's predilection for facts, something of the spirit of Miss White's 'possibly but not probably', and was to cherish the ironic smile of Talleyrand, the subtle stare of Chekhov, against exciting zealots in a hurry. 'The trouble with Mr Gladstone,' Disraeli said, 'is that he has no redeeming defect.' For all my awe of 'progressive opinion', I knew from Hampden Jackson that in the last free Russian elections, the Bolsheviks had decisively lost, yet kept power, exterminating or enslaving their opponents. This fact could be, and indeed was, explained away, but not wholly convincingly, even for me. I would have exemplified Marx's stricture that the English were deficient in the spirit of generalization and revolutionary fervour. I smiled, when reading, in a book by Philip Guedalla, that in 1848 German politics suffered from a rush of professors to the head. In music halls, I could have bawled with the others the gusty old song:

> Damn their eyes
> If ever they tries
>   To rob a poor man of his beer

— delivered with a lack of rancour which Lenin so deplored. The unprecedented concept of legal, and later, paid Opposition, still seems to me our most signal contribution of the arts of living.

Looking about me at certain prefects, a few masters, I could see that if power, as Marx claimed, was a responsibility, it was also an appetite. Ivor Cousins, Robespierre, Napoleon. Terrible figures were gripping the world's throat, in the spirit of Lenin's letter to Gorky: 'It would not matter at all if three-quarters of mankind perished; the important thing is

155

that the remaining quarter should be communist.' That intelligent people should seriously accept such rubbish does sometimes suggest that deep in mankind lies a desire to be hanged.

I myself was scarcely immune to the reckless promise and the big drum: sometimes I wanted to lead the dance, wave a banner, sometimes I responded to the local poet, the eighteenth-century John Scott of Amwell:

> I hate that drum's discordant sound,
> Parading round and round and round:
> To thoughless youth it pleasure yields,
> And lures from cities and from fields,
> To sell their liberty for charms
> Of tawdry lace, and glittering arms;
> And when Ambition's voice commands,
> To march and fight, and fall in foreign lands.

Not until 1940 did I hear E.M. Forster's Rede Lecture on Virginia Woolf: 'She reminds us of the importance of sensation in an age which practises brutality and recommends ideals.'

With the crushing political defeat of Labour in 1931, and the need for that party to evolve new ideas, new leaders, and renewed electoral support, the Communists were grabbing more effective publicity, and appeared to be in the lead against the dictators. Communism seemed to promise, or had perhaps actually achieved, a fresh start. The traumatic influence of previous eras, people's inability to escape genetic inheritance, the abnormal temptations of power, even belief in magic and astrology were still unfamiliar to me. I believed in spontaneous conversions, changes of heart, genuine revolution. I joined the Left Book Club, founded in 1936 by Victor Gollancz, who was one day to reject *Animal Farm* on political grounds. His chief associates were John Strachey, Mosley's former colleague, and Professor Harold Laski of the London School of Economics, later the Chairman of the Labour Party: both were, at least, near Communists. I was, I admit, attracted less by the books' arguments than by their externals. Self-importantly, I would walk holding some bright orange volume so that all could see the black *Not for Sale to the Public* on the cover, and imagine me in the secret councils of the realm, and indeed I did feel part of some vigorous, barely legal conspiracy, particularly at Hampstead LBC parties, where solemn subversives denounced Chamberlain, extolled Russian education, art, morals, abused the New Deal as paternalist and, in comfortable chairs, over brimming glasses, demanded arms for the Spanish Republicans. Those orange books still restore past days as swiftly as cricket legends, the recorded hoot of a steam train, a flake of Harry Roy's racketty music.

'On December 5th, 1936, a new form of democracy was born into a world where tyranny, in the form of fascism, openly scorned the democratic idea and threatened the democratic States . . . the present Soviet Constitution stands in a worthy line with our own Magna Carta and the democratic Constitutions of France and the United States.'

Thus the Red Dean for the Left Book Club in 1939. Others were jabbering like mad birds. GBS pronounced that Stalin was no dictator but a mere party secretary liable to dismissal at ten minutes notice. 'Stalin has delivered the goods to an extent that seemed impossible ten years ago, and I take my hat off to him accordingly.' Julian Huxley told of Comrade Stalin sometimes leaving the Kremlin to walk down the road to assist local railway workers. H.G. Wells, though briefly, rated him 'kindly', as did Beaverbrook. Anthony Eden praised his 'natural good manners' and 'felt a sympathy which I have never been able entirely to analyse'. FDR was one of my heroes, and on the whole still is, and I would have believed whatever he said, not least his wartime rebuff to William Bullitt.

'Bill, I don't dispute your facts, they are accurate. I don't dispute the logic of your reasoning. I just have a hunch that Stalin is not that kind of man. Harry [Hopkins] says he's not and that he doesn't want anything but security for his country, and I think that if I give him everything I possibly can and ask nothing from him in return, *noblesse oblige*, he won't try to annex anything and will work with me for a world of democracy and peace.

The peoples of Latvia, Lithuania, Estonia are unlikely to be grateful.

Gullible and, within my shyness, an inverted snob with short-lived flashes of conceit, one of those who wanted to swim without getting wet, I bowed to the LBC sage, John Strachey, commending Stalin's Russia as 'The Kingdom of Freedom'.

Dead horses, resuming their ghostly lives. Soon, the Hitler-Stalin Pact, soon the World War. 'It is not only insensate but criminal to fight against Hitler and disguise it as a war for democracy,' Molotov trumpeted. Stephen Spender was learning more directly about Party politics:

> But what amazed me was to find that Communism could not only control a party member's theory and behaviour, but also his awareness of actuality. Indeed, I have never ceased to be astonished by the extent to which Communists are indifferent to awkward facts. For example, one day I asked Chalmers what he thought of the most recent Moscow Trials in which Yagoda, who had been largely responsible for incriminating the victims of the previous purge, had himself been sentenced to death. Chalmers looked up, with his bright glance like a bird-watcher's, and said: 'What trials? I've given up thinking about such things ages ago.'

2

What I did learn from these political books, while in the Haileybury History VIth, was the recasting of rebellion and famine, slave trade and institution, heroes and villains, in terms of class-struggle, material assets and deficiences, instead of individual ambition and failure.

All these, however, lay with me for two decades, before, with some help from Huizinga, erupting in my novel, *The Tournament*, dedicated to Hampden Jackson, and concerned with the illusions of splendour, what Ralegh called 'seeming', the role of ceremony, titles, pageantry, imaginary beasts, bluff, in the incessant business of power. External extravagance implied inner decay.

More armoured forms were standing together in the Great Yard. Momentarily they were silent, staring at a row of cannon pointing outward toward the city. This was the Duke's celebrated Iron Family. Slender, elegant in their tracings, ominous in soundless restraint, they tugged at the eye as if from the other side of a mysterious frontier. For all their glitter they were solitary, in sinister virginity.

In contrast, the lords, transfixed before them, appeared over-bulky, over-magnificent in their armour; their breastplates, iron inlaid with silver, with gold, were thicker than ever; their helmets were plumed and lavish; one casque was topped with a green, jagged dragon's wing, another with a golden globe supporting a throne with crimson crown aloft, another was double-turbaned with coils of black and silver. More heads, seen against the sky, stared down, beaked and slitted from beneath golden stags, jewelled lions, wide fretted teeth, dark hammers. Some were as if hard Saracen birds had alighted on their helms.

I was displeased to learn from an academic that this passage was a substitute for masturbation.

3

During 1937–8, together with my muted war-whoops against *Führer* and *Duce*, and my announcement 'I have come into the world in order to disagree' which I had, to others' irritation, appropriated from Maxim Gorky, and repeated too often and too loudly, was an interest in pacifism, then attractively presented by Canon 'Dick' Shepherd and the Peace Pledge Union, which he started in 1935, with support from Aldous Huxley, Vera Brittain, Rose Macaulay. Not only self-interest was involved: the ignorance, romanticism, and idealism of youth left me open to the arguments of Huxley, Gandhi, Bertrand Russell, Fenner Brockway, Eric Gill, Joad.

Huxley's *Ends and Means* provided many suggestions which common-sense queried, yet they nevertheless appeared attractive and indeed moving. Non-violence, I read, had succeeded in Deak's Hungary; among Catholics and Social Democrats in Bismarck's Germany; in Finland against Tsarism; in Norway against Sweden. Peaceful debate had settled a frontier dispute between Britain and America over a century ago, and between Chile and Peru. Gandhi would succeed in India, boycott was more effective than guns. Beyond doubt, Huxley, Dick Shepherd, Cyril Joad, were going to make Hitler and Mussolini look extremely foolish.

Famous thinkers appeared at this time to believe that Alexander, Caesar, Wallenstein, Napoleon, Ludendorff, would have been shamed into geniality by cups of tea smilingly presented, by humanist sympathy and reasoned argument. It was all in the spirit of the effective German film, *Kamaradschaft* and I failed to realize how easily Hitler and Stalin could ban it. I was particularly affected by G.P. Baker's biography of Hannibal, which showed me a personality and career quite new to me, that of Timoleon of Syracuse; a career which still seemed, though decreasingly, relevant to the situation that had created the Dictators we now faced.

If it is possible for a man to be a political saint, Timoleon was one. He possessed the simplicity, the sincerity, the power of working miracles, which only two or three political idealists in world history have shared with him. The Greeks came at last to the astonished belief — not wholly unreasonable — that Timoleon was under the especial protection of the divine powers. He came to Sicily with a forlorn hope just when it seemed as if Greek society were about to dissolve into barbarism. In a series of the most romantic and improbable adventures he captured Syracuse, received the surrender of young Dionysius, sent him to Corinth to be a wonder of all beholders, and almost refounded Sicilian Hellenism. He capped his feats of successful political idealism by the military triumph he won at the Crimesus, when he met and overthrew not merely a Carthaginian mercenary army, but the veritable 'Sacred

Band' of Carthage herself.

Later,

> He resigned his power into the hands of a restored Syracusan democracy which repaid him with a devoted affection which few men have ever had the privilege of enjoying – especially from the Greeks. Old, blind and retired, he remained a dictator without a body-guard, without a secret police, and without a privilege, who swayed his fellow citizens purely by moral prestige.

I was fascinated by idealism harnessed to responsibility and action, and have always been uninterested in idealism alone. The Kingdom, as Christ taught, was not to be built by half-measures from the lazy. A classical dictionary informed me of a further action of Timoleon. 'His early life was stained by a dreadful deed of blood. We are told that so ardent was his love of liberty, that when his brother Timophanes endeavoured to make himself tyrant of their native city, Timoleon murdered him rather than allow him to destroy the liberty of the State.'

So! Vindicating the Old Testament, individual murder could be sanctioned for the public good, as, not very far ahead, Pastor Bonhoeffer was to conclude. Here was a situation that engrosses me yet, and was the theme of my novel *The Game and the Ground* (1956) in which a doctor-idealist murders a fugitive SS officer, his own brother, in the interests of the refugee children whose lives he is restoring.

I sought in these figures the practical sense of Timoleon and the good humour of Socrates. The idealist so easily degenerates into a Robespierre, Saint Just, Himmler. 'Be not righteous over much, neither make thyself over-wise. Why shouldest thou destroy theyself?' The husband in Somerset Maugham's 'The Colonel's Lady' reflects that 'if Evie hadn't been such a good woman she'd have been a better wife'. 'Worldly' is not the most disgraceful of the world's words. Florence Nightingale, Chekhov, Nansen, did not seek perfection, they acquired goodness.

4

Yet nearing eighteen in 1938, I was still seeking the absolutes: the Best Friend, the Champion, the Supremo. I knew from Acton that absolute power corrupts absolutely, but would also learn from Steven Runciman that absolute powerlessness does likewise. My own idealism did not long survive. Knowing a little of how some of my friends had died under the Japanese, ignorant of apparent Japanese peace-feelers, indeed of the Japanese mind itself, and expecting a prolonged Far Eastern war, I rejoiced at Hiroshima, and at the Socialist government's insistence on making Britain an atomic power, as much to prevent American monopoly as to threaten the Russians. Even famous pacifists could emerge with unexpected proposals. In 1948, Bertrand Russell himself suggested that a destructive arms race might be prevented by the threat of immediate nuclear war, by America, to enforce nuclear disarmament on Russia.

Meanwhile Auden's poems were exhorting me to brace myself to resist Fascism, though when his own chance came he rejected it. Gandhi was being applauded in cinemas throughout Britain, between bouts of imprisonment. His apparent simplicity seems now to have veered between the subtle, the crafty, the naïve and the foolish. He supported Polish resistance in 1939, but informed the Viceroy in 1940 that Hitler 'was not a bad man'. Against the Japanese he advocated Indian non-resistance, though recommending that the invaders should be made to feel 'unwanted'. From safe quarters beyond the Atlantic, devotees of the Perennial Philosophy seemed to be teaching that deep breathing, meditation, spiritual exercises would worst the Gestapo.

Corder Catchpool, the saintly Quaker delegate in Hitler's Berlin, had already pleaded that 'different forms of government were not a reason for hostility'. I myself loftily explained to those who would listen – very few – that economic sanctions would prevent the war. War and Empire were plainly due to no more than the need for potash, manganese, iron, teak . . . Man's natural goodness would ensure the survival of the good.

I envisaged a visionary world in which human dignity linked men in the spirit of Antigone; of the fifteenth–century Aragonese Cortes' reply to the Spanish King: 'We, who are as good as you are, take an oath to you who are no better than us, as prince and heir to our kingdom, the condition being that you preserve our laws and liberties, and, if you do not, we do not.'

I was to live to believe, after the war, that Maximilian Köbe, Bonhoeffer, Elizabeth Pilenko, Enzo Sereni, Jacques Moulin made the Russells and the Gandhis seem rather small beer. Martin Wight, grave and humane, was a pacifist, but I never had a chance to discuss this with him. My flimsy and wavering beliefs were never to be seriously tested, due to yet another mysterious and adverse medical examination, at which a military doctor, addressing me as 'Sir Robert', ignoring my weak eyes, scribbled and pondered, prodded and shook his head, and suddenly, in mid-afternoon, switched me into his car, drove me from Camden Town to Hampstead, abandoning the glum file of naked youths, then shook my hand without a word, and vanished. I was left for fire service, civil defence, teaching, while my friends waited or fell at Dunkirk, drowned off Singapore; Wilfred Bristow vanishing above the North Sea, Byng struggling at Arnhem, George Rothery and Michael Rouse winning spurs in Asia, Alan Ross sailing through minefields to Murmansk. By then I could not really convince myself that Gandhi's magnetism was crushing a ruthless tyranny, that bombs were glancing off the glittering charisma of Huxley, that Russell was on the frontier primed to blunt the SS and the *Wehrmacht* by irrefutable argument and wit. Until the newsreels of Belsen in June 1945 – those striped, lurching half-corpses, those blank eyes and unfleshed claws, those streaks of gaunt flesh once smiling and alive – I had accepted Hitler merely as Churchill's 'wicked man', an outsize Bismarck. I have often pondered A.J.P. Taylor's assessment of him as 'a very ordinary German'. He now seems to me to have had a flake of genius, no talent, a crazed logic proceeding from a jittery centre, or no centre at all.

I read today of a sense of boredom and futility pervading the thirties. As a schoolboy, during holidays in London, Brighton, Buckinghamshire, I saw none of this. History bristled on all sides, with threats and promises hanging like planets. The streets of the late thirties remained theatre, now filling with hunger-marchers, street-corner Caesars, Neros, Blackshirts. The crowds themselves seemed heritage of an older, angrier London, of Hogarth − his name, Baudelaire wrote, fills the memory like a bomb − of Dickens, 'Hogarth in words'.

Shouts of 'Biscuit, Biscuit' would greet Ramsay Mac, before Baldwin replaced him as Premier of the National Government in 1931, jeering at his alleged sale of a title to some biscuit merchant, for £30,000 and a Daimler. 'Baby-starver,' yelled the unemployed. 'You cannot,' said Ramsay Mac, 'clip the wings of the rising tide.' And yet, and yet, he may have been a great man. Churchill was denounced, even after Munich, as a warmonger, Baldwin hooted at for 'Safety First'. On walls was daubed, chalked, nailed 'Arms for Spain', and at an LBC stall I bought George Barker's *Elegy on Spain*. I have it still.

Madrid, like a live eye in the Iberian mask,
Asks help from heaven and receives a bomb:
Doom makes the night her eyelid, but at dawn
Drawn is the screen from the bull's-eye capital.
She gazes at the Junker angels in the sky
Passionately and pitifully. Die
The death of a dog, O Capital City, still
Sirious shall spring up from the hill.

In bed, I recited:

Thunder and Mussolini cannot forbid to sing and spring
The bird with a word of determination, or a blossom of hope,
Heard in a dream, or blooming down Time's slope.

Still not wholly convinced of the absolute righteousness of

republican Spain, I thrilled to 'No pasaran', and remembered Val reading us Auden:

> Tomorrow for the young the poets exploding like bombs,
> The walks by the lake, the winter of perfect communion;
> > Tomorrow the bicycle races
> Through the suburbs on summer evenings: but today the struggle.

On pavements, in shops, I was seeing sharper profiles, hearing unfamiliar accents, mutters against refugees, anger at Britain accepting far too many Jews, or far too few. I understand that Britain accepted, if scarcely welcomed, some 40,000 between 1933 and 1939, France 30,000, USA 63,000. This does not suggest generosity. Malcolm MacDonald and Bishop George Bell found the Dominions apathetic. From these refugees I was to collect many friends: Erich Heller, Rudolf Nassauer, Wilfrid Israel, Constance Neurath, Mario Dubsky, Michael Hamburger. The last, for whom my affection is suitably tinged with awe, for his knowledge and practice of literature always far exceeded my own, has, in his autobiography, paid fine tribute to his adopted home. American Jewry, like the Administration, showed emphatic uninterest in Wilfrid Israel's pleas to increase the Jewish immigration quota.

Koestler had already noted the Berlin parade of 15,000 Jewish Great War veterans, wearing their medals, holding banners enscribed with the Kaiser's thanks, in protest against Hitler cancelling their war pensions, the crowd jeering as they passed. Auden had written:

> O it's broken the lock and splintered the door,
> > O it's the gate where they're turning, turning;
> Their feet are heavy on the floor
> > And their eyes are burning!

6

Life, of course, was not only thunder and Mussolini. I remember, on my holiday walks, a death's head street-singer croaking through the ruins of a fine voice, on windy Hampstead High Street; an old man, visibly dying, almost a skeleton, standing by one lemon on a dirty sack outside the General Hospital. In Heath Street a fishmonger, with hook instead of hand, reigned over vast, glistening marble slabs where between piles of crushed ice lay fish and crustaceans of all hues, beneath glowing, subtle-tinted game-birds; scallops and salmon trout, silver herrings, pale delicate ovals and darkly-shining crescents; fish with lemon between their lips, lobsters twitching in buckets. The fishmonger was obsequious to the rich, for whom he ran a despotic wartime black market; brutal to the unimportant and to the children — he once shoved a live crab down a small girl's back. There he was, in his glory, until the day when, in bright boater, long blue and white coat, he climbed the hill to the Heath and drowned himself in a pond, the boater drifting from bubbles to the reeds.

At eighteen, I could now wander further, beyond the Dark Arches, making my petty discoveries. Cheyne Road was haunted, and I might have seen other ghosts on Highgate Hill, Primrose Hill, Gloucester Avenue. In St George the Martyr, Holborn, was the 1834 memorial to Captain James South who gave £1,000 in Consols, 'for Christmas Dinners to Chimney Sweeps from all parts of London'. I could be submerged in the great London 'pea-soup' fogs, so beloved by Monet and, presumably, Jack the Ripper, enveloping without warning the chattering markets, locked and leafy squares, high-walled gardens, flaring slums, the broad filthy river, along which were nightly huddled vague, hopeless shapes, terrible heirs of those seen by Shaftesbury, Mayhew, Dickens. They were cared for by the soup kitchen of the philanthropist, Betty Baxter, the Silver Lady, who regularly appealed for funds in the *Morning Post*. I imagined that she was a leper, not altogether absurdly, for the young Masefield had seen a leper selling hot pigs' trotters outside Charing Cross Station. Once, from a pile of verminous rags, an educated voice addressed me, 'In Paris, we used to prefer boys.'

My earlier visions of old spectral London remained, remain still. Who could not be aware of it? Anti-Reform bishops, wigged and mitred, booed away from Westminster, dandies quizzing through St James' windows, the din of slap-bang supper rooms, uproar at the Goat and Compasses, the Star and Garter, the Marquis of Granby; the flutes, violins, and the hare that played the tabor at Vauxhall Gardens, where Leopold Mozart remarked that the music in London's pleasure gardens was unequalled in the world. Spirited repartee enthused London: in popular drama, caricature, chance encounters. A drunk accosted Lord Chesterfield, 'I never make way for a scoundrel.' 'Ah!' Chesterfield stepped off the pavement, doubtless raising his hat, 'I always do.'

It is the spirit, sharp, immediate, independent, of a later joke:

'Hey, my man, would you like to take me to Piccadilly?' 'Wouldn't mind, but I don't think the 'arness would fit yer.'

A twelfth-century monk, Fitz Stephen, required a city to be not only commodious and serious, but merry and sportful. Lord's and the Oval were open to me: Patsy Hendren, like Tim Pember, unexpectedly bowling an orange, Alf Gover, tirelessly pounding up like a railway engine with full head of steam. An open car stationary outside a dubious café, containing seven nuns, slanting like coffins. Cinemas, theatres, music halls.

In the thunderclap year, 1870, London had nearly sixty theatres, and some four hundred music halls aswirl with humour and drink, unbreakable weapons against the hoity-toity and the lah-di-dah. The comic, having played *Macbeth*, accepts fiasco with a joke and transforms it to a sort of triumph:

They made me a present
Of Mornington Crescent,

They threw it one brick at a time.

Hearty, patriotic, coarse, brutal and tuneful, the songs, in the thirties, were still being put over with gusto and style, wryness and stoicism.

> Tell them that my true love is far, far away.
> Here's your nice heads of celery.

The lachrymose, commonplace and melancholy within a breath. The intrusion of 'Ta-ra-ra-Boom-dee-ay' into Chekhov's *The Three Sisters*, at a moment even sadder than usual, was startling, yet grimly appropriate to actual conditions of existence. Vulgarity was redeemed by personality, and personality was big in the thirties, the voice not yet flattened by amplifier and deceiving machines and knobs. 'My wife, my wife,' shouted Max Miller, 'I'll tell you about my wife. She's so ugly that it's easier to take her out to dinner than to kiss her goodnight.'

With Byng at the Brighton Hippodrome, with Michael Rouse at the Kingston Empire, by myself at the Bedford, Camden Town — pease puddings and Guinness — I would see rowdy, sentimental Gracie Fields, Nellie Wallace with her crumbling feather boa, Will Hay, George Formby, Max Miller the Cheeky Chappie with his gaudy suit and bookmaker manner:

> I told her a funny tale,
> Made the Moon turn quite pale.
> Tore my pants on a rusty nail,
> Sitting on a stile with Sarah.

Billy Bennett, 'Almost a Gentleman', dangled time and events in fool's vision:

> Think of what we have done in the Future,
> Shall we do what we should do in the past?

He evoked timeless and loving response as he leered

confidentially over the orchestra pit – those tinny, crash-bang, slap-along orchestras. 'We want work – and not much of it.' Will Fyffe followed, with an echo of Sam Weller, 'What do the rich *do*? I'll tell you what they do. They do *us*.'

Songs, some quite dead:

It's very labour-saving when the dinner party comes,
You place it on the table and it eats up all the crumbs,
Gorgonzola, Gorgonzola, Gorgonzola,
   Three cheers for the Red, White and Blue.

I see Norman Long at the piano, with his Londoner's voice and chatty verses:

Lady Astor's bonnet
Had a Guinness advert on it
On the day that Chelsea went and won the Cup.

And the drawling, monocled Western Brothers,

Gandhi's loin-cloth
Fell off,
But it was perfectly all right,
He was wearing his Old School Tie.

Some songs linger, and much better than the Spanish general bawling 'Long Live Death' and docile mobs intoning 'Mussolini is always right.' I remember Turner Layton singing the virtually meaningless yet teasingly *There*:

'East of the Sun – and West of the Moon.'

Older songs survive in the eighties, from the days of Victoria and Edward VII, 'Lily of Laguna', 'Champagne Charlie', 'Boiled Beef and Carrots', 'Any Old Iron'. That Irving Berlin, composer of 'Alexander's Ragtime Band', is still alive in 1985 makes an extraordinary link with what seems to me a seething, violent yet good-natured world, which both sighed and laughed at the Great Big Shame of Jim, six feet three, married to a girl four feet two, and under her thumb in a month. The halls had some link with Bartholomew Fair, Mistress Quickly's Eastcheap, with Moll Flanders and Mr Vincent Crummles. The northern theatres I never visited and, with their fierceness, their intolerance of whoever displeased them, and with my memories of Whispering Jack Smith, I was glad to forgo them. Even the gentle Neville Cardus, when young, would, with his friends, bring in eggs, to reinforce disapproval.

8

I remember long lost London cinemas, those shining Regals, Roxies, Galas, Bijous, Plazas, Paramounts, Empires, Astorias, Granadas, Metropoles, Odeons, Palaces, Pavilions, Grands, Rexes, Capitols, Regents . . . twisted into pinnacled pagodas, straightened back into Greek temples, flaunting their sham boxes, mock-rococo ceilings, gilded flambeaux and caryatids, the Gothic, the Moorish, Byzantine, Venetian, recklessly entwined, the plushed crimson carpets, mauve tassels, the Wurlitzer rising from shadows through a bizarre procession of lights, like a gigantic Neopolitan ice. One organist was billed as 'Wyndham Lewis', which would have reinforced the more famous Lewis' rank suspicions of the world around him.

I loved the pre-war cinema in all its spurious grandeur, like Philip Toynbee before me:

And who shall pierce Old Muffler, old swaddler of the dulled senses, except those flickering giants who love and kill in the light, out of our darkness?
Your eyes gleam in the flickering light of the screen
On huge heroes; famous, fabulous women.

Villa, the warted hero with a nose like a burst plum, lolls in the conquered palace, scoring with his spurred feet the polish of a royal desk:
His barbarous lips pout on a vast cheroot,
Then push at our faces rollicking gusts of smoke.

Or all of those bandoliered sailors who mount the steps of
Another palace and fall stiffly to the silent jabbing of a
White machine-gun:
And the czar tilts in the sky, his horse careens
In stiff deference, unyielding, ludicrous submission.

At the Hampstead Everyman Cinema I too visited the Paris
of Clair and Renoir: Jouvet, Gabin, Suzy Prim, Pierre
Blanchard, Raimu, Michel Simon, Michele Morgan, Danielle
Darrieux, Harry Bauer, Corinne Luchaire . . . some with Herr
Otto Abetz's pleasant manners and the shadow of Nazi
collaboration almost upon them. For weeks I imitated Louis
Jouvet's deliberate step, spaced hands, high aloof stare.
   Chaplin I found more sinister than funny: sly, nightmarish,
jittering with vengeful cruelty. Keaton I only saw years later.
The slow-motion *non sequiturs*, stately misunderstandings,
solemn slapstick of Laurel and Hardy, were more to my taste.
Figures even stranger passed before me: Erich von Stroheim, of
whom John Huston's wife said that he wore his face on the
back of his neck; George Brent, always captaining the liner
from the cocktail bar; Eugene Pallette, all chins astir, Friar
Tuck to Errol Flynn's Robin Hood. More songs — Carl
Brisson's 'A Little White Gardenia'; Astaire singing 'The Way
You Look To-Night' to an invisible Ginger Rogers, her head
blank with soapsuds. And still, from China, Spain, Russia,
Austria, Germany, America, the inexorable newsreels and
their appalling glamour: a rollcall of the doomed illustrious,
ignoble   heroes,   and   the   quietly   forgotten.   Marshal
Tuchachevsky,   Prince   Humbert   of   Piedmont,   Hermann
Goering, King Leopold, Tsar Boris, Baron von Neurath,
Prince Starhemberg, Field Marshal Mannerheim, King Carol
and his Lupescu, Marshal Pétain, Stalin dim and motionless
above Red Square while thick columns goosestepped into the
sky. Curious futures dangled: the feet marched, the drums
beat, and at home we had three Kings in one year.
   Cecil Day Lewis' 'Newsreel' puts it for me:

Enter the dream-house, brothers and sisters, leaving
Your debts asleep, your history at the door:

This is the house for heroes, and this loving
Darkness a fur you can afford.

Fish in their tank electrically heated
Nose without envy the glass wall: for them
Clerk, spy, nurse, killer, prince, the great and the defeated,
Move in a mute day-dream.

Bathed in this common source, you gape incurious
At what your active hours have willed —
Sleep-walking on that silver wall, the furious
Sick shapes and pregnant fancies of your world.

There is the mayor opening the oyster season:
A society wedding: the autumn hats look swell:
An old crocks' race, and a politician
In fishing-waders to prove that all is well.

Oh, look at the warplanes! Screaming hysteric treble
In the long power-dive, like gannets they fall steep.
But what are they to trouble —
These silver shadows to trouble your watery, womb-deep
sleep?

See the big guns, rising, groping, erected
To plant death in your world's soft womb.
Fire-bud, smoke-blossom, iron seed projected —
Are these exotics? They will grow nearer home:

Grow nearer home — and out of the dream-house stumbling
One night into a strangling air and the flung
Rags of children and thunder of stone niagaras tumbling,
You'll know you slept too long.

Even Hollywood was turning to a real world. Not only
Marie Antoinette and *Destry Rides Again*, but also *The Grapes of
Wrath* and *Confessions of a Nazi Spy*. The film that most affected
me was Russian, Donskoi's *The Childhood of Maxim Gorky*. Old

172

Russia seen through a small boy, the Russia of toadying priests, bizarre affiliations, government spies, fairs, an atmosphere of the Lower God, Bishop Hatto, Baba Yaga and the hut moving on chickens' legs. The convicts dragging boats up the wide, shining Volga gave images to my novel *The Overseer*. Two uncles murder a favourite servant whose skills will save the family business, by making an abnormally heavy cross, forcing him to carry it up a hill, rejoicing when it fatally crushes him. Children play their immemorial games and tricks, the sadistic, tyrannical grandfather excitedly teaches young Gorky to read, and, crammed with ancient lore, magic charms, peasant stories, the wise, indomitable grandmother, so hauntingly acted by Massalitinowa, gravely declares: 'Behind another's conscience thou shalt not hide.'

9

Though loyal to Graham, fixed star in an ideal sky, I was tramping streets, parks, Heath, for the vague yet fateful encounters with girls from which would stream galaxies. Slender impossibles glimmered beyond reach, seemingly forever. LBC parties might possibly assist, though in anticipation only, for, on arrival, I would almost always find evidence to support the character in a Koestler novel, who maintained that one could see the fallacies of the Left by the ugliness of its women. Unfair, of course, and refuted by the handsome Alexandra Kollontai, though even Chekhov asserted that female liberalism was intolerant, pitiless and harsh.

At last, in the late summer of 1937, after an ascetic cocoa and biscuits evening in honour of Lord Addison's *A Plan for British Agriculture*, I walked home through Belsize Park, which in moonlight, pillared and tall, seemed a passable imitation of St Petersburg's white nights, though I was uncertain whether these meant snow or marble. Beside me was a slim dark girl in red corduroys, a genuine refugee, Fritzi Lehmann. This name I considered uncommon to a degree of brilliance, being that of the poet and editor, John Lehmann. Could she be his daughter, thus a passport to the published Elect? Guarded enquiries suggested that this was unlikely.

The evening swiftly faltered. She spoke, she spoke well, but only of Vienna, mentioning Major Fey. Of him I thought I had not heard, but said heartily that he was a good show. She replied shortly that he was a hungry wolf. I walked like Louis Jouvet at his best, but, irritated, she inquired if I had a hole in my sock. Dictators, I said, with increasing crassness, at least humanized authority. Her father and brothers, she said, were imprisoned in a camp. I wanted to take her hand, but one hand held a bag, the other a batch of yellow leaflets. I nerved myself to brush her shoulder, and she muttered something further about Emil Fey, whom, I now recalled, was mentioned unfavourably − 'Fey's strong white face' − in Spender's 'Vienna'. He was an Austrian Fascist leader, supported by Mussolini. 'We'll go to work and do a thorough job' he had promised in February 1934, before savaging Viennese workers' homes and lives, leaving over 2,000 dead by fighting, and by hanging. Rather desperate, I told her that I had written a life of Mazzini. She had not heard of him. I added that I was a poet, she shrugged. I was tempted to recite 'Squelching through the Gulch' but prudence intervened. The red trousers glimmered in pale air, making roselight; the dark eyes drooped, lifted again; the sharp lips pouted. She was already turning aside, I dared not ask her telephone number, she had disappeared into the basement of a house which, in the early morning, I was unable to find.

At another LBC gathering, a young man addressed us on the relative benefits enjoyed by American, Russian, German and British workers, Russia easily leading the field. A future Cabinet Minister and peer, I met him two years later, eagerly justifying the Hitler−Stalin Pact, which destroyed most of the LBC assumptions within seconds: and yet again at Oxford, demonstrating with impressive facility the justice of the Russian attack on Finland, which would secure the defences of Leningrad, presumably against Britain and France, following the Reds' fulsome praise of their new comrade, Hitler. Myself he ignored, but a thickish woman of about thirty detached herself from a morose husband with decided views about the

174

current situation amongst American garment workers in the larger towns, and suggested a break for fresh air. We walked on the Heath. She had a tired prettiness and a strong scent. She took my hand as if picking up a plate. We sat on a wooden bench — it still remains — the warm night fresh with rustling trees. After cursory, though obligatory reference to the International Brigade, I remarked on the iniquity of marriage. She sighed, said I was very understanding. Emboldened, a man's man, I kissed her chin, aiming too low. She sighed again. Highgate lights glittered from a hill. 'Like stars,' I said, testing a line that had regularly bobbed up in my aborted novels, 'like stars in a fisherman's net.'

'Ah!' Her sighs now seemed firm steps towards nowhere, 'That's very poetic and intense.' At this I kissed her more accurately and we had a minor struggle on the seat which at once proved too narrow. Before she fell off, I was already scared, ignorant of how to continue. Back on her feet she murmured, with the poetic intensity she had admired in me, 'You're very young, aren't you!' then giggled, my last hopes falling around me in blunt bits.

Like many of my contemporaries, I found the progress to full sexual initiation protracted, rather laborious. A dance band refrain, 'I Want to be Smashed and Grabbed', made me ponder. Had I known Freud's belief that copulation was an act between four people, I would have pondered still more.

Next year, on Primrose Hill, guns would be poking skywards, silver balloons hovering over London. Virgin, oppressed, restless, I would stand at midnight by the Heath pond where girls reputedly bathed naked, slithering between rushes, flopping on rafts, gliding over turf between trees, lowly calling, lowly calling; breasting tiny waves, diving down long, polished shadows. Girls in woods, girls on islands, girls outstretched and dazzling on grass, single, or in the eager, beckoning hordes of an Eddie Cantor or Dick Powell musical. Girls: Sylvia Sydney, Betty Field, Carole Lombard, Ruby Keeler, Ginger, Michelle, Danielle . . . Dorothy Hyson, still lovely today . . . but dancing away, dancing away to Gosport, leaving me in a pack of dwarfs, cretins, Woosters.

175

I would see, but never dare follow, slick-haired big-shots, hot-shots, with their sparkling floozies passing into dance Meccas where gaudy lights and throbbing drums suggested alloyed bliss, 'hitting the high spots'.

Eight

Pale Ebenezer thought it wrong to fight,
But Roaring Bill (who killed him) thought it right.

Hilaire Belloc

Dictators ride to and fro upon tigers which they dare not
dismount.

Winston Churchill

The Second World War was the noblest task to which the
British people ever set their hand. We alone on the Allied side
entered the war of our voluntary choice and stayed in it till the
end. Yet it was hardly over before it was set aside and soon
forgotten.

A.J.P. Taylor

Perfection, of a kind, was what he was after,
And the poetry he invented was easy to understand;
He knew human folly like the back of his hand,
And was greatly interested in armies and fleets;
When he laughed, respectable senators burst with laughter,
And when he cried the little children died in the streets.

W.H. Auden

1

The Czech Crisis had been settled, though 'settled' could have
been uttered by Apollo at Delphi. We had drilled fiercely on
Big Side, rushed about Quad with stirrup pumps, sat on

sandbags awaiting bombs to smash the dome that Wilfrid Blunt so deplored. Eventually our fears dissolved and a mature voice announced over our bent heads: 'We owe our presence here tonight, in lasting peace and honourable security, to two great spiritual forces. I will not call them men: I repeat, I call them two great spiritual forces. I refer to the Prime Minister, and. . .er. . .God.'

Returning to Haileybury that autumn, 1938, I was struck by a personal bomb. Without warning, Graham had left. Mathematical deficiencies, shared wholeheartedly with myself, had removed him to a Brighton crammer's, to prepare him for the army. Desolate, I nerved myself to write, and was astonished to receive a reply, short, matter-of-fact, friendly. More letters were exchanged, a relationship established on absences, a palace of air. Nightly I prayed for his return.

I was working for an Oxford history scholarship, though lacking genuine scholastic inquiry and application, reading more round the subjects than the subjects themselves. Denis Mack Smith was bound for Cambridge and inevitable success which, unlike much that is inevitable, agreed to occur. I believe that Italy is now strewn with Via Mack Smiths, befitting our senior Italian specialist. Denis already had knowledge, discernment, an objective; I had considerable though unco-ordinated reading, a feeling for the bizarre, a reliable memory, and now trusted to glibness and a flair for occasion, and another prayer, to see me through.

My notebooks were stored with facts, picturesque but by no means essential. An eighteenth-century German Elector had composed 52,365 military marches, on two fingers. '*Boudoir* descended from the French 'to sulk', thus 'A place where ladies can retire to sulk'. Fourteenth-century noblemen kept jesters to ward off not only monotony, but retribution. Cellini insisted that musical skill was essential for architects.

I arrived at Oxford for a trial run, having another year at Haileybury in reserve. December was cold, wet, raw. Fellow candidates stood about with expressions of importance and appeared forbiddingly well-informed. One of them said in an off-hand way that a glance at the Roman export trade and at the Middle Eastern trade routes would explain the origins of

Christianity. Only a dark, romantic-looking boy, Sachnowsky, would, I felt, like me, never win anything, and I demanded, though silently, his instantaneous intimacy.

This I did not receive. I slept in an undergraduate's rooms, so much more spacious than my college study, and lined with books of stupendous, scarcely imaginable intellectual quality. Humiliated further, I sat up late, bemusedly reading Havelock Ellis' essay on the Dance, which dispersed all my loosely held beliefs and left me, some two inches high, to face the papers, with no more in my head than Charles V and his swarthy, grave commanders.

Of the exams I remember only an English essay, on 'Beauty'. I sat helpless, while a hundred heads lowered determinedly, pens scratched with authority, confident smiles were swapped. The moments dropped away, water in sand. Beauty! Should I merely describe Sachnowsky? But I could not see him, and indeed never did again. Perhaps he had already summoned his troika and returned to whatever glimmering fastness had bred him. Beauty! What was there to say?

Evidently plenty! The pens were like a regiment marching. I was desperate with vacancy. I considered handing in my paper blank save for an elaborate fretwork of dots and dashes designed around it. The beauty, I could today have reasoned, of an empty canvas, a creamy flatness spread over innumerable possibilities. Finally, crushed, I glanced at my neighbour's paper. Hoggish, red, a man of violence, he held his pen like an electric drill. Cautiously, I inspected his opening line: 'Beauty is of two kinds.'

I drew breath. This simple statement ripped away my blankness, tore away surfaces, revealing separate splendours, waiting to be linked, to create the new, indeed the unprecedented. It was, I felt, a supreme example of how not to write, how not to think. Roads met within me for an instant's embrace, then swirled away over the hills, to the Estramadura, to the Wartburg, down Esplanades, past Ambassadors, past Hilaire Belloc, reaching Gosport with ease, lunging towards the Khanate of the Golden Horde and the Dome of Mohammed Abdin. I cannot remember what nonsense I wrote, save for recklessly quoting, while omitting marks of quotation, from Spender, from Leigh Hunt.

I was, many years afterwards, to realize that I had despised
my neighbour unfairly. Baudelaire, whom neither of us were
likely to have read, had himself divided Beauty into two parts,
the eternal and the relative.

2

Aptly, 'precarious' derives from *preces*, prayer. That winter, my
prayers were as usual answered. A telegram arrived from
Worcester College, Oxford. I had won the top scholarship. A
letter came from Graham. Next term he was returning to
Haileybury.

I was desolated, buckled, and would remain so forever.
Why? Because when Graham arrived, I would have departed.
With horrid irrefutability, Edgar Matthews declared that,
having the scholarship, there was no further need for me to
remain at school, costing my mother considerable fees, not all
of which she had as yet paid. Neither she nor he were possible
recipients of my grief.

Graham agreed to meet me on the platform of Tottenham
Court Road Tube Station, but there were many platforms on
several levels, and while he waited two hours on one, I trudged
for three hours up and down another.

Eventually, we did meet occasionally. I sold my stamp
collection, to meet him in Brighton. We were happy, and
calmly, in friendly sequence, he came, I think, to like and
trust me. 'I can write anything to you . . . My trouble is that I
cannot express myself. But one day we will walk the streets of
Paris, you talking. You will always be talking. You will have
written your first book'. That book was at last dedicated to
him, but he never saw it. For him too the war came as a
release. Awaiting call-up, he worked in a bank. Then his
father, powerful in India, had him offered a regular commis-
sion in the Indian army. To go to India? To remain in London,
near me? He asked my opinion. I was moved that he did so,
but I had, in all honesty, and in renewed sadness, to advise
India.

There, like Percival, he died, within months. In the best traditions of the Breed, he drowned, swimming back from safety to rescue his native batman, having been directed into a flooded river on foolish orders from an absentee commander. A column on a lonely Scottish moor bears his name.

Perhaps, though Martin Wight discerned rather more, 'a grave, graceful and rare sense', he had been no more than what Dick Hannay had called 'the typical English boy, good at games, fairly intelligent, reasonably honest and clean, the kind of public school product you read about in books'. I cannot know. Occasionally, in a dream, a turn of the street, far off in a theatre, he reappears: he walks out to bat, vanishes round a corner, sits absorbed, stands very still, about to melt into a wall. He never turns his head.

I left Haileybury with sadness, and gratitude for having been treated, not perhaps with full understanding — who is? — but with tolerance and good humour. I am now surprised to learn from Wilfrid Blunt that mine was 'The Iron Age' of Haileybury, cautious, puritan, suspicious, as against 'The Golden Age' which was from 1923 to 1928 and which had indeed nourished Arthur, Chris Bullick, Hampden Jackson, Daddy Dawes, Wilfrid himself. The Iron Age, if it was so, must have owed something to Canon Bonhote's inaugural address, in which he announced that coming to Haileybury had not been from personal pleasure but from a sense of duty. Certainly, I saw F.M. Heywood, Lionel Gough, Henry Havergal, the vigorous music beak, Dawes, Jackson and Wilfrid himself depart. 'They were replaced by men of guaranteed soundness, and dining in Common Room was no longer any fun.' From a boy's view, this scarcely sums up Val Rogers, Martin Wight, and a devotee of the Marx Brothers, Geoffrey Wright. Bonhote I remember with more affection than Wilfrid. After I had once given him a torrent of ill-judged lies, he shamed me by replying, 'Since, as you are a gentleman, what you have told me can only be the truth, I of course accept your explanation.'

I now had a year free, before Oxford, where I was due in the autumn of 1939. Part of this I spent on the staff of an Essex prep school. My employer was a Mr Blake-Blake, whose parents, with scarcely imaginative taste, had given him the Christian name of Blake, a distinction which the more irreverent of his pupils, with a liking for rhyme, did not allow to pass unnoticed. He was youngish, stoutish and rich, though the riches were not for me. For the term's work he paid me, in advance, ten pounds, explaining that I would have the advantage, not easily estimated in mere cash, of working with an exceptionally distinguished staff. Teachers no longer received tips. There resulted a misadventure apparently common, indeed classic, for later I found it reproduced in *A School in Private*, by Philip Toynbee, not yet known to me. It was not criminal, but decidedly worse than when Michael Rouse appeared and quietly, though unnecessarily, dug up his private tennis court.

In my first week, my 'tenner', a useful sum then, disappeared. Obvious theft from smiling, polite, over-fed boys. So I complained. Irritated, Mr Blake-Blake publicly invited the thief to confess. Of course, this was declined, so he proclaimed a state of emergency. Until the money was restored, all half-holidays would be cancelled, including school football matches. I was swiftly unpopular: even the staff were forced to work. The outcome is already obvious. After seven weeks of resigned misery, I put on an old coat which I seldom wore, and in it, of course, was the missing note. An interesting moral problem had then to be tackled, but I lacked the nerve to confess, so that misery continued unabated. A number of ageing gentlemen may still remember me with hatred, particularly the athletes. I am grateful again to Wilfrid Blunt, in whose book I have recently encountered a remark of Sir Walter Scott — applied by Wilfrid to the Haileybury Common Room — 'No Schoolmaster ever existed without having some private reserve of extreme absurdity.' Mr Blake-Blake, usefully disguised in my novel *Broken Canes* as

'Mr Drake-Drake', was unexceptional in his occupation. He had once been 'out East', which he spoke of as a single and deplorable country. 'Not as bad as Russia, mind. There the people go about in gangs!' His wife, more of an intellectual, spoke respectfully of a former minister, 'a Jewish version of Professor Einstein'. Blake-Blake was slightly deaf, which rather rationed intelligent conversation. A beaming child would approach, and say gently: 'I say, sir, you are a rotten old fool, aren't you!'

'Yes, yes, whenever you like.'

With his wife he tended to use only two replies, doubtless hacked out from his dealings with parents: 'Yes, yes, of course,' and 'it simply can't be done.'

'I see the Royal Family are back home, dear.'

'It simply can't be done.'

'Do you think Canon Outram dislikes me, dear?'

'Yes, yes, of course.'

He could be sententious: 'It is my considered opinion that fresh fruit is good for growing boys.' This entitled him to charge extra for providing two windfalls a week for each pupil, together with permission to share out any fruit sent from home. Social responsibilities he did not neglect: on Ascot Gold Cup day, he would stand motionless in his study in full morning dress, holding his grey hat, for boys and staff to file past, observing what a gentleman looked like. On Sports Day he regularly intrigued for a titled personage to give away prizes. Whenever failing, he would readjust his own speech. 'Had her Ladyship been present, she would have said how very glad she always is to visit the school, cheap in none of its ideals and fittings, though far from expensive. She would have added . . .' Parents, as was usual in prep schools, would present silver cups for events their sons were likely to win, sometimes turning nasty when they failed to do so. One winner had his cup snatched back by an aggrieved couple.

The exceptionally distinguished staff were several melancholy figures, the sexes unevenly distributed. Despite my financial insecurity, they treated me amiably enough, once they discovered that I too lacked a degree. The oldest would invite himself as often as possible to the homes of wealthier

183

boys, and could wreck Christmas festivities by blurting out such remarks as 'If it wasn't for people like you I'd have spent the holiday wandering about in the lanes.' A rival had some talent in coaxing boys to undergo private tuition, the profits to be shared unofficially with Mr Blake-Blake. In a friendly way, I imagined all of us as the lunatics hired to enliven Tudor weddings.

From this experience I derived the conviction that teachers should either be very young and enthusiastic, or very old and very cynical. The boys I remember less, though one of them on Naval Service, died in an unusual way, being apparently blown to pieces by a Royal Salute; this caused red faces when it was noticed that his own was no longer among them, though he was honoured as a war casualty on the school's Roll of Honour.

Blake-Blake himself qualified as experienced. He catalogued parents as the well-born but poor, the common but well-connected, the rich but not quite gentlemen, and the dangerous. School reports, he insisted, must be doctored, in the knowledge of these nuances. They were exercises not in truth, but in diplomacy. To praise Lord X's lazy or foul-minded son might induce his friend Lady Y to send, or transfer, her son to us. My own reports were revised by Mr Blake-Blake, though he failed, where a mother did not, to notice one elementary error. 'His spelling,' I wrote severely, 'must develope'.

Mr Blake-Blake would speak resolutely of the approaching war. 'And when it comes, you know where you'll find me!'

'In Chapel?'

'No, no, they'll all be closed down. No. You'll find me, of course, in the Front Line.' A forecast made inaccurate by his subsequent wartime sojourn in the Ministry of Information.

I was to have some twenty-five years school-mastering and have friendly memories. That terrible word 'Project', those 'Open Days', with the art teacher hurriedly painting dozens of pictures and signing them with children's names, the children in a progressive school, anxious to attend lessons, but forbearing, being still more anxious not to offend the staff. I must have learnt more from my pupils than they did from me, and noted several unusual features. The presentation of a hippo's foot caused queer feuds and anxieties amongst the boys. The popularity of one boy was transformed to contempt, when his father was killed in Korea. Another father, wholesale grocer, achieved brief fame by being imprisoned for manufacturing wooden pips for sale in his own branded marmalade: for some days, school opinion wavered between admiration and disapproval, the latter finally winning, the son, hitherto much liked, being sent to Coventry. Certain boys and girls, of high but frustrated intelligence, jealous of younger siblings, turned to truancy and petty crime.

One school story I particularly enjoyed. A very rich parent, the Headmaster announced, was going to give the school a most unusual treat, for his son's birthday. For weeks, everyone speculated what this could be: a trip in the Graf Zeppelin? To Brooklands, to see Sir Malcolm Campbell race 'Bluebird'? To the Zoo? A submarine voyage? The son fattened on gross toadying and flattery. The great day came, and, on every breakfast plate was a square of smoked salmon, fresh from Fortnum and Mason, very small, very expensive. Several boys were quickly sick, the son was ostracized for months, only the staff prospered, eagerly grubbing up the remains.

During that unhappy term with Blake-Blake, the hours of extra work I had contrived for everyone were mostly given over to 'prep'. Supervision duties were unexacting, enabling me to begin a novel. I wrote the last chapter without having begun the first, having read of too many aspirants abandoning their books through inability to finish. I copied this out in longhand, supposing that publishers would pay me, and pay me well, to complete it at leisure. In this I was mistaken. Another job was necessary.

From Chekhov and Turgenev, I coveted the role of young tutor in a country house. It was temporary, it held sexual prospects, the work would be negligible and the meals delicious. This was unexpectedly easy to procure; a West Country family had a backward daughter facing the School Certificate examination, and, over the telephone, her mother urged me to hasten with all speed. This was in late July, 1939.

She was small, chatty, seemingly ineffective. The father was tall, tanned by foreign suns, taciturn. The daughter, save at meals, I seldom met.

The house was large, old, comfortable, well-staffed. On my arrival we had tea on a patch of scrub called, though not to its face, the croquet lawn. A little maid appeared, staggering under the heavy tray—cups, butter, scones, sandwiches, cream, jams. Then another, better-muscled, with a crowded cake-stand. Then the housekeeper, bearing silver tea-set on glittering tray. Finally, the butler, with a tiny tea-jug on a silver saucer. This promised well, though the mother spoke of Latin, mentioned arithmetic, not my favoured subjects. The daughter must have been present. The father, slumped in a deckchair, said nothing and seemed to sleep, awaking only when I mentioned that I had brought a tennis racket.

At dinner, only he and I were allowed wine. He doled out lemonade, rather grudgingly, to the women. The wife periodically mentioned the villagers, as she might a tribe of uncertain habits and vile disposition, akin to Mr Blake-Blake's lowest rung of parents. Next morning, the father appeared, surreptitiously in my bedroom. He was in blazer and white flannels. 'Don't tell the others, but there's tennis at old Clavering's.'

So began a daily routine. On those sunlit, windless, August mornings we breakfasted alone, after dawn, before driving to tennis: tennis at Places, tennis at Parks, tennis at Halls, tennis at Lodges, tennis at Manors. My service, his volley, made us an effective pair. We were seen at Bath and Chard, at Lyme Regis, Norton, Fitzwarren, Frome, Shepton Mallet, Taunton, Bridgewater, as if charting the Monmouth Rebellion.

Beauty hovered. Flat, brilliant lawns, darting, captious players, the roses, butlers polishing silver behind tall windows, old red walls, old grey walls, huge brooding elms, silver tankards on sidelines, gracious dinner tables, slim shining bottles, rising harvest smells, old moon over new ricks, distant homesteads lit and decorated as archdukes.

The daughter was being given ample inducement to remain backward, occasionally wondering aloud when lessons would begin. The mother was beginning to watch me more narrowly, sometimes with deceptive wistfulness, sometimes talking to me, usually about flowers. Tulips, I learnt, had a cruel streak, violets were over-sensitive, roses the most fulfilled, pansies had apparently been responsible for much violence, 'like poppies, I suppose'. Once, observing me writing my novel, she said, 'If I ever write a book, a real book, I mean, not a novel, I think I'd call it *Up There*. That's about the most wonderful picture anyone can imagine. I don't mean to suggest that I don't read novels. I have read *Destiny Bay* three times. As you know, that's the finest novel ever imagined.'

Her relationship with her husband appeared at best a mutual assistance pact against the villagers, with off-shore support from a hefty bank balance. She always referred to him as 'The Boy'. The Boy, she continued, had considered entering Parliament, but they had eventually decided that it wouldn't be fair.

The butler, who doubled as the gardener, was the most interesting. His 'Sir' to me was frequently accompanied by a wink. More importantly, he was prone to rape local girls, which only slightly detracted from the Boy's status as a magistrate. Another magistrate, a retired major, had political yearnings more explicit, and enjoyed putting PC after his name, admitting rather reluctantly that this meant Parish Councillor.

Driving back from a long day's tennis, the Boy had, in his gruff way, begun to confide, mentioning two previous wives, though impersonally, as if they had been previous editions of a rather dull book. He did once declare that marriage was a sheer drop. 'Old Compton Mackenzie yarns his head off about love.' He chuckled unexpectedly, as if at a bar-room joke. Off court, he would usually sit alone in his library, leaving me to wonder what he did. He certainly did not read, though I think he knew how to. Sometimes, he may have wept.

I did give a few lessons, mostly reading aloud from *The Wind in the Willows*, when the Boy jammed his fingers in a door. These lessons were unsuccessful. My pupil was loyal to her school, or bored, or merely obstinate. 'I've been taught differently,' she would say, reminiscent cunning flitting over her thin, spectacled, rather hang-dog face. She did once volunteer that Chaucer was no good. On another occasion, when the parents drove to a funeral, I had to take her out to lunch. She spoke three times. 'The last time I was here I didn't get my fair share of the stuff,' followed, after a long interval, by 'It looks as if it's going to be the same this time,' rounded off with 'My father says fizzy orangeade's foul' before resuming not so much silence as nothingness.

I was being paid fifteen guineas a week 'all found'. A useful advance on Mr Blake-Blake. My tennis was improving fast, though my novel flagged, from the many books in the house that I needed to read. I was moved by Chesterton on Dickens: 'He did not dislike this or that argument for oppression; he disliked oppression. He disliked a certain look on the face of a man when he looks down on another man. And that look on that face is the only thing in the world that we have really to fight between here and the fires of hell.'

It all ended abruptly. September skies darkened, the rains came, obliterating the courts. The season was over; with war about to start, so perhaps was Britain. The Boy was retired to the library, until next summer. The wife, larger, sterner, produced a coach ticket to London and, with scarcely a word, sent me on my way.

Already, the Hitler-Stalin Pact had been signed in Moscow, acclaimed by GBS as 'Joyful news . . . Hitler is now under the thumb of Stalin, whose interest in peace is overwhelming. And everyone, except myself, is frightened out of his or her wits. Why?' Not until 1941, when Hitler invaded Russia, killing, torturing, enslaving, did I realize the full enormity of this treaty, and ever since I have regarded Militant Left and Right as identical psychological types. In 1939, I tended to blame Anglo-French apathy and suspicion of Russia for Stalin's new policy.

Oxford was an anticlimax. I realized anew that, lazy, ill-educated in languages, I would never be a historian. I had notions, but no ideas. I was gullible enough to join the Oxford Labour Club's demonstration in support of the Russian attack on Finland. I attended not lectures but cinemas, explored a few gardens, attended a few parties and knew I was in the wrong place. Half-knowledge, unanswered questions, never-theless, could assist my novel. I could be suggestive without responsibility. I quit Oxford very soon, having made only one friend, James Bailey, a Slade student evacuated from London, later a successful painter, who designed a *Giselle* for Covent Garden. My only solid memento is a letter from Dr Lys, Provost of Worcester, in reply to one from myself, thanking him for my scholarship.

Dear Mr Vansittart. I have received your letter: it is very ill-written. A letter to the head of your College should begin 'Dear Mr Provost'. *Not* as yours does, and you should learn what are the proper ways of concluding a letter, and a letter to any officer of the College should be written in black ink, not in red. Your very truly . . .

My novel must be written, and I really believed that, were I to fail, the prospects of civilized society would be gravely undermined, notwithstanding that we were all expecting London to be obliterated by the mass-bombings and worse, foretold by H.G. Wells.

I felt characters thriving within me, like bison and aurochs painted in the darkness of ancient caves and awaiting the light. I felt myself, not an emperor gazed at by the mob, rather that the mob was within me, and, proudly, I wrote at the top of page 1, 'I am the World.'

Unfortunately, I did not leave it at that. But my head was clinking with words, incidents, landscapes, demanding their freedom. Memories destroyed time. John Armitage, Wilfred Bristow, Graham, watched approvingly. The kingfisher flashed across water. At Sedan, starving horses ate each other. Gulls tore Baltic skies to shreds. The German sat on the beach; rats approached the Rhine; eyes met with messages that spoken words would never serve. I would never forget the giant on the ladder, the White Horse on the hill, and they must serve my ends.

Nine

The archaic Greeks, like the modern Indians, recorded events pictorially, in art and poetry, and when the original meaning of pictographs was forgotten, a new meaning was invented that satisfied curiosity. A poetic pictograph was called a myth but with no connotation of untruth.

Robert Graves

I love my country
its myths and legends,
its tin symbols
and other lies.
Francisco Carrillo

When litters are upset by the whirlwind and faces are covered by cloaks, the new republic will be troubled by its people. Then the reds and the whites will rule wrongly.

Nostradamus

We as Jews, I feel, are merely a *part* of the human race and not *apart from* the human race. Humanity has to re-educate itself to realize this simple truth which has been questioned so long, and we ourselves should begin to re-educate ourselves likewise. We have been stampeded into reacting as a separatist body all over the world since 1933. This must lead up to a destructive solution in the 20th century. I think we must serve the cause in persevering to save every one child and every one adult we can get hold of during this disaster. But only a great humanist revival (which I believe must associate itself and merge with a wide socialist endeavour, at least on the continent of Europe) will be able to find a true global situation.

Wilfrid Israel

1

My tepid career at Oxford in 1939 and 1940, as a history student, never made me doubt the value of history as a necessary part of adult life, or wish to join some African tribe that keeps no annals and punishes whoever attempts to do so. History, like fate-tales and gods, kept me at home in the world, and corrected me whenever I forgot that evidence of the times is not evidence of all Time. It was the speech of some Shadow Cabinet loudmouth, attacking a minor educational bill as an error 'unparalled in history', that helped me to write my novel set in the Britain of the disastrous AD 367, which, had he read it might have startled the politican into some awareness of what has lain beneath British politics for so long.

The past I see sometimes very clear, sometimes dream-like, but always with the future curling backwards towards me, the past ever reaching forward. Both give drama to the common-place: herrings, mosquitoes, rats, can transform society more thoroughly than ironclad knights or tanks; a stone circle on a windy moor addresses me more convincingly than Mussolini.

Too much stale knowledge, of course, oppresses, and, writing a historical novel, I may have to attempt descriptions of flowers, stars, people, as seen by remote illiterates ignorant of classical and biblical lore, thus seeing and naming them freshly. Pablo Neruda has written of Latin America, 'There are in our countries rivers which have no names, trees which nobody knows, and birds which nobody has described. It is easier for us to be surrealistic because everything we know is new.'

Movement always fascinated me, and, as I grew older, the movement which is only apparent. I was arrested by a passage in Thomas Mann's *Buddenbrooks*.

Often the outward and visible material signs and symbols

. . . only show themselves when the process of decline has already set in. The outer manifestations take time . . . like the light of that star up there which may in reality be already quenched when it looks to us to be showing at its brightest.

GBS has defined evolution as a pond of amoebae changing into the French Academy. What starts as human sacrifice may end as income tax. My own hand suggested a stage between prehistoric claws and the building of an unimaginable tower in a mineral as yet unknown, on a planet still to be discovered. Dylan Thomas had written:

> The hand that signed the paper felled a city;
> Five sovereign fingers taxed the breath,
> Doubled the globe of dead and halved a country;
> These five kings did a king to death.

Palms had grown in Middlesex, elephants had roamed the south of England, when the North Sea had been a trickle. Alexandria replaces Babylon, Amsterdam supplants Venice, Antwerp falters, London recovers her Roman powers. Quietly, quietly, the desert moves on. The dispossessed become supernatural presences, haunting lost lands, like Anne Boleyn deposing Katherine of Aragon, 'the Wronged Queen', and degenerating to an *ana bolena*, Spanish witch.

Currency precipitated me towards fashioning *Lancelot* (1978), a novel of post-Roman Britain. In museums lay the fine, Greek-style Belgic coins, the broad, clear, first-century Roman gold mintage, then, gradually, with periodic recoveries, declining into the late fifth-century *minissimi*, 'of which fifty could be spread on a halfpenny'. A sombre image. Cannibalism is now sacramental, now mere greed. Spartans taught their children to steal, to stimulate courageous resourcefulness. Christian Fathers ferociously debated the permissibility of loving one's wife.

Movement was incessant but I could see that its direction was not always predictable. What should happen often did not. A.L. Rowse's family possessed only one book, *The Home*

Preacher. Rowse could have become an illiterate ranter: he has written some sixty books. The bravest opposition to Hitler should have been from the Left: embarrassingly, it came from Jehovah's Witnesses. I pondered, and still do, the Greek magistrate, Aristides, exiled not for tyranny or incompetence, but from popular weariness of hearing him called 'the Just'. More than ever I was distrusting the neat, the packaged, the schematic, and today I see history as a matter of loose ends, but loose ends that tingle.

Near my friend Wilfrid Israel's weekend villa outside Berlin was a slab of the Tuileries, imported after the German invasion of 1871. It bore the words, 'This stone from the Seine banks, planted here in German earth, gives warning, traveller, how swiftly fortune changes.'

There could be what Victor Hugo called progress backwards. An Academy can revert to the witless and 'jungleloid'. In Stalin's Russia, 'the first state ever envisaged on scientific principles', Ernst Fischer's friend Klara was introduced to 'a special apparatus to obtain a systematic sincere confession'. Orwell mentioned that the Nazis used science in the cause of superstition. In my own development, Robespierre moved from childhood villain to potential hero, before settling down as symbol not of hypocrisy, moral cowardice, even bigotry, but of lack of imagination.

Theories of myths as misinterpretations of ikons, as symbolic conflicts and fusions of old and new beliefs and peoples, found in Reinach, Arnold Toynbee, Graves, excited me. That they were not final or irrefutable did not matter. One learns from learning, from querying one's favourite oracle. A poem, Auden declared, is a tall story, but if it is tall enough, it makes you go out and find the truth. Myths, while incapsulating tribal change, must also express psychic challenges and dilemmas, sexual conflict, legal restrictions and social custom.

Simultaneously, literary hints, critical allusions, at last began cracking some of my ponderous literal-mindedness. Hugh Kenner claimed Hamlet's words 'makes mouths at the invisible event' is a triple metaphor. As the cannon elevated to a target beyond the horizon. As the shouting face of an officer.

As a nose thumbed at Destiny. Again, the truth of this was less important than my resolve to read texts more carefully, and write my own more scrupulously.

'Well, actually I'm reading a historical novel. But only because . . .' I was to write several historical novels, a genre which is often scorned as a form of delinquency; sentimentality, embroidery, rough stuff, masquerading as serious writing. It can indeed be charged with rudimentary psychology, ornate special effects, bespoke plots, undue emphasis on royal weight-lifting. Dialogue can invite ridicule. Alfred Duggan, spurning the Tush and Prithee school, may have overdone the casual: 'King Romulus is a splendid fellow and we must support him. He really believes all that stuff about Rome being something special, a city destined to endure till the end of the world. As far as that goes he may be right.'

Even plain statement can induce the comic. I always chuckle at Stefan Heym's chaste sentence, without wholly knowing why, '"I understand you." Engels poured off the dirty water, refilled the basin from a pitcher, and invited Marx to have a drink.'

Nevertheless, a historical novel can set pertinent questions about movement, conflict, power, the 'otherness' of people, the relationship of past to present, our kinship with primitives, with animals, the role of free will, the changing functions and personalities of words. To write of the past wholly for its own sake seldom interested me. Writing a war novel, *Enemies* (1948), mindful of Graham's death, I deliberately set it not in the war which had destroyed him, but, in effort to realize the nature of all wars, in the Franco-Prussian war of 1870, on both sides of the frontier.

Philip Toynbee considered the historical novel akin to poetry. Certainly it must use the poetic, discern the mythical within history. This latitude enabled me to manipulate Time, so that Merlin, in *Lancelot*, obliquely refers to Robespierre, to Goering, and, I hoped, enlarges the scope of this novel: by discarding conventional historical notions of time, historical truth could be sought more thoroughly. Merlin had a convincing fable of a dictator, far in the past or future, overthrown because, in popular belief and academic theory, fierce rain dispersed his troops at midnight. Generations later, a minor historian at last consulted the annals, and found no such rain.

Erich Heller has distinguished between 'interesting stories' which end in death, and 'mythologies', which concern resurrection, transformation, metamorphoses, using the 'moon-grammar' of symbolism and astral allusion, as in Mann's *Joseph* cycle. For my historical novels I had to try and recast the ordinary. Shadow, gate, bird, stars, jewels, trees, blood, pedigree, circle, music, chessman, oaths, the dead, disease, a jug, thresholds, the left hand, foot prints, cripples, were alike hung with myth, legend, the imagery and ritual of ancestors often forgotten, used and performed dutifully but without comprehension. Huizinga's medieval studies affected me. 'Nothing was too humble to represent and glorify the sublime. The walnut signifies Christ, the sweet kernel is the divine nature, the green and pulpy outer peel is His humanity, the wooden shell in between is the Cross.'

I believed that the historical novel proper needed less research than speculation, sometimes too daring for the academic, and with luck rather than documentation, sometimes inspired. Speculations could be articulated through characters, seen both alone and in conflict, whose dilemmas, mysteriously urgent, became themes; and themes solidified to plots. Lack of scholarship was actually useful, allowing room for the impact of my own chance encounters, glimpses of random faces, unresolved quests. From historians, from my own observations, I learnt that there are no neat answers and few solutions. 'Revolutions,' Pasternak wrote, 'are made by fanatics with minds narrow to the point of genius.' But also, surely, from mythical inheritance, chance, lack of sleep, and sheer confusion.

Too much knowledge could corrupt the novel, making it essay, tract, thesis. No one will read a novel of mine for exact information about Roman belts, Bismarck's cigars, the length of Hitler's penis. Detractors would see an Impressionist who had never learnt to draw, and I have been rebuked by the Bulletin of Joint Association of Classical Teachers for causing 'flashes of pain' by wrongly dating a Roman coin, misspelling

Near Eastern towns and allowing a bird to fly eight miles.

For *The Tournament* I played long records of late medieval Burgundian music to assist thought in 'moon grammar'. I envisaged each character as most truly himself when alone. Alone, in the dark, Time is telescoped; wolves howl, the giant stands on the lawn, a god with animal head glares from the yard. I strove to disclose an unindustrialized age, largely illiterate, where omens clustered everywhere and in everything, the soul is live, occasionally visible tissue, to be felt, shared, occasionally exchanged, as in folk tales: a short cut to the gleaming invisible. The divine was accessible, through harsh effort, or fluke; a song was chipped from celestial Song; the golden hero was vulnerable to the evil eye of the universe; sacraments were as necessary as eggs.

My hero, the Duke, presided over a society whose music, paintings, literature, are part of modern consciousness, yet existed from different angles. Obscenity had protective powers; numbers, colours, bodily parts were strung to planets; short haired women could not perform magic, the owl was a baker's daughter; the year was strengthened by the blood of great ones; it was perilous to address ghosts by name, to touch twins and the red-headed, and to build a bridge without first placating the river or road with flowers, coins, a virgin. Wisdom could be learnt from centaur or unicorn, which were simultaneously known not to exist.

Duke Simon is youngish, healthy, but always, like myself, faintly perplexed: 'There had always been so many questions, ever since that day, years ago, when he had been puzzled at being forbidden to sleep under trees at noon by an old nurse who had eventually been hustled away, screaming, with all her head shorn, and never seen again.

Childhood questions, but even now never fully answered, accumulating new meanings through the years. Would a river *feel*? Could music *live*? On the other side of music, *what*? Why must dukes sometimes limp? Suppose you slept and never awoke? Or touched a priest with your left hand! Always that weird nausea at left-handedness. Grandfather with his magic spiders and silent furies, the terror of priests and robbers, who had closeted himself with lodestones and mandalas, collected raven-stones for invisibility and understood birds' speech by allowing his ears to be licked by the Snake, had had twins and the left-handed slain. It was said in the Palace that a left-handed baby Robert would have become Duke but for this, so that for young Simon certain passage ways, certain shadows, certain turns in the way were unpleasantly haunted, and in certain moods he felt a gap in himself, hollowed out by the accusing stare of his lost brother.'

A theme over which, as a man of the thirties, I particularly worried was that of people's surrender, sometimes voluntary, to the powerful but seldom all-powerful few: to the self-styled Elect, Inquisitors, Gauleiters, Central Committees. The following, from Friedrich Sieburg's *Robespierre*, is so perennial that its date is unimportant. It prefaced my Anabaptist novel, and, much later, pervaded *Pastimes of a Red Summer*, describing the hot Paris summer of 1794: year Two of the Republic.

Hardly ever did one of these unfortunates try to struggle against his fate, even at the last moment. This curious paralysis testified to their consciousness not only of the immense power of the State, but also of the elemental force of the Revolution. 'The condition of paralysis,' said a contemporary, 'was so strong that if one had said to a condemned person, "Go home now and wait for the cart which will come round to-morrow to fetch you", he would have gone home and next morning, at the appointed time, would have climbed on to the cart.'

The paralysis affected leaders and led alike, the sheep surrendering their wool, as Mussolini once said of his Italians. The genuine revolution, in which, in Saint-Just's words, punishment is a free pardon, will disperse it forever, though no sign of it can yet be seen.

A novel has many compulsions, and *The Tournament* (1959) owed as much to my personal preoccupations – marriage, middle-age, failures – as to problems of history. I was also prompted by guilt over lack of purposeful war activity, my exclusion from the men's men, while Graham and Byng, George and Stanley, Michael, Alan . . . Philip Toynbee, Perry

Worsthorne, Raleigh Trevelyan, Bill Letwin, Ben Nicolson, Drummond Allison, Freddie Ayer . . . rode out to dangerous pasture.

A pupil once asked me, with who knows what malice, whether talent was needed to write a novel. Actually, the question is serious. Looking back, as student, teacher and literary lounger, I now see that initial, sometimes spectacular talents were often misleading, or ultimately deflected elsewhere. I have also seen talent, negligible at the start, fostered or even invented by self-confidence, curiosity, and stamina. 'Without curiosity there can be no literature.' Ezra Pound also mentioned that he had seen young men and women of the utmost ability, who had come to nothing because they had failed to calculate the length of the journey.

Ten

Waiters, whom a provincial youth would have mistaken for diplomats but for their youth, stood about with the grave deportment of men who know themselves to be grossly overpaid.

Balzac

The important thing is to keep going and to appreciate that even one small improvement is infinitely worth making. It is the multiplication of many people each working in their chosen field and in their individual way that brings about genuine change.

Leonard Cheshire

If we want things to stay as they are, things will have to change.

Prince di Lampedusa

There is a third way between Utopianism and despair. That is to take the world as it is and improve it; to have faith without a creed, hope without God. The Western World is committed to the proposition that rational man will in the end prove stronger and more successful than irrational man. If the Western World abandons this proposition, it may conquer communism but it will destroy itself.

A.J.P. Taylor

1

Throughout war-time changes of address, I had maintained a Hampstead base. Returning permanently in 1947, I found few very startling changes. Sunday morning bugles still rang for some unseen parade. Each day I was awoken by unseen horses trotting up Heath Street to the Whitestone Pond, where, later, raucous Mosleyites would gather, as they had done in the thirties. Tennis courts, the Everyman, British Restaurants, Salvation Army, people in dressing gowns buying early bread in the High Street, small tea shops managed by genteel ladies, old-fashioned drapers, still remained, apparently un-threatened. On a Heath bench, as if he had been sitting there throughout the war, was the dirty-bearded, red-eyed, many-coated and well-papered tramp I had long known, a graphic reminder of Rebecca West's observation on the Paris con-cierge, 'How realist are the French to keep at their doorways a perpetual reminder that the body of man is contemptible and his nature fundamentally evil!' The Heath was as ever: the kites still floated above Parliament Hill, the blue and yellow balls rose and fell behind a dark copse. A woman paused to tell me that, when a child, she had imagined that 'going on holiday' meant living in a distant ash visible across the Heath from her bedroom.

Like a stage-producer, the Heath can alter my life. In 1939, under a rough, blue sky between Kenwood and the Leg of Mutton Pond, a slender, tallish man, neither young nor old, but an enigmatic mingling of both, had sauntered towards me, asked the time, nodded, as if confirming some vital, though private complexity, then departed. A few minutes later, we met again, on another path, and, as if resuming a discussion of some weeks previously, he inquired, rather diffidently, about some French notable, of whom I had not heard but found myself pretending to recognize.

I inspected the stranger more closely. He was pale, blue-eyed, not quite English, not wholly alien, not obviously anything very pronounced, elegant but not smart, smiling but not grinning, grave but not solemn. In my pocket was Isherwood's *Goodbye to Berlin*, and later, in the stranger's apartment, at Riverside Drive, Golders Green, I was startled to discover an almost exact reproduction of a room in Bernhard Landauer's home, as described in that book. I gaped at paintings precise and imprecise, oriental statuettes, Persian bronze tigers, a Buddha's head, H.A. Vachell's Harrovian novel, *The Hill*, a maquette apparently carved, or assembled, by my host. He was simultaneously tentative and fluent, controlled yet mysteriously apologetic, talking in soft but emphatic English which, I felt, uneasy yet flattered, was too finely phrased, too civilized and allusive, gliding from Pissaro to English public schools, from Bismarck to the derivation of a local pub-sign, the Naked Boy.

He opened a book, touched a record, glanced at a pot of flowers as if to soothe their anxiety. 'And you, sir? A poet? One must guess these matters while, at the same time, knowing them.' This was better. 'A novelist, actually.' I felt important, and thankfully, and as I was to realize, typically, he forebore to demand the name of my publisher; instead, he glanced briefly yet firmly at a line of volumes – Tolstoy, Turgenev, Thomas Mann, as if to confirm that I was amongst them.

'Ah! The Novel! How I wish . . . and how enviable!' Wide-eyed with respect he inquired where I usually dined, and meanwhile, as a favour, would I judge for him a wine which might prove to have unusually special qualities. 'Though of course . . .' he sighed, as if disappointments were inevitable but could be redeemed by sharing.

He was Wilfrid Israel, London born, with German Jewish father, Anglo-Jewish mother, a friend not only of Isherwood but of Stephen Spender, Adam von Trott, Chaim Weizmann, Philip Noel-Baker, Hugh Cecil, Einstein, Tagore, Martin Buber, Norman Bentwich, of Nansen himself – Nansen who denied the impossible but conceded that it might take slightly more time – and of George Bell, Bishop of Chichester, whose doubts about inherent German villainy, saturation bombing, and much else, so irritated Churchill and Eden.

All this I was to gather more by inference than from blunt disclosures. Mr Israel, never exactly devious, yet had reasons, from temperament and from enforced strategy, to avoid personal disclosure, together with a fastidious distaste for name-dropping. Gradually I learnt that he must be, or have been, a business man, possibly a commercial traveller, an undoubted sculptor and connoisseur, with duties at Oxford, presumably academic. I had sufficient sense not to mention Isherwood's book, but, allowing for the novelist's free-wheeling, it probably contained some aspect of his personality: 'gently inquisitive, mildly satiric, poking his nose into everything: Jewish settlements on the Black Sea, revolutionary committees, rebel armies in Mexico'. My own literary hopes shrivelled and foundered under Isherwood's unnerving eye which saw so much that escaped me in a personality humorous, barely translatable. Elusive, ironic, obliquely powerful, teasingly covering his tracks, Wilfrid was a Merlin without the malice.

I took long to understand that Isherwood's description was as partial as my own, though from a jumble of half-truths some pattern of truth can emerge. Isherwood himself, in 1931, could well not have known that far from being a weary, over-sophisticated dilettante, poking his nose about with no very obvious results, his unspectacular companion was exceptionally practical, well-informed and, in a special way, adventurous, intervening with quietly decisive initiative in many directions, some of them of historical importance.

There was a largeness about his home, quite detached from its literal size, which was small. It found room for a personality restrained yet withal outsize. Khmer Buddhas glimmered from private worlds. Also Assyrian and Cambodian carvings, classical and pre-classical heads, jars, plates, a Cézanne, Wilfrid's own drawings and mouldings. His collection he left to the Hazorea Kibbutz. He loved the eclectic Ghandasan sculpture, baroque music, quartets. Flowers deftly, unflamboyantly arranged, threw shadows from slim silver vases. Everywhere were clean, trim books in several languages by authors unknown to me yet whom, without fuss or condescension, he suggested I might care to reread or assess: L.B. Namier, Plekanov, Emil Ludwig, Klaus Mann and his friend, Frederick Prokosch; Kleist, Jacob Wassermann, Koestler, reaching to infinity. His first gift to me, Rilke's *Later Poems* began transforming rooms, fruits, arches, roses, dogs, gardens, parks, statues, horizons, and, I hope, myself. They soon led to the *Sonnets to Orpheus*, and continue today.

Oh, but in spite of fate, life's glorious abundance
foaming over in parks and splendid estates —
or in stone men, with all their straining redundance,
under balconies built over lofty gates.

Even I, a hobbledehoy here, could sense a radiance penetrating, then enveloping the day, which, with tuition and hard
work, I might dimly comprehend. These poems helped me
listen more attentively to Wilfrid's records, during which he
might occasionally glance up, as if fearing my displeasure.
When I mentioned Glinka, he nodded thoughtfully, asked
questions, always enjoying giving me a chance to inform,
explain, carve out an opinion, an identity, from my wayward,
impressionable flux. I did not mention that my interest in
Glinka came more from pleasure in the name than from
musical experience. 'Glinka', as dainty, as sweetly chiming, as
'rococo', as 'summer-house'.

Amongst those to whom he introduced me, cosmopolitan,
varied, mostly forbidding, I became aware that I had acquired
some reputation as a musicologist, with particular status in
Glinka studies. Also, as an unorthodox authority on
architecture, which I traced to my imprudent assessment of
Selfridge's as the most marvellous building in London.

He took me to 'a most unusual film. One of those foreign
movies you've taught me to enjoy.' It featured Mickey
Rooney. In the questioning way which implied he had very
much to learn, he would speak of Chinese painting,
Wordsworth and Southey, Namier's view of the role of our
early Hanoverian monarchs, though occasionally, as when I
referred to Myra Hess as a virtuoso, my ignorance or crassness
provoked a polite yet emphatic dissent. That I must have
seemed younger than I was, probably created a bond for,
uneasy with children, for whom he did so much, he had
exceptional sympathy with adolescence, its ambitions and
rebuffs, its dilemmas, eagerness, distresses, bewilderments
and disappointments.

We shared many evenings with books, music, talk, wine,
Wilfrid bird-like in a kimono of intricate patterns, though,
quietly masterful, he insisted that I spend a regular part of

each day working on my novel. I protested that I would never dare show it him, but he only smiled, 'But surely, that is all the more reason . . .'

Often the telephone rang, little voices from out of the night, clearly wanting information, advice, money, comfort. To each he was strictly attentive, patient, helpful, always with some useful answer before making some remark, never obviously funny, always gently amusing, before ringing off, sending me a rueful smile for the exorbitance of the world.

That some of these calls were from Palestine, unoccupied France, Spain and Portugal, Sweden, Switzerland, America did not occur to me, nor that they might be from ministers, senior civil servants, members of Parliament, famous writers and dons, from the Ministry of Information, Foreign Office, from exiled governments, from the refugee internment camp on the Isle of Man. I was to be astonished, too late, at the live history within my reach in that small room from which, while I read and wrote, Wilfrid negotiated ransoms and escapes, resettlements and funds, issued requests, probed appeals, and advised on post-war Germany, the reconstruction, and reconciliations. Even at the very worst, he always believed in an older, enduring Germany, open to reason, to spiritual enlightenment, of which the Nazis were not the representatives but merely the occupying power. On behalf of von Trott, Bonhoeffer, Dietrich Schonfeld, he was striving to convince the influential Stafford Cripps and Robert Vansittart of this, at the first stirrings of the Stauffenberg Plot. He opposed the various Allied plans to dismember Germany as unworkable and unjust. 'The simple but significant fact that the German people — not only the Jews — were the first victims of Nazi oppression is still too often ignored,' he wrote to Bishop Bell, who quoted him in a famous speech in the Lords. He was totally at odds with Lord Vansittart's pamphlet, 'Black Record' which saddled all Germans at all times with all criminal enormities and criminal aberrations.

Isherwood evokes one side, not the most significant, of him brilliantly, though this word is unsuited to Wilfrid's muted elegance, restrained persona:

He called for me about eight o'clock, in a big closed car with a chauffeur. The car, Bernhard explained, belonged to the business. Both he and his uncle used it. It was typical, I thought, of the patriarchal simplicity in which the Landauers lived that Natalia's parents had no private car of their own, and that Bernhard even seemed inclined to apologize for the existence of this one. It was a complicated simplicity, the negation of a negation. Its roots were entangled deep in the awful guilt of possession. Oh dear, I sighed to myself, shall I ever get to the bottom of these people, shall I ever understand them? The mere act of thinking about the Landauers' psychic make-up overcame me, as always, with a sense of absolute, defeated exhaustion.

'You are tired?' Bernhard asked, solicitous, at my elbow.

'Oh no . . .', I roused myself, 'Not a bit.'

'You will not mind if we call first at the house of a friend of mine? There is someone else coming with us, you see . . . I hope you don't object?'

'No, of course not.' I said politely.

'He is very quiet. An old friend of the family.' Bernhard, for some reason, seemed amused. He chuckled faintly to himself. The car stopped outside a villa in the Fasanenstrasse. Bernhard rang the bell and was let in: a few minutes later, he reappeared, carrying in his arms a Skye Terrier.

Our days were filled with small, though pleasurable shocks, minor readjustments to a routine orderly but unpredictable. He invited me to 'a glorious swim', I arrived with a flamboyant towel, and was driven to a Tchaikovsky concert. When all our friends were talking of 'the French paintings', Wilfrid carefully noted the gallery, and the next day said we must go to 'those pictures'. These proved to be *Gone with the Wind*, during which he left me. In the interval I found him, concerned, meditative, intent, listening to the manager, who was weeping.

Wilfred Israel was shot down over the Bay of Biscay in June 1943, returning from Lisbon after a mission for the Jewish Agency on behalf of refugees, mostly children. This destruction of a civilian plane was possibly due to German error, part of an effort to waylay Winston Churchill, due back from North Africa. Another passenger was the actor, Leslie Howard.

At that time I was teaching in Devonshire, and had received one of Wilfrid's non-committal cards. 'I shall be away a few days . . . these things occur. They may take a few days to arrange.' What things? He had always half-revealed, then withdrawn, like a novelist reluctant to overimpose himself on his characters. That his world travels had been largely humanitarian was unknown to me, and indeed I rather enjoyed his lack of explanations: I could build up a 'Merlin' from speculations, fruitful gaps, cryptic allusions. There was, I reflected, plenty of time.

'Wilfrid, do tell me . . .' He glanced aside, smiled instead of answering, then asked his own questions, shrewder than I then realized, and always seeming surprised, grateful, entertained by replies. His flattery was not seduction, but a subtly contrived sharing between unequals, a tactful form of tutoring. His artistic talents I cannot now judge, but he was an adept in diplomacy, friendship, perhaps love. Today, I sometimes feel ashamed at my lack of active curiosity, though shyness and reluctance to intrude had some part here, and of my almost total lack of help to him. More often, I fail to see myself through his eyes and to identify his personal needs. Sometimes, and it must have jarred horribly, I sought refuge in dire facetiousness.

After many months a small booklet reached me, compiled by certain friends – Bell, Einstein, Buber, Weizmann, Harold Beeley, and others, astonishing me by its range of facts. This is now far more substantially supplemented by Naomi Shepherd's biography, *Wilfrid Israel: German Jewry's Secret Ambassador*, to which I am much indebted.

The family business, N. Israel, the great department store, founded 1815, was the last big Berlin Jewish store to survive, until 1939, a model of benevolent paternalism, to which Wilfrid introduced Owenite undertones. At cost to his cultural and artistic tastes, he entered commerce through duty, though as always on his own terms, working assiduously, particularly amongst the young. An idealist with a streak of mysticism, he nevertheless showed unexpected flair for administration, policy, personnel management. He founded a unique Berlin business school and, after 1933, arranged the emigration of some 3000 employees.

He had worked with post-1918 Quaker relief for starving and destituted Europeans, having already written, with the Great War still raging, 'Now we still hear "The Battle continues". When will we hear "Humanity has awakened"?' Years later, as a matter of course, he responded generously to a young Nazi employee who had begged his help. In 1922, he was assisting Nansen in the Russian famine. He sat on a score of committees, not exclusively Jewish, for youth, education, pacifism; travelled to India to meet Tagore and the Gandhists, to Russia, America, Poland, China, the Baltic States, speaking of Zionism but alert for social experiments and artistic discoveries, investigating philanthropic, humanistic, internationalist cells, communities, projects — agricultural, artistic, scientific — and the endless needs of refugees. A capitalist with socialist convictions perhaps rather romantic, very urbanized yet with agrarian yearnings, he never seems to have paused from work. He helped found the Ben Scheman youth village in Palestine, was a sponsor of the Kibbutz Hazorea, to which he remained profoundly attached. The planting of a forest, a tree, was dear to him. He was governor of a German private school. Margot Klausner called him 'Pathfinder for the Habima', the Hebrew National Theatre in Palestine, for which, in ways usually unknown, he helped advise and judge, and gave money. I see him linking cultures and generations, religions and sciences, arts and trades, Jews and Arabs, Jews and Gentiles. After 1933 he was intermediary between German Jewry and international interests, between conflicting Jewish factions, between Einstein and Weizmann, between British government departments and the aliens interned in the Isle of Man. Foremost, he negotiated and promoted European emigration, mostly Jewish, bearding Eichmann himself, arranging ransoms from the camps and, usually vainly, urging on Western governments his plans to rescue many more. He was attacked in the obscene *Die Sturmer*, was beaten by SS thugs, and, quietly but obdurately, doubtless with his usual courtesy and reticent charm, resisted further assault while he bargained with the Gestapo. In 1938 alone, Wilfrid helped rescue and resettle some 10,000 children, 8,000 adults. 'I played the Scarlet Pimpernel,' Leslie Howard told him, 'you *were* the Scarlet Pimpernel.'

Throughout our friendship he was submitting memoranda to Chatham House, to the Foreign Office, to Ministers, on German history, psychology, future; on mass deportations from Belgium and Czechoslovakia, the annihilation of the Jews of Bessarabia, 250,000 Jews murdered in occupied Poland. In Austria, where he wrote, 'strong anti-semitism has always been prevailing, certainly within the ranks of the middle-class', the remaining 40,000 Jews were 'probably only waiting for their deportation to Poland.' This was seven months before the Allies officially acknowledged the existence of the Final Solution.

Pledged both to Palestine and internationalism, with instinctive loyalties both to Britain and Germany, Wilfrid had much in common with the more astringent Hampden Jackson. Both believed not in authoritarian socialism but in small, co-operative bases for reform and well-being: a village, farm, school, kibbutz, firm; a gallery, theatre, certain households. Each desired social change, without destroying organic traditions, believing not in panaceas but small advances on many fronts. Wilfrid hoped for a Palestine, not merely one more national state, but a pioneer in new concepts of work, belief, education, citizenship. 'You know,' he wrote to Adam von Trott, 'that I feel responsibility towards the future.' It sounds sententious, but no man was less so. Pacific but not quietist, he headed a British anti-aircraft research unit. Uncompetitive, he was often in the lead. Never a father, he worked endlessly for children. He had active relations with the International Red Cross and the League of Nations, and his unexplained trips to Oxford were to a Chatham House research department, stationed at Balliol. 'The ideals of the League of Nations,' wrote Norman Bentwick, 'and the International Labour Office, which was to usher in the new order, were to him dynamic motives of action.'

Unhurried, yet seldom inactive, Wilfrid would in a single

day draw a picture of himself, grapple with piles of typescript, contemplate sunlight on blossom, chair a committee, dictate a dozen letters filled with statistics and carefully docketed information, listen to a Mozart record from some out-of-the-way shop, telephone his mother in California, arrange a dinner for ourselves, the painter David Haughton, the Tamil writer, Subramamian. We would discuss comparative religion and he introduced me to the precepts of Lao Tsu, often akin to his own, though he did agree that 'The Sage accomplishes everything without doing it' might at times be dangerous.

Behind his serene amusement, calm smiles, he must often have been seething with frustrations, disappointments, and physical strains yet, curious, encouraging, he appeared concerned not with his own life but with my own strivings to get published, my reactions to Bach, Mozart, Tchaikovsky; to Bismarck Herring, which he guaranteed as of Medicean splendour and proved, as he knew it would, disgusting. Often, if only for a few minutes, he would sit on a bench in Brent Park, under drowsy trees, watching swans and ripples, talking of books, friends, past lives, trees, Hermann Goering, the last objectively, as if Goering were a force of nature rather than a political force, the former boss of the Gestapo. We must have discussed almost everything save what actually obsessed him.

That he had some emotional lack I suspected, but could not precisely locate, and my sensation of being a favourite pupil still somewhat on probation inhibited me from seeking further. No sign of self-pity betrayed him. In worldly terms he was doubtless a failure. His pleas for Europe and Jewry were largely disregarded, he saved only a fraction of those millions of condemned; he died virtually unknown and was lost in the aura of Leslie Howard. His artistic hopes were aborted; Palestine evolved in directions far from what he desired. Yet for me, and for others far more important, he survives as an example of how the dedicated individual can still grapple with the bureaucratic, the selfish, indifferent and wicked, and what Naomi Shepherd calls 'the immorality of pessimism'. In my life he was another of those who, by some fluke of temperament and bearing, some trick of eye and mouth, a disciplined display of friendly conviction, a sophisticated aloofness, conceals infinite reserves. Power, asserted Saint-Just, dandified in high white stock and golden earrings, belongs to the impassive. There are those who can lose with a shrug, win without fighting, perhaps – perhaps – accomplish without doing. I have heard, somewhere, that the Gestapo once came to harass and bully Wilfrid, but were seen to depart speechless, in a sort of shame, demoralized by some undefined potency delivered by a man unarmed, apparently frail, yet fearless; courteously hospitable, interested in all that was said, yet unyielding.

Does it sound unreal, too lofty, and, in my telling, pompous? If so, I have only to meet his eye, then envisage his ironic, smiling gratification when cheering Indian crowds mistook him for his host, the Maharajah of Baroda. That brings him to life better than I can. And, had he been with me at Marlborough House, he would have routed Ivor with a glance.

Martin Buber's verse obituary begins:

He was lonely as a star, yet resolutely belonging to all.
He lived with us as if with a stranger, yet
Was the most faithful of our friends.
He was shy when even the shyest are free,
Yet infinitely determined.
All of him was vulnerable, yet withstanding all blows,
Battle-torn, yet still unblemished.
All open to life like a victim, yet appearing
A lord of existence.
To him, though, suffering was not food, more like breathing
Which passes unnoticed.
He was always young, though he had undergone all.
His sadness of spirit was not dark, not bitter;
Its stringent clarity was that of finality.
Within it, the will to sacrifice himself to inescapable
Necessity.
Western the sparing gesture, eastern the wise eyes –
And the voice? . . .

To his mother, Albert Einstein wrote, 'Never in my life have I come in contact with a being so noble, so strong and as selfless as he was — in very truth a living work of art.' He was part of what E.M. Forster called the aristocracy of the sensitive, the considerate, and the plucky.

To drag myself in here might seem an impertinence, though self-importance is not involved. A writer, says Silone, must bear witness, though it is only through others that I can capture anything of Wilfrid: elusive, not devious, very quiet, yet neither stealthy nor unobstrusive, slightly mocking, but not at us. My novel, *The Overseer* (1949) is dedicated 'to Wilfrid Berthold Israel, a great and beloved European, killed 1943, serving the Jewish people and humanity.' But already it sounds sententious, embalming him with pious and dead phrases. In *Enemies*, a little earlier, I drew on some of him for the character of Herr Oberfelt:

> About this time it became understood that Herr Perfekt had returned from his travels. His real name was Oberfelt but, both in jest and affection, the citizens called him 'Perfekt', the Perfect Man, because of his sympathetic and generous disposition. He was a link between the wealthy squares and the darker, fever-ridden quarters: the poor knew him and the Grand Duke invited him to the monthly banquets. Periodically he departed suddenly, and it was never known where he had been.
>
> He had wide, lustrous eyes and an indolent expression that would flake unexpectedly into a smile. He seemed neither young nor old and his voice too was unusual, very precise, yet also hesitant, slightly querying.

A small boy, Conrad, residue of that long-ago Red Town, listens to Oberfelt at the piano:

> His hands moved across the keys in brief, emphatic motions, assembling a quick, jerky little tune, like something the peasants sang in the fields. The woodwork was very polished and it was as if four hands were moving swiftly over ghostly keyboards. The notes streamed out,

persistent as running water, now wandering away, fading, now returning in the odd, insisting rhythm that made Conrad half-expect the cool, poised dancers to spring from their frame on to the roses. He had never heard anything so quick and airy, it was minor revolution, he thought of Haydn and at once wanted to be a musician.

Quickly the notes succeeded each other, were caught in the tune, locked for an instant in a struggling medley of sound; then emerged, passed on, fell away and died like petals on the dark table.

'Is it finished? It was very unusual.'

'But did you like it?'

'Yes. It fitted in here. This room. What is it called?'

Oberfelt was still at the stool. His voice was light. 'It is an old French tune, "The Times are Gay".'

'French!' Conrad stared back in dismay, the thoughts threaded by the tune now mocking and ugly.

'Entirely French.' Herr Oberfelt rose. He was very slim and pallid in the dusk. A sudden tensity appeared in him. His eyes questioned. Conrad spoke, indistinct:

'But I thought the French were wicked.'

Oberfelt looked at him quickly, but his voice was still quiet, even humorous, 'Did the schoolmaster tell you that?'

'No . . . or not exactly.'

He knew he was disappointing, awkward, featureless, and now spoke with difficulty. 'Isn't it true?'

The Perfect Man reflected, then, brushing the roses, walked over, a strange light, both ironical and compassionate, breaking upon his eyes. Then he gently touched Conrad's bent head.

'Don't you know, my friend, that no one is wicked? That it's all an invention of interested parties?'

2

During that period between 1939 and 1943 I had finished *I Am The World*. None of it was planned. Daily, I grabbed a pen and followed its lead, imagining that I was hacking out the vast and momentous. There emerged massed rhetorical blocks of description, without the advantages of dialogue, character, humour, social and sexual relationship. Colour, I thought, hundreds of words, overwhelm the reader with torrents, avalanches, whirlwinds of words. Like Gershwin's father, I judged works by their length. *Anthony Adverse*, *I Claudius*, *Bevis*, were long, therefore they were good. My novel was a mish-mash, not of myself, but of other books, the dregs of my indiscriminate borrowings – the work, a reviewer wrote, of a young person who had read too much Baron Corvo and misread too much Herman Melville. I suspect that Wilde's *The Birthday of the Infanta* was more apposite than Melville, of whom I knew nothing.

In this novel, in a muddled, frantic way, I was seeking to penetrate the ornate trappings of power and revolution and find the flawed, various individuals within, but it was wordy fantasy, without the inspiration of genuine nonsense. I had not yet learnt from Alain-Fournier, 'I like the fantastic only inside the real,' that bizarre 'fairytales' endured because of their solid core of psychological validity. Man, with body, language, architecture, adventures, choices, sets proportion to the universe.

I had started, not from the flashpoint of personal vision, from overheard questions, ambiguous expressions, a sudden inset of sunlight on rain, colour in darkness, but from vague sonorities about violence and self. I could not trust my real feelings, was unable to believe that my own experiences, simply described, could be anything but puny. I attempted to storm readers by force, by melodrama, instead of grappling with the wolf, with Admirals, with a blind pirate on the winter road; with Graham, beside the River Lea or in a London fog; with the White Horse outspread as if by magic. I was to pay severe penalties.

I had it typed and methodically dispatched it to publishers in alphabetical order. Edward Arnold returned it without comment, Arrowsmith considered it impossible. Basil Blackwell rated it slightly higher: unpublishable. Batsford disdained it, Jonathan Cape, in a harsh letter, referred to

'Wardour Street English' and abused one of too many careless sentences, 'the meal was replete with food and drink.'

As always, prayers were answered. Chatto & Windus accepted it, on a report from V.S. Pritchett, but suggested I should meet Mr Pritchett to discuss changes. The prospect scared me. I read Pritchett's weekly *New Statesman* literary essay, and had had more real education from this man than in my three terms at Oxford. He himself was a one-man university, and I envisaged a gigantic and unanswerable polymath, ruthlessly censoring my marvellous script. Very foolishly I refused, and the book was published in its entirety, with its mistakes of spelling, syntax, meanings of words. Years later, I met VSP. Modest, genial, unfailingly friendly and encouraging, a smallish man of all the virtues, all the kindnesses and tacts, and finally realized the extent of my mistake. A few years ago, he and his wife Dorothy accepted a dedication in another novel, which at least derived from a real experience.

The reviews were mixed. They were either bad or very bad. John o'London was relatively mild. 'I cannot say this is the worst book ever written . . . I can without hesitation say it is the worst book ever published.' I would go round public libraries, sneaking the book under my coat, then dropping it into Heath ponds. 'Writing,' Frank Swinnerton wrote of it, 'should always begin with a distinct knowledge of what one wishes to say.'

It had one melancholy distinction. During the war, everyone read. People read prone in bunkers, crouching in ARP shelters; they read between fire-watching stints and between battles; in the NAAFI and the mess, in food queues, in dimly-lit trains, on blueish, echoing platforms, on rafts and in prison. They read on, above and under the earth. They read Trollope and Dickens, Walpole and Hay, Shakespeare and Ethel M. Dell. They listened to Felix Aylmer reading *War and Peace* on the wireless and to V.S. Pritchett reviewing books. One book, and one book alone, they did not read. With that indefinable sense of the fitness of things that sometimes infuses the public – over a scandal, a reprieve, a change in the law, an election – my book was ignored. It was deservedly and

214

promptly forgotten, if indeed a book can be forgotten without having been remembered.

I had prayed frenziedly to be published, and I had been. Six years followed before I could get another book accepted. A testing time, with instants of numbing despair as my contemporaries and juniors hurried into the light. I had to write, write incessantly, yet forget all my early attempts, train myself to see people and things, not so much new, but as I had seen them in the days of Dr Golder and Miss Howe. To emerge from books even while writing a book. Persist like a Mystery candidate through degrees of being, in a journey which could take years even to find the path, which could vanish at a touch.

3

Thus deflated, I, like so many youngish aspirants, roamed the statutory Soho literary pubs, saw, occasionally spoke to, statutory celebrities, momentarily hoping to win some sort of reputation without earning it. That Soho frieze I still find poignant. The Coffee 'an, the Black Horse, the Wheatsheaf, the Fitzroy, the Duke of York's, by now so often and variously depicted. At the Fitzroy, old-timers still cadging drinks for their recollections of the Great Beast, Aleister Crowley, surely a dreary imposter; Nina Hamnet jeering at a bald woman; the piano notes flying like chips from a woodcutter. There too would I unexpectedly meet Alan Ross, to my surprise, envy and irritation not only a fine cricketer, art-connoisseur, war-poet, traveller, but already much published, far more skilled, sophisticated and desired than myself. Once, borrowing his *Observer*, I saw, almost with alarm, a lengthy review by Denis Mack Smith, and, then, in a nearby shop, a book of poems by Gerard Irvine, and another book by Wilfrid Blunt. Anthony Curtis was already an authority on the theatre; John Heath-Stubbs and Michael Hamburger seemed to be published daily. I wandered through the pubs, disconsolate and boring even for those quarters. There, a much-married novelist was said to charge royalties for the use of his previous wives.

(To such as he, Mae West remarked that the wedding bells must now sound like an alarm clock.) An Indian dancer offered me a game of tennis; after five broiling sets I just managed to win, after which, one of his aides whispered that he had never before held a racquet. In this twilit shrubbery of talk and claims, denizens accepted to the limit Shakespeare's 'There's beggary in the love that can be reckoned'. One man, youthful under the paint, consistently and rather convincingly claimed to be two thousand years old. 'I remember Domitian always standing in the exact centre of the room . . .', 'Socrates never seemed to notice the wine-stains . . .' A Mr Scott, on active service abroad, had once met a Maharajah, which, he asserted, entitled him to free meals in Indian cafés. 'The King of Poland', an ubiquitous personage, was undeniably royal, in that he never carried money, unendearing in pub-land. I sat in corners, with my notebook, alert for high talk: 'I don't know . . . people like Chekhov . . . Cole Porter . . . types like that . . .' 'Rupert Croft-Cook . . .' 'I'd prefer Debussy. Unplayed, of course.' 'Did you read James' ode. Ode to Proust. "You and I, Marcel . . ." Rather clammy.' 'He did know Norman Douglas.'

I saw Paul Potts, who once bought a hat so that he could raise it to a man currently unpopular. I once stepped over Dylan Thomas. From a safe distance I watched the gifted but unpredictable Robert MacBryde and Robert Colquhoun. I dodged, for many weeks, buying a drink for Julian Maclaren Ross, seated at the bar in mid-July, encased in furs, fondling his ornamental cane, talking to his subordinates about Laird Creager, the movie actor. He had apparently read everything, even *I Am The World*: 'Chatto book. Yellow cover. Title blocked in blue. Very pompous.'

Meekly I surrendered. 'Would you like a drink, Julian?' He did not look round. 'Indubitably. Pints all round. A double brandy for Monica.'

The cash in my pocket was always in inverse proportion to my misgivings and fears, though I still imagined I was breaking into London's answer to the Left Bank. I was impressed when a haggard, threadbare man showed me his poem beginning, 'The People of England have asked me . . .'

In this atmosphere I was led to discover Dostoevsky, which induced a minor incident on the last night bus from Hammersmith. My companion, a young art critic, suddenly nudged me, and we both gazed at a man sitting near us. I looked at Tony, Tony looked at me, then we turned more formally to the man. Tony said, very politely, 'Excuse me, sir, for addressing you, but, has anyone told you that you look exactly like the Idiot?'

'Yes,' I joined in, 'you know, Dostoevsky's Idiot.'

But our enthusiasm for Prince Myshkin was absurdly misplaced, the stranger began shouting to such effect that the conductor ejected him from the bus.

More profitably, during the later part of the war, I had written to George Orwell, then literary editor of *Tribune*, not mentioning our previous encounter, but requesting books to review. He kindly sent me a book on Danish Folk High Schools, which I covered with the massive authority of supreme ignorance. Later, I was occasionally permitted, in his absence, to write his column, 'As I Please'. I was proud of my first effort, was convinced, wrongly, that it would erase *I Am The World*, not least for Chatto & Windus, and marched about London, *Tribune* in hand, awaiting a chance to boast. At the end of a weary day, this occurred. An Indian seated himself beside me in Hyde Park. Rather ostentatiously I began reading *Tribune* with small grunts of approval, nods of assent, sharp intakes of sheer delight.

'May I ask you, sir, what is the journal which you so plainly admire?'

I handed it to him, casually mentioning that it was my preferred vehicle in which to write. He looked at me with grave respect.

'Ah, sir, you are a writer. How much I envy you! It has always been my ambition to write, and yes indeed, to write well. How, I often wonder, does one do it?'

He need wonder no more. I spoke of form and balance, of spatial relations considered verbally, considered musically; I mentioned the several uses of dialogue and the techniques found useful from the cinema. He listened, with gratitude, respect, even reverence. Sighing, he rose, passing me his card. 'It has been a valuable lesson. You are my example. You will be hearing more of me.'

I did hear more of him. I can only here call him Mr KS. He is still very much alive but charges for quotation and has a taste for litigation. In the next *Sunday Times* was a full length article by Sir Desmond MacCarthy praising rather fulsomely the virtues of that talented and prolific man-of-letters, Mr KS.

The literary editors of *Tribune*, Orwell and his post-war successor, the wise and benevolent, T.R. Fyvel, could pay little, and I had less than £4 weekly. At best, I could occasionally afford a Charlotte Street meal, at Bertorelli's, or the even cheaper Schmidt's. The latter recently extracted a gaffe from me. My dinner companions were lamenting its demise, and thoughtlessly, I said that I had indeed found it useful, chiefly for entertaining girls, though only those I could regard as belonging, as it were, to the second eleven. There followed a considerable silence, during which I realized that all the ladies present had, long ago, accepted my invitation to Schmidt's.

'Subra,' I demanded one day, 'why am I so poor?'

Subramamian winked. 'Because you don't take my advice.'

'But you've never given me any.'

'When have you asked?'

'Oh, well! What is your advice?'

'If you want money, you write to the Prime Minster. A Mr Attlee. Mr. C.R. Attlee.'

The atmosphere suddenly coarsened. His broad, smiling face and brown eyes became interested, 'I always take,' Subra said, 'fifteen per cent.'

'Utter nonsense!'

He smiled again, sleekly complacent. Later, I reconsidered it, and wrote very carefully to the Premier, mentioning as if in afterthought that we had been at the same school, and referring to my love of cricket. I added that I had published fiction which had been reviewed in high places, and wished to write more, but could not afford the ink and paper. Then I showed the letter to Subra, who said, 'Perfect. It can't fail. You'll have to wait a few days.' I posted it to Downing Street.

The months trailed by. I glared at Subra. He winked again. 'I shall take,' he reminded me, 'my twenty per cent.'

It was too ludicrous for me to bother to pray. Finally a crested letter arrived, stating that the Prime Minister acknowledged my communication. Subra looked still smugger. Finally, another statement. The Prime Minister had examined my situation very carefully, and, after consultation with the appropriate departments, had advised His Majesty to grant me £150 from the Royal Bounty. The writer was instructed to add that in no circumstances could the grant be repeated.

I was pleased to envisage the Monarch and his Premier pacing the lawns, pausing between sundials, listening to peacocks, wrapping away Marshall Aid, Berlin Airlift, African Independence, Ground Nuts, Lancashire Cotton, to discuss my future.

4

In post-war café society at the Cosmo Café, Swiss Cottage, I met writers more or less contemporary. Michael Hamburger I already knew elsewhere, but here were Joan and Dannie Abse, Rudolf Nassauer, Emanuel Litvinoff, Bernice Rubens, Arthur Boyars, from all of whom I had much to learn. Much older, much revered, was the future Nobel Prize-winner, Elias Canetti, whose novel *Auto da Fé* won a huge critical success. With women I was still something of a man's man. The most lasting was A, who had been ill-treated by a musician of some fame. She was a teacher always, often on inappropriate occasions, referring to her employer as 'The Holy Head'. She would slice away a discussion hitherto cogent and enjoyable, with 'The Holy Head would totally disagree.' I began to be mildly jealous of this reverend implement. All was rather well with me until one day she widened my experience by leaving me not for the Holy Head but for Clara.

'Clara?'

'Clara.'

Still, two novels were precipitated by these sexual relationships. The title of one, *A Little Madness* (1953) explains the theme. The other was more substantial, an affair, when during the sixties my own marriage was cracking up, with a woman married, ostensibly on unequal terms, to a more obvious man's man. Elegant and purposeful, she had fine eyes, dyed hair, dark, spun-glass delicacy, faint, even dying voice, but she must have been impatient with my bemused inability to exploit every opportunity she allowed me. There were plenty. The husband I knew only as a fellow of some fame.

One day, when our meetings were at their most torrid, when I was convinced that I was valued almost as much as her house and dog, news came that the husband was dead, killed in Asia during further heroics. Her feelings were inscrutable, but mine were not. I found, to my horror, some sadness at never having met him. This boded ill for my relations with the widow. We said nothing, but some hours later another message arrived. He was not dead and had beaten some record or other. Subsequently, she promised me marriage, then vanished for months. An anonymous letter then reached me in Sweden, perhaps from a Holy Head, announcing that she was back with her husband, a postscript adding that she was pregnant.

Pain, outrage, despair. I sat all night on a frozen hill pondering alternatives. The easiest, cheapest and most accusing would be suicide, perhaps on her doorstep, though this would enlarge her vanity. The other, lengthier, tedious, exhausting, would be to transform our tale to a novel, allowing myself the best lines. The art of life, after all, is the transformation of set-backs to assets.

This I preferred, though it needed caution. Autobiography is a useful way of paying off old scores, but it also creates new ones. The man's man had powerful resources and was no fool. Indeed, my first job on returning to England was to give a radio talk praising his latest book.

For *The Story Teller* (1968) I devised a man born in 1362, and aged only sixty-two in 1962. Other plans went awry, for, as always, my imagination declared independence; the best lines fell to the husband, with myself rather absurdly pursuing a silly, exacting woman through a medieval peasant revolt,

Wallenstein's palace, Directoire Paris, the Kaiser's Berlin, and a thirties progressive school in Sweden.

I did not send her the book, she would not have read it, and, cherishing my secret, I was proud of my restraint, feeling that it qualified me for Lord Chesterfield's definition of a gentleman as one who knows how to play the trumpet but doesn't. But the writing succeeded. I pass that house, hear their children, but they are only characters in my own book. Good luck to them.

5

During the fifties, sixties, seventies, not girls, but London itself remained my keenest teacher. Walking, walking, I could be alone with myself. An empty bandstand, toy pleasure-dome sedate in its park, supported an anthology of memories. I had listened, slanted dreamily in a deckchair, inhaling sounds largely unchanged through eighty summers. Sullivan, Rossini, Lehár, Lionel Monkton, Sousa, Suppé, Strauss . . . 'Greensleeves' arranged for xylophone, for cornet. Children gesticulating like traffic cops or cricket umpires, an old lady, toqued like the prevailing royal widow, sleeping peacefully, with a resemblance to a dead hen strong enough to infringe copyright. A scene captured by Harold Rome in a 1937 revue staged not by Ziegfeld or Berkeley but the International Ladies Garment-Workers' Union.

> On Sunday in the Park
> All week long we keep on looking forward to
> The happy things we do . . .
>
> It's our summer home where we can play and sport,
> Our fashionable resort
> Until it's dark . . .
> On Sunday in the Park.

Moonlight made the bandstand vaguely Byzantine; in full darkness it seemed more like a cave glimmering in a black cliff, a primitive temple from which unearthly music would sound in crisis. I wandered far, seeking parks not yet supervised by armed police, heavy planners, gigantic nurses, though losing the mystery that had glamourized the attics, dirty but dazzling fairgrounds, jungle gardens, queer side streets and little shops, the wild commons of childhood.

The old Broad Street Railway, like the Canal, disclosed the backstairs London of marshalling yards, uncanny furnaces, gigantic weeds left over from Blitz and eviction, people threatening or loving each other in impoverished rooms, then sliced off as if a page had been torn; tiny desolate woods, old sheds, stacks of broken furniture and tyres, half-covered with roses; sprawling allotments and drowsy bonfires, mountains of rusted cars, children playing cowboys, real amid the blight, sheets flapping like trapped swans. They still remain, though, at furtive times, trains rush through carrying atomic waste, or worse.

Stories remained to be gathered: Mrs Tofts, 1726, giving birth, to rabbits; dockside London jeering at the infirmities of the dying Fielding. Today, outside Belsize Park Station, a security guard shot dead, for £864. Tottenham Court Road recalled the old Italian nationalist who, ignorant of English, trundled a cart across England and America to exhibit the torture implements used by the Bourbon King of Naples, 'Bomba', so vehemently condemned by Gladstone. This veteran spent his last coins to hire an interpreter, and a Tottenham Court Road meeting-house, for an oration on Italian Freedom, and killed himself when no one came.

London's language interested me, as I tramped the streets tracing lost villages under the ponderous rind of post-war rebuilding. Kennington and Southwark, Camberwell and Stratford, the huge cranes swinging above dark gaps and bombed walls. Something of the old speech still remained. 'Cockney', I was told, was Old English, 'cock's egg'. To Chaucer it meant a silly or tiresome child. Later it became 'ignorant' or 'foolish', then was applied to a town-dweller; finally a Londoner. Shakespeare used it for a timid woman, with Lear's Fool: 'Cry to it, nuncle, as the cockney did to the eels when she put them into the paste alive.' 'Arse', I heard from Charles Chiltern, is the oldest known Cockney, 'Booze' the second. 'Clobber' is Jewish. The huge verbal mint of the great city writers, Shakespeare, Dickens, Joyce, had early origins, though J.R.R. Tolkien denounced the first for ruining traditional English. In Mark Lane, Bermondsey and Stepney bars, on the foreshore at Rotherhithe, at Deptford and Whitechapel, a patois existed: 'Hampton Wick' (penis), 'Mince Pies' (eyes), 'Tommy Tucker' (supper), 'Holy Friar' (liar), 'Goose's Neck' (cheque). Familiar cries survived war. 'Tuppence a pound! I'm *givin'* it away, come on, don't mess yourself aroun',' though less vivid than shouts heard by Dickens. 'Here's the sort o' game to make you laugh seven years arter you're dead, and turn ev'ry 'air on your 'ed grey with delight.'

<h1 style="text-align:center">6</h1>

John Hampden Jackson's influence remained and, throughout the war and because of the war, I sought the small, co-operative community, self-reliant, more autonomous than the fire service and civil defence departments from which I was invalided out. For three years I taught under the stimulating, sometimes fiery Howard Thomas, at Wychwood, Bournemouth, where Wilfrid Blunt had once studied. Howard, like my pupils, Paul Tory and the late John Atkinson, remained a valued friend, but the school itself, rather a very effective one-man show than a pad of idealistic virtue, offered few chances. Howard and I enjoy recalling a junior master unhinged by a formal occasion. He had to say a mealtime grace, but overnervous, began instead Hamlet's 'To be or not to be . . .', eventually realizing his error and uttering a resounding four-letter word, at that time unacceptable.

Back in London in 1947, after a drift through the Middle East, where pacific geniality was not noticeable, I at last fancied I had found the Good Place, the free estate for moral regeneration, for freedom, love, wisdom, and, of course, free sex. The last was the most evident.

From then for some years I taught, or was at least present, at

Burgess Hill co-educational School, Hampstead, somewhat to the left of Bertrand and Dora Russell, and of A.S. Neill; indeed providing a safety-net for some of his drop-outs, whose existence was not implied in his own books. On rare meetings, I found him dour, somewhat authoritarian, apparently anti-intellectual. My employer, Geoffrey Thorpe, had himself taught at Summerhill and disputed Neill's view that an ill-written, badly-produced and unfinished play written by children was preferable to an enthusiastically acted play by Shakespeare. I did appreciate Neill giving a shilling to a delinquent each time he stole, understanding the loneliness and rejection underlying actions ostensibly anti-social. Years afterwards, I was abashed to receive, following my own curt note regarding copyright, an affectionate and calligraphically beautiful letter from Neill, and only his death a few days later prevented my replying more graciously.

Tolerant, conscientious, periodically alarming, Geoffrey Thorpe was a Great War survivor, fellow-pupil of Robert Graves, teacher of Stephen Spender, friend of Hampden Jackson, of H.G. Wells, and, in legend, had entombed his father under the inscription 'Thorpe's Corpse'. Our pupils were of all ages, the concept of age itself being treated with lavish unconcern. One, a Turk, rheumatic, heavily bearded, must have been about thirty, which provoked comment on sporting occasions with schools more conventional. A Mr R. Jackson offered his services as resident psychologist with ability to cure homosexuality, alternatively as table-tennis instructor, though eventually he agreed to enrol as a pupil.

From headmaster to char, all staff were paid, very badly, the identical salary. Earlier, influenced by its thirties founders, which included the anarchist poet, critic and war-hero, Herbert Read, the school had denied itself a headmaster, on libertarian grounds. The staff in general apparently judged applicants by the temerity with which they withstood a barrage of obscenities and insults calculated to test their tolerance and maturity. During the war, when I had visited it with my former Haileybury teacher, Neville Bewley (who was, unwisely, to submit his own cancer to the healing properties of a Reichian Orgone Box), a headmaster did indeed exist, but for some misdemeanour had been condemned by the children's committee to eat in private and refrain from teaching.

Rules were few, and largely established, amended, cancelled, by the weekly School Meeting, at which a seven year-old had equal voice with a teacher, let alone the Turk. This had authority over everything save, I think, the question of whether to pay the rates. Such assemblies tended, in the spirit of creative improvisation, to be inconsistent, overturning within seconds some decision previously agreed on after hours of sometimes savage partisanship. They tended to bossiness far more than had John Hampden Jackson, Val Rogers, Edgar Matthews. On matters of kindness, forgiveness, injustice, majority opinion, often irritating, was fairly trustworthy. Regarding teaching methods, curriculum, attitudes to neighbours, local shops, property, less so. Contradicting the habits of Mr Blake-Blake, the children wrote reports on the teachers, with considerable freedom of thought.

Lessons were voluntary. Some teachers were dedicated and stimulating – Glyn and Ruth Richards, Elsa Boyd, Joan Veltman, Jack Gibson, Erna Gal, Bernice Rubens (now a widely read novelist) together with the unfailing kindness of Jacqueline Goldsmith, whom I later married, and our cook, Helen Byrne, mother of the actor, Michael Byrne. Others were authoritarian anarchists, a forbidding breed. Offering small salaries and haphazard organization, such schools tended to attract cranks, crooks, idealists and the oversensitive. I possessed minor elements of all, which I could usually control. In the early sixties, however, I felt that I had now said my say. Public opinion had, a little later, one if its rare chances to express itself, and Burgess Hill itself faded; I abandoned the profession.

Remembering Nansen, Chekhov, Timoleon, Wilfrid Israel, I had really been seeking some elegant Hercules who wins without fighting: new words for a new time, armour for some figure who, with a single glance or phrase, dismisses his assailants, and for whom the angel opens the prison gates. I scarcely saw myself in such armour, but hoped that a purposeful and harmonious community could pioneer the rivets. This was leading to yet another novel about Germany, about discipline and authority and necessary change, in the turmoil of 1945–6. This was *The Game and the Ground* (1957).

He paused, then said conversationally, 'Frankly, I don't know. It's the perpetual dilemma, is it not, of people like ourselves? How to resist. How to find a new weapon, a new technique, which saves the citadel without destroying our souls. To find the single word, irresistible as sarcasm used against children, that will make the killer throw away his gun.'

As none of us moved, he leaned back, head raised, 'I wonder if you remember the story of the Chinese general defending the city against the Mongols? All his weapons were broken, all food gone, all hope abandoned. One night, as his people despaired, the general stood on a tower and, on his pipe, played Tartar tunes, there in the darkness, the lonely desolate songs of the steppes. And in the morning, the Chinese crowded the walls and found that their enemies had gone. Betrayed by song, they had packed up and stormed their way back, desperate for home.'

I remember Burgess Hill with wonder, fluctuating affection, and a sense of lost chances. Undeniably we helped children abandoned by parents, orthodox State schools, and those other establishments of which a north London writer, Dickens, voiced an 'ancient suspicion touching that curious coincidence that the boy with four brothers to come always gets the prizes.'

We gave no prizes, marks, punishments, and sported the obligatory decor of dirty feet, bare or sandalled; beards of fanciful cut or no cut; pacifist, sexual and anarchist pretensions. Adults, often with pronounced ill-will, vehemently debated Freud, Wilhelm Reich, love, freedom, self-expression, while brightly clad children drifted in and out, yawning, swearing, contradicting, with expressions of importance, making general observations: 'What pansy voices the birds have!'

Significant IQs and advanced theories jostled with facts open to varied interpretations. A rumoured adolescent pregnancy was deplored by one faction, applauded by another as undeniable self-expression. An incest-complex, a mother-fixation, a malfunctioning gland, were blamed for a child's incessant weeping, eventually traced, to her mother's surprise, to shoes two sizes too small. 'Divide and rule,' the childen said. Another mother commanded that her daughter, at set periods, should publically address her as 'old cow', to ditch the inhibitions.

Fortunately, we lacked a staff commonroom, which rots so much zest and promise, but old arguments return to me from small, bristly parties:

'Beastly dictators! How can you expect even the least human decency unless you allow freedom to be free:'

'But surely children should be taught to wash, or at least encouraged to?'

'Why?'

'Oh . . .'

'You must remember that the strongest animals in the world, the hippo and the pig, are also the dirtiest.'

'But it's unnatural!'

'So are good manners. Also poetry.'

'Yet all animals clean themselves.'

'There's no recorded case in history of a puma washing.'

I was forced to admit that the most elaborate reasoning, the most convincing theses, are only as strong as the personalities behind them. I read a finely reasoned, humanitarian pamphlet, 'The Chains of Slavery', by the terrorist, Dr Jean-Paul Marat; a sensible denunciation of cruelty to animals, by the mass-murderer, Heinrich Himmler; and some impeccable moral philosophy from Albert Speer, who has been called the greatest slave-owner since the Pharoahs. Demanding Peace, Women's Rights, Racial Equality in voices like those of ill-natured policemen, people murder their spouses, children and friends daily. Good causes can not only extract the best of our qualities, they as often extract the worst.

Despite noisy theories, we shied from intellectual discipline and from personal modesty and we provided insufficient mental or physical activity. 'What shall we do this afternoon?' was a familiar question, more often a moan, seldom very satisfactorily answered. Listlessness could dampen quick wits and energy, and teachers were so dismayed by fascist leaders (less so by communists) that they shrank from giving a lead. One lively teacher successfully vetoed our cricketers wearing whites, reminding us of the totalitarian implications of a uniform appearance.

Permanently bruised by the Hitler-Stalin pact, which more experienced brains than my own should have expected, I was finding, rather late, that professions of love, co-operation, freedom, can accompany spite, intolerance, vicious antagonisms. In the larger world, socialism was being proved compatible with secret police, capital punishment, censorship and elitism. Ordinary Londoners queued down Oxford Street for a film of Nazi brutes publically hanged at Kharkov. A Haileyburian friend, Desmond Stewart, novelist, Arabist, biographer of Jesus and T.E. Lawrence, told me that a London mock-up of a concentration camp sexually stimulated him; men are likewise aroused, he told me, on their way to the gallows. It was Desmond who introduced me to Gerald Hamilton, for whom he seemed to be pimping. Allegedly the original of Isherwood's 'Mr Norris', Hamilton was the ugliest and wittiest man I have ever encountered, though I was relieved not to be invited to return my visit.

The anarchist hero, Bakunin, had written in 1869, 'we recognize no other activity but the work of extermination. In this struggle, revolution sanctifies all.' I realized that no revolution was likely from Burgess Hill where envy, rivalry, absurdity ranged as freely as in the institutions we so despised. That a child had to address teacher and parent by Christian names was no real advance on having to call Martin Wight 'Sir'. Lack of rules and directions could mean liberation, it could also mean apathy, cowardice, toadyism to the young, and could induce chaos, for which few pupils were ultimately grateful.

In all circumstances and countries, whatever the prevailing conventions and ethos, I have continually met those whom F. Scott Fitzgerald called Tom and Daisy and must, I fear, include myself, though without the enviable handicap of their wealth. 'They were careless people, Tom and Daisy — they

228

smashed up things and creatures and then retreated back into their money or their vast carelessness, or whatever it was that kept them together, and let other people clean up the mess they had made.'

I still believed in private education, not for the merely rich, but for those who cherish colour, variety, oddity. Contemporary Lenins and Saint-Justs will destroy it, but a society that can, by electoral vote or ministerial ukase, dispense with Currey's Dartington Hall, Neill's Summerhill, with a Bertrand Russell, a George Lyward – with Arthur and Hilda, Wilfrid Blunt and Hampden Jackson, even Gertie, is reckless, arrogant and probably malignant, despite screeches about equality and decency.

Memories, however, are untrustworthy. In retrospect, Burgess Hill can become a sunlit idyll of innocence, purity, charm, testifying to Hugh Kenner's remark that teaching is an act of generosity. It is certainly an art of sharing. It can also be an amateurish gamble with the lives of others. These pages could be rewritten with divergent results by my tolerant and charming pupils: John Fortnum, Gillian Nicholson, William and Edward Kacynski, Ben Bardi, Mick Hatterway, Nicholas Tucker, Mario Dubsky, Constance Neurath, Mike Byrne, Sonia, Kika, Petra and Jehanne Markham, my stepdaughter, Mary Stephens, and, from an earlier school, Derek Robinson. In fairness, the painter and writer, Mario Dubsky, recorded (in X Factor 1984): 'The school was remarkable in many ways, small in scale, comforting and homely, with more than a touch of spartan shabbiness. It was a wonderful place, ideal for me, and . . . gave me both stimulus and direction'.

For a novelist, the experience could scarcely be improvident, and, encouraged by Tosco and Mary Fyvel, still my very generous friends, I wrote Broken Canes, intended as a major challenge to the academic establishment, serious, nay, profound, and supremely original, very possibly unique. In the New Statesman, John Raymond reviewed it as 'uproariously funny, a rough Godwinian eclogue set in an Arcadia of stucco and long grass . . . borrowing wholesale from Isherwood, Rose Macaulay, Woolf, Lehmann, Bowen and Auden.' It had a minor critical though not financial success. Few of my friends and none of the public observe to the letter Bishop Heber's recommendation that a gentleman should buy three copies of any book: one for his library, one to read, one to give away. Thirty years on, I still meet those who, with a conspiratorial leer, a quiet wink, murmur such remarks as 'Ah yes. I remember your novel *Broken Canes*. Indeed, I often wonder whether it was that which made you give up writing.'

<h1 style="text-align:center">7</h1>

Whatever the plight of my pupils, I was slowly acquiring a certain self-knowledge, a trust in my own feelings; slowly unblocking my head-on approach. The past was revealing other faces. A snow-fight, years back, at school, suddenly re-emerged, a white turmoil through which I could now see masters and boys nakedly exposed as lovers and haters, cringers, victims, bullies, desperate heroes. Hitherto, more-over, a timid literary snobbishness had prevented my natural humour seeping into my writing, though I always hanker for laughter and generally find it. The absurd, the witty, the inconsequential. It had been necessary during the war, essential in the classroom, as, so long ago, Ian Stewart and Arthur Harrison had known so well. It was fortunate that our wartime leader had been a wit and I still treasure his remark that a certain noble lord had reached senility before reaching maturity, and, in his History, writing that Bishop Beaufort, in 1414, opened a parliamentary session with a sermon on 'Strive for the Truth unto Death' and the exhortation 'While we have Time, let us do good to all men'. This was understood to mean the speedy invasion of France. There came a freezing night when, impelled by what I could not coherently explain, I joined a two-mile queue, stretching far into the South Bank, to reach Westminster Hall where the old Chatterbox at last lay silent.

'Humour,' Milton asserts, 'hath off-times a sinewy force in teaching and reflecting.' Ralegh spoke of wit turning huge kingdoms upside down. Talleyrand reflected that in France, nothing eased the strain of obedience as easily as an epigram.

Enjoying the humour of observation and incongruous personal encounters, I would not have enjoyed the 1976 Cardiff International Conference on Humour, which sprouted papers on 'A Genetic Analysis of Humour Preferences' and 'Perceptions of Equally-Different Computer-Drawn Schematic Faces'. Freud and Bergson, in the territory of laughter, are not for me. Of stand-up comics, I have enjoyed few, save Max Miller and Billy Bennett, but I enjoy the slyer wit of E.M. Forster, Sybille Bedford, Rebecca West: 'This Orestes was an Illyrian adventurer who had at one time been secretary to Attila the Hun. It can never have been a satisfactory reference.' But, for me, an eminently satisfying observation.

8

Houses have always fascinated me: shrouded, deceptive, candid, suggestive. Swedish manors with generals going mad in the library; a dark lodge, apparently doorless, in a bright park; 398 Rue St Honoré, commonplace in appearance, which, during the late fifties, contained a jazzy bar. On its first floor was a tightly closed door once seen by Sir John Elliot, a former transport magnate.

When I first saw it, it was painted a dark green, almost black, cobwebs hung unbroken over its two large panels and over the grill at the top. It looked what it was — old, neglected, but important; and from it exuded that strange apprehensiveness which haunts the places from the past. It is small, it hides itself away in this corner, it belongs to a great epoch yet is marked by no plaque or monument. Only a few yards away the noise of modern Paris comes strangely through the passage, halts confusedly, and eddies weakly back from whence it came.

Here, on a hot steamy evening, a cart filled with bound men once passed, and a heavy atrocious face cursed the man hidden within. Three months later, that same man departed, perhaps in the same cart, to the same end, passing the same house, on which a child then splashed ox-blood, with a broomstick. The man was Robespierre, and this, in his last years, was where he had lived, nominally engaged to the daughter of his admiring landlord.

In opulent Avenue Road, Hampstead, a woman shivered in her jewels. 'My father never punished me enough. Never once took the stick to me. I should have been made to bleed.' From such comments, outskirts of novels fall in shoals, to be stored in notebooks which become, like memory, not untruthful but seldom giving the whole truth. An indispensible liability.

Behind many smart doors, soft-spoken men have entertained me for years: they have no discernible occupation, enormous cars, vast overdrafts, tables permanently reserved at expensive, obsequious restaurants; they sit surrounded by the ornate and glittering, offer exotic drinks, yet vainly ransack their pockets for a common coin and drift off when the postman rings. 'Furnished Room for Gentleman of Refined Habits' earned me many rebuffs when I applied. 'Strictly Single, Strictly White' has period tang. In one dingy lodging house, still festering on Haverstock Hill, clandestine legends throve. The landlady never cared to admit death, so that when a lodger died, he was said to be shoved into a certain hollow sofa, which was then removed for 'repairs'. As winter chilled each loveless room, whispers stole between tables that mildewed Mrs Shepherd, covered with cracks, dirty Mr Art Weekes who managed a cinema and invited me to trade shows, gaudy Miss Van Raalte who drank ink and nasty Mr Wood who talked with some eloquence, though to himself, were all 'ripe for the menders'. I heard of Monte Carlo Casino disposing of suicides, with more style, in grand pianos. I would hear without zest of the cat that slept on baby Terry's face, and slept too long, the parents subsequently renaming the cat 'Terry', which apparently readjusted the balance.

Hotels absorb me: short stories sit at each table, questions are left unanswered on stairways, people die in lifts from some secret complaint, unlikely partners gesticulate, curse, lament, just out of earshot. This transient world displays us at our most artificial, light with mock-amiability, imposture, greed, and, as if in distorting mirrors, the grandest of us join a parade of buffoons. Here, among spurious gold and plastic flowers, among the lonely and overfed, anonymous refugees, swollen celebrities and widows with cats and boiled legs, we are spies and authors. Here, wartime ladies dreaded scandal more than bombs, were avid for news of killings, refused to apply for ration books to avoid disclosing their age. Here the barman was dazed with admiration for his own story, of a youth with an extravagantly long nose, rebuffed by girls whom his romantic spirit embellished beyond their station. Where, the author demanded, faintly accusing, could he get it published? I suspected that he had upstairs a poem, beginning,

> Hail to thee, blithe Spirit!
> Bird thou never wert.

Once, not recently, I tried to kiss a maid on the stairs, but at once, like a god, from several landings above, a deep voice tolled, 'Try higher up, old man.'

Behind doors, voices murmur, protest, scream. Confidences are exchanged at bars: 'I haven't much faith in the Pleiades, Mercury may well lose me my mother . . . but will give me fame after death.' 'Guest owed me five hundred. One day I went to him and gave him a cheque. For five hundred. He looked a bit queer and asked me why I'd given it him. I said that it was customary at this time of the year for money to change hands. Well, it succeeded.' 'I've only one desire left. Do you know what? To die in Hampton Court. Can true imagination go further than that? If you ask me, No.'

Sometimes, as I stand alone at a window or slink into a world gone mouldy, I seem to be awaiting that far off sound in *The Cherry Orchard* which Chekhov described as, 'as though from out of the sky, the sound of a snapped string.'

I acquired a house of my own, in Hampstead, in a way that some may consider unusual. In the early fifties my bicycle collapsed and I entered the Haverstock Arms, new to me, and I was at once accosted by a short, beery man. 'Ah sir, you look like one of the boys.' This had not occurred to me, and it made me uneasy, but he continued with inexorable and crafty relish, 'I like doing business with your sort. Boys in my own stream who know a bargain when they see one.'

The thought was hideous, but my expression and silence did not deter him. He tapped my chest as he might a barometer, blinked, sipped, looked at the bar as if to offer me a drink, but it was crowded by those who must have already rebuffed him, and he desisted, swore softly, then spread grimed, bitten fingers over my sleeve.

'Nice bit of cloth . . . not fancy, but nice. Now . . .' his manner sharpened, his rather boiled-looking eyes lost their sogginess, 'Now, you don't have a house. You may have a home, but you don't have a house.'

I could not deny it. He was pleased. 'Boy, you're wrong! You've a house, a very fine house, all your own, and it's through me you've got it. Mind . . .' the fingers pressed, warningly, 'there's ground rent. But nominal. That's the word. Nominal.'

'Nominal?'

'Yes. You pay the Church. The Church of *England*. The . . . commissioners. No trouble from that quarter. Love your neighbour, isn't it? All is charity. You can't ask for a better thing. With their influence upstairs you don't even need insurance.'

Dazed, I was being pulled outside, was already halfway down a side-road. 'Look!' He was proud, even swaggering, 'there it is!' I could not dissent. A tall, ramshackle house of about 1830 stood above a tattered garden and derelict pathway.

'I'll vacate at once. Instanter, as the Marines say. Mind, I've a family on my floor. All girls, of course, about fifteen, beside the regulars. But I'll see to it. I'll get them out. I keep my tongue in my strong right arm. Coloureds pay double, of course. Nothing like it. You're in millions already. Mind, I prefer cash. I can't avoid telling you that. I prefer cash.'

He got it. So now I had a house, stuffed with aggrieved tenants and suspicious clients, mostly Caribbean, one family, each paying large rents, in every corner of large rooms, themselves adorned with stolen furniture. The vendor, of course, soon vanished into prison, almost followed by myself. Meanwhile, picking my way between children, pregnant girls, large men in threatening mood, I travelled from floor to floor in anticipation of the delights of property, recklessly naming the rooms: Sun Room, Breakfast Room, Studio, Library, Still Room, Gun Room, Orangery, Retiring Room for the Laundry Maid's Gentleman Friend. At the end of the long scrapheap beyond the windows, much resembling a cemetery gradually transformed to a builder's yard and butcher's repository, I placed 'The Summerhouse'.

The aftermath was like a dated novel of small misadventures, which indeed it became. Reducing the population to proportions more temperate and legal, dismantling the dubious residue of my predecessor's sublettings, I rejoiced in prospects of an income virtually unearned. This was very largely misconceived, for to avoid payments, the tenants wriggled into attitudes that I found impressive but unremunerative. An unemployed salesman gratuitously painted the hall bottle-green, then harshly demanded recompense; an artist handed over her appalling abstracts ('They're such a good investment that you owe me fifty pounds'), a woman appeared daily with dead flowers, dead tea and seemed disposed to hand me the bill. Mrs Cousins, dire name, always addressed me in verse,

> I can bear thunder and rain,
> I can bear the darkness,
> But the wind, the wind
> I cannot bear

while her husband handed over dead mice, each, it seemed, with a price on its head. A Bengali invited me to read his manuscript.

'Graham Greene has read it. Not Graham Greene himself, but his brother. To Learned Mr Greene I pay two hundred pound, to Mr Greene I pay one hundred pound. To you, in your kindness, I pay forty-nine pound.'

'What did Mr Greene, the one hundred pound one, think of your book?'

'Well now . . . yes, and again, yes. Very much the thing. Not obscene at all. After you have read it, I should say, perused it, evinced a very considerable interest, I shall hand you over a slap-up dinner, which I shall share.'

'And you will also hand over the forty-nine quid!'

'Ah yes. The forty-nine.' The manuscript, perhaps a few pages shorter than *Crime and Punishment*, was handwritten, without shape, punctuation, coherence, but I read it, enticed by the forty-nine pounds, slightly less so by the slap-up dinner, which would probably be at the local Indian restaurant with the dustbin, emptied punctually at 9 p.m., in the far corner under the cardboard palm.

'Can it be published?'

'Well, it's perfectly possible. Technically possible.'

'Good man, good man. Just what I wanted to hear. Good news is its own reward.'

'Yes. But . . .'

'You must kindly wait for our mutual cash payment, when we can recoup from our first royalties.' Later, he relented, and presented me instead with *The Splendid Days of Bruce*, second-hand.

Indian tenants were more fluent than most others, notably on rent-day. 'Pray to God, whom you very much resemble . . .' Half anxious, half amused, another pushed away the rent-book, 'Old Man, a word in your ear. I don't want to upset the apples but I think my wife's gone phut.' My house, no more than Burgess Hill, became a commune of New Harmony, a show-piece for the tolerant, the free, the wise, though, becalmed in the equivocations of ownership, I could study, if not always personality, at least behaviour. Girlie and Mate, very unmusical, but responsible, endlessly played Mozart's D Major Flute Concerto to induce good taste in their baby, thereby offending their West Indian neighbour, who sported the resonant Christian name 'Crippen', presumably the heritage of some distant hero-worship. They further disgruntled him by giving him, at Christmas, a tin-opener on which he cut himself and, in riposte, he then swayed the house with rock music, seriously endangering the baby's cultural destiny. During the freeze-up in the early sixties, he manufactured ice-shillings for his gas-meter, with success modified by his need to boast of it.

236

Another room penned in a British Nazi, who trained on the Heath with wooden rifle, and was photographed for a Sunday paper in SS uniform. He covered the walls with anti-semitic slogans, and sat at a curtained window to spit at passing blacks, though, without the heroism professed by the Nazi creed, leaving me to answer the subsequent thunder on the front door. I believe, on the whole, in reasoning with monsters ninety-nine times, and then either hitting back very hard and very dirtily, or devoting myself to the offender, and the offender alone. This I have not yet done. After he had tied a label, 'Jewish vermin, please poison' to Girlie's baby, in a pram outside Sainsbury's I did try and eject him, to be at once assailed, in the local press, by Hampstead's famous liberals, who reminded me that the Second World War had been fought for free speech, and demanded that I should refrain from upsetting the peace settlement. There was some feeling that I should offer compensation.

This man was cowardly, lonely, boastful of untrustworthy intimacies in high places, though now living on National Assistance. He was about five feet high and cycled about London looking for boys.

'Tell me, Gerry, why do you so admire the Nazis?'

He was suddenly wistful, 'They were such fine figures of men.'

'Goebbels? Streicher? Hitler? Ribbentrop?'

'Yes. When you got to know them.'

When he owed me some £150, he gave notice. 'Jew-lovers should pay *me* for living in this ghetto. Anyway, I've been appointed to Government House, Hong Kong.' At which, in his absence on his bicycle searching for boys, I packed up his trunk and dispatched it to Government House, Hong Kong.

Mr Pearson bought a guitar, registered as an unemployed musician, lived for years on relief. I ejected him for unending theft and I hope he died in the snow. He once told me that it was he who had put Corsica on the map. Mr O'Lynne divided his room with plywood, sub-letting the other half at double the rent he always owed me. He admired, vainly, the Chinese girl whose name translated into 'My Father wanted a Boy'. Far my best tenant was a stylish youth who hired a room ('It must face South') only to house a pair of riding boots.

My own role was confessor, moneylender, scapegoat and, at times, protector, often needed but seldom welcomed. 'The new Rent Act,' Mr Ng hissed at me, 'is to deal with you personally. But it's not enough. Silly Queen and dotty Parliament!' I comforted, without consoling, ageing girls whose escorts jibbed at nothing save marriage and who sat long mornings before mirrors that whispered or cackled 'Others are Better', and to whom no marvellous telegram proclaimed 'You've Won'. One girl was beautiful, with family, admirers, friends, but, on her 21st birthday, received no card, present, call, and she spent it howling. Later, I found in her room a Marriage Bureau form, which shocked me more than the current public enormities: 'NB If the Gentleman does not write within 8 Days, there is No Objection to the Lady writing again, giving further information to arouse interest.'

I sat in the centre of petty crime, guarded resentments, foul cooking and floating pathos, random folk cherishing their own oddity, alert for each other's weaknesses, involuntary gestures, mail, awaiting calls that seldom came, chirping 'see you later' while dreading it. They seemed to expect dreadful verdicts. My bell was often rung by flat mournful ladies, applying for rooms they did not actually want and seldom bothered to see. They did want a cup of tea. 'You're not quite what I would call a gentleman,' a well-dressed visitor told me, 'but at least you pretend to listen.'

Another was scared of the coming Census. 'It's the Devil's work. Numbering the people. They're going to tattoo our wrists with numbers. Only the Blacks will be favoured.' She was obsessed by her failure to get a war-veteran's pension, her husband having been convicted, or honoured, for supplying bad jam to the armies in 1916. She had further worries, having read a German Manual of Artillery, published in 1907, with some instructions on how to bombard London from Dover. She left me £150 for a Requiem Mass. Her diary entry for each day was merely 'Nobody came today'.

For joyous companionship I preferred Mrs Cousins:

> You'll need looking after,
> Young Man,

238

Especially with all these people about.
So I've asked my friend to do so:
Mr Odenanka,
Who passed over five years ago,
In the summer time, mercifully.
I'm sure you will get along together,
Very well.

9

Now in my sixties, I still wander Hampstead streets, which may dwindle to lanes sodden with French Letters, alert for the random, the overheard, the scrawled. 'J.B. Priestley Hates Christmas', 'James Dean. Dead and Eternal', 'Michael Foot's a disgrace to the sheep that gave him birth'. I am too old to do other than shudder at a shop window advertisement: 'People come together in party-like atmosphere to play co-operative games, dance, sing, share their humour, create improvised theatre and to entertain and be entertained. To reconnect with the innate sense of playfulness of early childhood to the appreciation of the ridiculous and sublime.' Unable to forget that paper clown suit of my childhood, which would have qualified me for entry, I move on, and read elsewhere: 'The soft and yielding overcomes hardness and force.' I would hesitate to test that against Himmler, Stalin, Amin, the gentlemen of Katyn, Dachau, the IRA. 'Possibly, but not probably.' Likewise I shy from an invitation to test Biodynamic Massage.

The past, too, is putting on weight. The long grass of my Burgess Hill Arcadia is now, in 1985, a lawn for rich spaniels beneath a millionaire heap of flats and penthouses. Of swinging London, I remember only eleven noisy streets and some unusual clothes, couture without style, huge hair and pretentious idleness, and a lot of hearsay.

From wine bars, cafés, pubs, resonant statements abound. *Twelfth Night* is disclosed as an unconscious plea for republicanism. I hear of an opinion poll to decide whether Cézanne knew how to paint, and learn that a North American

University computer has found that the Great War could not have occurred.

'Aren't we all God's children?'

'Certainly not.'

'But the liver only needs three days to recover completely.' People slump beside me, 'I'm not a sex-maniac but I like them medium-rare,' to tell me their life stories, departing only when I start telling mine. For £750, professors of TM will enable me to levitate. A psychologist-novelist instructs me that the Nazis were the first to make killing an art.

Obviously, I am under siege from personal torpor, indifference, timidity, declining sympathies. Temptations abound to muse too long over eccentricities, literary small talk, bad films. Much conversation, reflects Ezra Pound's Propertius, is as good as having a home. Sometimes — recounted not here but in my novels — I have fled, to Russia, France, America, Spain, Austria, Germany, Poland, the Middle East, Italy, though essentially I have never strayed very far from the White Horse. No sightseer, dogged by interior obsessions, I love foreign streets, incomprehensible languages, small tables on sunset quays, narrow lanes winding to the Old Town, the ruined castle on the headland, the dusty village. I am a survivor, from bombs and pain, girls who bore twins, from funny men turning terrible, while cherishing my return to the tousled garden, the untidy desk, to telephones and tennis.

Eleven

I don't know whether
You will agree, but novel writing is
A higher art than poetry altogether
In my opinion, and success implies
Both finer character and faculties.
Perhaps that's why real novelists are as rare
As winter thunder or a polar bear.

W.H. Auden

In this big London, all full of intellect and business, I feel
pleasure in dipping down into the country and rubbing my
hand over the cool dew upon the pastures, as it were.

Edward FitzGerald

. . . a wild amphibious race
with sullen woe displayed on every face,
Who far from Civil arts and social fly,
and scowl at strangers with suspicious eye.

George Crabbe

1

In talk and while writing, I tend to assert, often from
inconclusive evidence; but inwardly, I am a 'Perhaps man'. I
must try and explain. Browning mentions, 'the Grand
Perhaps' but *'perhaps'* is seldom grand. Apparently mild,
almost insignificant, it can be sloppy, evasive, cautious, and as
such is a word I use so frequently that it must suggest my

essence. Yet, as much as 'rather', 'quite', 'but', it can be a small hinge on which turns the solid, the provocative, the transforming. Unlike, say, 'Eternity', and 'Never', which usually introduce the pretentious or downright silly, 'perhaps' can be deceptively tentative, modest, if sometimes teasing. E.M. Forster could write, 'Perhaps like many amateur's problems, there is no problem' intending us to realize that there is no 'perhaps' intended. Like such soft-spoken words as 'ah' and 'really', 'perhaps' can turn nasty, spiteful, sarcastic. 'Perhaps I am mistaken, but . . .' Lytton Strachey used it to jeer, quite untruthfully, at Dr Arnold, 'His legs, perhaps, were shorter than they should have been . . .'

Nevertheless, I cherish 'perhaps' as civilized and civilizing, and have embedded it in myself. 'Possibly not probably' echoing down my years. It suggests alternatives to the neutral and conventional, the despotic and disgusting. Oliver Cromwell, whom I now admire, unsuccessfully yet valiantly seeking government not ideal but workable and improving, surely spoke for all perhapsers in his famous plea to the General Assembly of the Church of Scotland — not renowned for genial politics and religious jocularity — to consider 'in the bowels of Christ' the possibility that they might be mistaken. But no, bigots to a man, they knew that they were absolutely right, they condemned 'perhaps' and suffered accordingly. I think, though, that Cromwell himself erred in invoking Christ. No 'perhaps' is uttered in the Gospel. The Kingdom was either-or, all-or-nothing. 'He that is not with me is against me.' 'Sell *all* that you have and give to the poor.'

Only in our own country, I think, does 'perhaps' dramatically enter theology, with such martyrs as Bonhoeffer who, as a pastor, faced the agonizing question whether he could, on Christian grounds, sanction assassination. He came to accept it, and could have pondered, understood, refuted, then, I believe, accepted John Buchan's remark about Calvinism: 'A religion which becomes Perhaps will not stand in the day of battle.'

Stalwart Jehovah's Witnesses would have shied at 'perhaps' as they would at a quart of brandy. Another obdurate spirit, Winston Churchill, had some gifted perhapsers in his 1940

Cabinet, intelligent appeasers. He was never one himself, nevertheless he saved the element of 'perhaps' for Britain and part of Europe. No 'perhaps' existed in Hitler, in or out of the bowels of Christ, any more than in the public statements of Clemenceau, Dr Johnson, Cobbett, GBS. Party politics necessarily ignores it, for it presupposes that final truth is not yet established. Chekhov, Turgenev, I suspect Chaucer, and surely Shakespeare, knew this. So did most, though not all of my own closer friends. Probably Hampden Jackson and George Rothery, fine mixture of sensitivity, tolerance and competence, certainly Graham, Wilfrid Israel, Philip Toynbee, Justine Brener. They did not, like Tolstoy, demand absolute and drastic consistency. Another, less impressive yet singular perhapser was Louis Napoleon, who is reputed to have shown early skill in Blind Man's Bluff. This, certainly a perhaps game, foreshadows his later foreign policy, with catastrophic results, for Bismarck was an unhappy choice on whom to test the political and military virtues of 'perhaps'. These virtues are not, however, the deepest, and need not have the final say. Poets, while remaining speculative, questioning, often uncertain, can make this quiet word positive, exciting, bold. Auden's 'The Prophets' moves from the tentative and seeking, to the fulfilled and assured:

Perhaps I always knew what they were saying:
Even the early messengers who walked
Into my life from books where they were staying,
Those beautiful machines that never talked
But let the small boy worship them and learn
All their long names whose hardness made him proud;
Love was the word they never said aloud
As something that a picture can't return.

Wilfrid's gift of Rilke's poems showed me a writer who, for me, is the greatest poet of 'perhaps', mediating between multitudinous worlds, articulating the infinite, his 'perhaps' an abiding and incessant ingredient in the incessant flux:

There remains, perhaps, some tree on a slope,

243

To be looked at, day after day

and elsewhere, grandly, challengingly:

We, hearers at last, perhaps the first ones to hear.

Pacific Islanders, apparently, lack 'because' and 'why'. I
hope they possess 'perhaps', impish, demanding or elegiac, a
reminder that we are human, flawed, liable to be distressed
yet, perhaps, prone to be rescued.

2

For many years now I have divided my month between
Hampstead, and a cottage bought by my mother in 1953, in a
Suffolk village, Kersey (perhaps 'Cress Island', possibly 'Caer's
People', probably neither). Here I can escape wheels, bells,
transistors, and test myself against marvellous silences. This,
like writing a novel, is some quest for identity.

The cottage, like most of the village, is some three centuries
older than the United States. The garden, designed by my
mother, leads you forward through three successive arches. It
reflects what I enjoy in books: the half-heard, half-seen, the
allusive and ambiguous, a sense of sly disclosures which makes
spaces seem larger than they really are. Arches, hedges, trees,
an old wall create concealments, almost conspiracy. Small
glimpses, hints, checked vistas. A blob of colour may be lupin
tips, a patch of light, a pheasant feather, a red admiral, a heron
or private insets of blue behind a wall of roses. Nothing is ever
quite complete, secrets are always waiting within the open
pattern. It can be detached units: rose garden, herbaceous
crescent, fuschia bed, iris bed, or a continuous flow through
the arches, revealing other hues, other lawns, while remaining
part of the whole. Here, long-lost lines return refreshed:

> Seeking the food he eats,
> and pleased with what he gets.

I can see, below, other gardens, tiled ochred roofs, thatch, descending, then ascending. One cottager planted nothing but left his plot open to allcomers, self-sown immigrants, many of which were borne on to my garden by wind and bird. Poppies, foxgloves, marigolds, cow-parsley, dockweed, hollyhocks, white-beaded nettles, snapdragons, dandelion. 'I'm only the umpire,' he told me, and from my apple tree his garden seemed a patched and vivid quilt. Like many of his friends, he called me by my first name, did not know the second. In London, people do know, but mispronounce it.

In London, grass, flower, tree, tend to have literary, symbolic and classic associations, graphic reminders of planes of experience and tradition. In the country, they exist for me, for me and Justine alone: old friends, quiet immemorial lives with genial nicknames, existing without chatter or grievance, uncluttered. Lacking the experienced eye of a Grigson, I must here, as in novel writing, build my imagination through ignorance, though I would enjoy seeing, rather than imagining, what I must often pass as if blind. On Breckland marshlands, I convince myself, almost certainly wrongly, that I have recognized Golden Dock, Sand Sedge, Yellow Vetch, Spanish Cat-fly, Centaury, the rare plants described by Olive Cook. Conversely, I certainly recognize destruction of trees, hedges, wild life, the blackened fields and vile developments and polluted waters. In my own garden, I cherish a frog, a mole. Refugees from progress.

Kersey is little more than a single fifteenth-century street crossed by a duck-crowded ford. William Addison compares it to the crook of a strong arm in which the whole village is firmly but gently held. It slants between two hills, a ruined priory topping one, and, on the other, the old church with one arcade left unfinished, through Plague, and its stone memorial:

> Reader pass on nor waste thy time
> On bad biography or bitter rhyme,
> For what I am the humble dust enclose
> And what I was is no affair of yours.

Through the centuries the family names persist. Squirrel,

Partridge, Spraggins, Farthing. My home was a weaver's cottage, probably just fulfilling the medieval insistence that domestic space should allow two oxen to turn round; and the village was a manufactory of a popular woollen cloth of standard excellence, 'Kersey true' approximating to 'Stirling value'. In *Love's Labour's Lost*, Berowne declares:

> henceforth my wooing mind shall be express'd
> in russet Yeas and honest kersey Noes.

In a Dutch War in 1672, Mr Commissioner Tippet lamented to Pepys, 'We have no flags, cotton or kerseys in store, the ships gone outwent without them, except colours, one of each so ragged as would hardly hang on the staff.' On his last day, Robespierre was wearing a kerseymere waistcoat. Dickens' Mr Weller tells a not very comic story of a fat gentleman with 'a great round watch almost bustin' through his grey kersey smalls'.

3

Ownership of these properties, socially reprehensible, entails, or caters for, a mildly split self. In London I am nervy, impulsive, forward-looking. There are books to review, pieces of music to hear, friends to be met, tennis courts to be booked. In Suffolk, I am calm, working laboriously in the garden and at the desk, orientated to the past, and hoping for a different sort of acquaintance. One day I may see Suffolk stone-curlews, redshanks, shelducks, coots, pipits, whinchats, stonechats. From the past, I remember Philip Toynbee and his no-nonsense American wife, Sally, during the fifties my neighbours, across the fields in Lindsay.

As a schoolboy, Philip wrote, 'Dear Mummy and Daddy, such a lovely thing has happened. An anti-Toynbee society has been started.' To counter this unpromising zest for notoriety, his father, Arnold Toynbee, read him Gibbon's account of an ambitious Roman careerist who bribed his way to the imperial throne, sat down to the dinner prepared for his immediate predecessor and was promptly murdered. 'I had hoped that this story would make an impression on Philip, and it did, but it was not the impression on which I had reckoned. "Well, you see, Daddy," was Philip's comment, "that emperor did quite right. He wanted to become famous and he did. He became famous enough to make Gibbon write this story about him, and to make you read Gibbon's story now to me." I had not thought of that, so Philip had the last world.'

Philip often had some disconcerting last word. For me, he was a very English, rebellious independent, buccaneering within a loose but traditional framework, alert for the new and apt to be over eager to accept it, while remaining rooted, sometimes unwillingly, in the old. He was always ready to swipe at solemn dogmatists who sacrificed human decency, human detail, for the abstract and statistical. He loved the richly organic: landscapes, gardens, country walks, fishing, sailing, cricket, rugby — which allowed the improvised, adventurous, experimental, risky, within accepted rules, while simultaneously, like that doomed Roman, hankering after the exorbitant and flamboyant. His intellectual sophistication secreted considerable simplicity. Through misunderstanding the purport of *Step outside*, he lost most of his teeth to a racialist pub bully.

More emphatically than Arnold, he claimed descent from a royal Bulgarian saint, Theophylact the Intolerable. I remember the invitations to share some of his enthusiasms, often short-lived: the fifteenth century, Offa's Dyke, a conception of God as inexperienced and clumsy, William Gaddis' novel *The Recognitions* in which modest Brother Eulalio rebukes himself for the extravagance of including all the vowels in his name. Postcards would arrive, with excited, not always convincing insights. 'I tend to think of Robespierre as being almost the licensed buffoon of the Convention.'

As a writer, he was readily identifiable, but less so in his central personality. He had elements of hunter, corsair, explorer, mystic, clown, boxer, with ample room for eccentricity, mischief, false starts, thoughtlessness, sympathy, excruciating pleasure and dramatic melancholy. An unfailing boyishness underlay those sudden crazes: once for a tape-recorder with which, unscrupulously, secretly, he recorded the arrival of John Berger and myself, John's greeting, which lasted one and a quarter minutes, contrasting with my single grunt; then for a new garden game; a ten-gear bicycle which I doubt was ever used; an infernal, home-made wine which briefly impaired his reputation for hospitality; and for make-believe. In Suffolk, he constructed a maze that resolutely refused to reach knee-level, though this he seemed not to recognize. He and John Bury once tramped Belgium disguised as wartime pastors. He would enter Suffolk pubs with false beard, falser accent, undeterred by the inevitable greeting, 'Ah, Philip! What are you drinking?' He would set up some high-minded, public-spirited, prophetic notion, only to blow it down with fractious change of mood or a furious joke which was seldom frivolous and never facetious. On his last appearance at the Bertorelli Wednesday Lunch Club (now Friday), he masqueraded as a veteran Russian emigré, yet still unmistakably Philip. Ivan Moffat long before had mentioned 'his ugly sort of beauty like a statue that's been left out in the rain'.

His uncompromising and experimental nature, lovable but maddening, erupted in intermittent hankerings for sainthood which was later to prompt his founding a rural Welsh commune, designed to exemplify, or at least foster, Tolstoyan fulfilment through work, thought, harmony. His trust in basic human virtue proved less than impeccable, and in his spiritual autobiography, *Part of a Journey*, he recorded an incident surely typical:

As I was starting the fearsome task of cleaning out the big front flower bed at Barn House, Phil came up and offered me a whetstone for my hook. Then he stood watching me work, with the full intensity of his shaggy earnestness. I gestured, as if whimsically, at a particularly tall clump of dock and thistle; and Phil thought this over for some time before saying, 'If you mean you want me to do some work, Philip, I'm afraid I can't because I'm just going up to meditate with Rose.'

And again, complaining about what we coarser spirits had told him at the start: 'This insistence on "doing one's own thing" can be simply a form of selfishness . . . Mary, for example . . . is going off for her third meditation course next week, just at the time when intensive labour on the land must be under way.' Marina Warner called the commune a crash-pad for freaks.

The energetic response he would have received from such pioneer saints as Benedict of Nursia, and Columbanus of Ireland, he did not receive there. Perhaps our greatest problem is how to love the unlovable and occasionally the unspeakable. A more enduring gift to social life was Philip's founding, with his closest friend, Benedict Nicolson in 1952, of the Bertorelli Wednesday Club, inspired, I suppose, by Buchan's fictional Thursday Club, frequented by Dick, Sandy, Leithen, Pallisser-Yeates and Nightingale 'a slim, peering fellow with double-glasses, who had gone back to Greek manuscripts and his Cambridge fellowship after captaining a Bedouin tribe'. I can still see him leaving the Bertorelli's Christmas Lunch, a Santa Claus hopelessly awry, shedding, one after the other, his children's parcels along Charlotte Street pavements.

Here occurred varied incidents which, back in Suffolk, we enjoyed recounting and doubtless embellishing. Of the bloody Hungarian Rising in 1956, a famous writer remarked that it was a pity, for no country in Europe more appreciated his work. A few weeks later, a Left Wing publisher brought as a guest a genuine Hungarian refugee. We were all much admiring and wished to be practical in our sympathy. Would he, we murmured to each other, be offended if we offered him a fur coat, a solid gold watch, jewellery, would he accept cheques? He sat throughout the lunch, munching solidly, drinking copiously, pausing only to order several double brandies. Finally satiated, he leant back, and remarked that he was, of course, departing to America, probably the West Coast, where all the action happened. There was a slight chilling of atmosphere, followed by real ice, a cessation of speculation about fur coats and cheques, as he said conversationally: 'Bad business of course, but Hungary's only had one good government since the First War. Hitler, of course. At least he knew what to do with the Jews.'

We remembered, more precisely than the others, A.J. Ayer and Father Martin D'Arcy disputing the phenomenon of miracles. In his usual fluent, incisive way, Freddie Ayer insisted on their impossibility: 'Nonsense . . . total fallacy . . . misunderstandings . . .' He was interrupted by a fan, which had hitherto been whirling, fixed on the high wall above the far end of the table. It now left the wall, passed through the air like a procession of the Holy Grail in more than usual hurry, and deposited itself between them. Even Freddie was momentarily checked, and D'Arcy looked supremely smug. 'Afternoon men!' Philip chuckled. From this luncheon club which survives its founders derive the male characters in *The Tournament* set in the fifteenth century but remaining, I think, true to themselves.

Philip's spontaneous enthusiasms and indignations, which had caused his expulsion from Rugby for departing to London, to assist in opposing a Mosley mass-meeting, prompted him to organize a protest march against the Suez invasion, preceded by a press conference, to which nobody came. The march itself attracted only limited response, despite a zealot accompanying us by helicopter. At Edgware I collected some further recruits by telling them that we were demonstrating against High Rents. Sometimes excessive, at times a littly silly, Philip's generosity of spirit was always galvanized by the hypocritical, pretentious, the overdogmatic and self-important. He enjoyed Auden's

> Clear from the head the masses of impressive rubbish;
> Rally the lost and trembling forces of the will,
> Gather them up and let them loose upon the earth.

To Jessica Mitford he wrote, 'I've always wanted to be a great writer and a good man, and I've nearly always believed that the second is more important than the first.' That *nearly* reveals his wry honesty, rueful humour, and perhaps his final status as a writer.

Impetuously, he wrote in his *Observer* column that if the survival of a single man, however atrocious, depended on the destruction of St Paul's Cathedral, the building of course must go. In early political heat he had been the first communist President of the Oxford Union and was barely deterred from opposing Neville Chamberlain at the hustings. The Hitler–Stalin pact outraged his party allegiances but not his political commitment. In family tradition he always believed in good citizenship, fiercely praising, in opposition to Edmund Wilson, the social justice of Income Tax, in which, as very often, he failed to carry all his friends.

With children he was stimulating, inventive, sometimes alarming, creating bizarre imaginary worlds and creatures. Jessica Mitford, in *Faces of Philip* published in 1984, quotes his daughter Polly: 'He invented wonderful games, the best, the cleverest, the most imaginative, and he was completely involved himself in a way grown-ups hardly ever are. His games were always more dangerous, more fun, yet horrifying.' For another daughter, Josephine, he was 'a dream playmate who would without warning turn into a terrifying, ogreish bad brother'.

His sympathy, perhaps empathy, with failures, drop-outs, off-beats, led to his editing *Under-dogs*, a record of unhappy lives, of which I remember a woman, clearly competent, lively, busy, with no obvious physical defects, who yet suffered from what she could only call 'un-charm', some mysterious personal element that repelled her acquaintances. Norah Otway, the old governess in *Pantaloon* is one of his most revealing creations, a tribute to values that nourish the lonely.

I once heard that, when a special correspondent in Iran, he scooped an interview with Dr Mosadeq through a waiter reporting his spirited defence of the radical leader, against some vehement colleagues. A story is also told of him at Cleveden, offending his hostess, Nancy Astor and doubtless others, by haranguing George VI and his Queen on the virtues of republican Spain. He himself was a considerable storyteller, though this talent he seldom used in print, save in *Friends Apart*, his one book that reached a wide public, rather to his own chagrin, for he thought of himself not as critic or biographer, but as poet and novelist. He liked recounting an episode that occurred during the last hours of the Second

World War. He was rushing round London trying to get the latest news, chiefly of the German surrender. He found it nowhere, and at last staggered into the Café Royal. There, at the bar, was a well-known novelist.

'Philip! Good! You've heard the news?'

'No, what is it? Come on, tell me at once.'

'I'm very surprised, Philip, and slightly disappointed, that you haven't heard the news.'

'Yes, yes, but for God's sake, what is it?'

'I've gone back to Secker and Warburg.'

A story told of Philip may not be true in all details, though it rings well enough. After the war, British and French writers hastened to renew contacts and a London editor held a cultural reception for them in his luxurious London flat. A French left-wing poet began to speak. He praised, he exhorted, he reminisced and he prophesied in rapid French, at great length. Hours seemed to pass, and perhaps did so. The audience's gradual but emphatic restlessness he interpreted as signals of encouragement, urging him to further laps. He continued, pleased, urgent, decreasingly comprehensible. Philip had, as usual, drunk well, and fatigued, wandered away into an adjoining room. There followed a resounding crash, the demise of a collection of rareish oriental porcelain. Momentarily, the speaker was halted and, as he drew breath to renew his oration, the captives grabbed their chance and applauded wildly but implacably, the uproar redoubling at the reappearance of Philip, slightly dazed, but finally gratified, accepting it as his general due, the audience then jumping up, stretching legs, indeed stretching hands for hard-earned refreshment.

Ayer compared him to Boswell in 'his lack of caution, his physical indulgence, his ease in making friends, his addiction to journalism, his profound changes of mood', and speculated whether it was his lack of a Johnson that perhaps made him find security ultimately in religion. I myself think that he had a Johnson, though an impersonal one, in his devotion to European history, its unambiguous lessons, its tremendous, untidy bulk of wisdom, grief, paradox, pain and courage, its incessant and magnetic hold on the imagination. Like Johnson, Philip contained something dark, even manic.

'Perhaps it's part of my dance to fall flat on my face from time to time.' Temperamentally, Noel Annan reflected, he liked to go too far. Devoid of malice, he could yet inflict pain. As a young man in war-time Cairo, he and Donald Maclean once wrecked, in her absence, a girl's flat, because they couldn't find anything to drink. There were other such episodes which I still find inexplicable, lacking as I do analytical insights and disposed to believe that people are more unknowable and strange than perhaps they really are. The suicide of a beloved brother Philip could never forget, and his barely tolerable wretchedness pervades *Two Brothers*, yet could scarcely have explained all. Philip himself, with his developing belief in the Christian soul, could nevertheless be baffled by his own mental vagaries until the end.

'I am conscious, Peter, of my good luck in leading a domestic and domesticated life which seems to get happier and richer every year. Yet I seem to spend much of the time in a sort of controlled agony.' Privately, I considered my own situation — with the married woman, and lack of literary standing and hard cash — far more agonizing, but the next day brought a typical Philip postcard: 'I've come across a minor henchman of Al Capone whose Christian names were Dominic Cinderella. We shall have to use him somewhere, sometime!'

Incapable of flattery, indeed his honesty could hurt, Philip managed to convey a sensation of having spent recent months reflecting about something you had said long ago. His capacity for friendship, at its most articulate in *Friends Apart*, remained intact for many years, though eventually faltering, through distance — he eventually left Suffolk for the Welsh borders — illness, personal and family preoccupations. For all his pungent anti-totalitarianism, it would not have occurred to him to desert the renegade Donald Maclean. Fashion and passing prejudices meant nothing to him. He rated *Anna Karenina* and *Sentimental Education* like *Dr Zhivago*, very bad novels. I gaped so much at this that I missed his thesis, and have been left gaping ever since. He wondered why 'Theatre of Cruelty' sounded so impressive, 'Theatre of Kindness' so ludicrous. He was pleased when I wrote of him, 'Emphatically, Toynbee is not *with it*,' that insolent phrase of top-tennery snobbishness, now seldom heard, though its attitude remains.

He declared that most contemporary novelists, notably Isherwood, had failed in nerve, were deferential and often frivolous. Deference was not for him. 'The novelist's deepest obligation is to discover novelty.' On the whole, I disagreed with this, but my critical opinions he told me were, at best, schoolboyish. He insisted that

the novelist's greatest crime is to repeat the discoveries of his predecessors. This is the imperishable belief of every true novelist, that there must be progression. Too often this belief is misinterpreted as a naïve confidence that the new is *better* than the old, whereas the truth is only that the new must be *different* . . .

Assume that a great novelist has explored and charted a hundred miles of new territory, then it is the duty of the minor novelist to push at least one yard further.

His own novels, the last four in verse, largely transmuting plot to myth, and displaying Jungian influences, were more numerous than was sometimes realized, and earned some respect, though he liked to maintain, 'there is only one review worth getting, and that's the one which says, very simply "this is the best book ever written."' This he never received, though T.C. Worsley's critique of *Tea with Mrs Goodman* was still giving him confidence twenty years later. Worsley, comparing it to *The Waves, Finnegan's Wake* and *The Death of Virgil*, claimed that its ripples would revolutionize English prose. Philip himself regarded the *Pantaloon* sequence, which he called a semi-ironical verse epic, as 'a new departure. What I have tried to do is to develop and change existing media for my entirely new purposes . . . a Bouvard-like procession through all the major ideas and idiocies of the age. Great fun!' These last two words are characteristic and help explain, I think, both his failures and successes. 'The swashbuckling element is very important to me, partly, perhaps, because most of our generation were so surfeited with school stories of sensitive youth . . . so a superficial coarseness seems like a splendid suit

254

of armour.' Much of himself, Dick Abbeville, alternately
staggers and swaggers throughout it, a headlong, ravaged,
self-mocking delinquent Peer Gynt, in helter-skelter between
Asgard and the gutter, vulnerable as a wealthy city whose guns
face the wrong way. Restless Dick is stronger than he
pretends, with reserves of talent, curiosity, dedication, though
always more eager to make amends than avoid repeating the
same blunders, excesses, maltreatments. He is ever aware that
the devilish abyss too often complements a brilliant sky dazed,
like Egypt, with too many conflicting gods.

His mind, like my own, was much drawn to the North and
riddled with avatars: the Buchan clubmen, Nansen, the
Marquis de Rose, Wolfe Tone, Danton, and

> The Führer's vast lieutenant, paraded through the
> Streets of Godesberg:
> Dope-fiend aeronaut in a grey Mercedes;
> A basking-shark riding the fleshy streets . . .
> Great Freibeuter, raised on the shields and bloody arms
> Of Kinder and Kamaraden — now an emperor —
> Some brief and reclining Caesar of the third century.

In these books he relished evoking political hooligans,
dreamers of perfections, perfect creation, perfect destruction
and small satirical imps gesticulating from the recesses of
mighty cathedrals. Also snapshots of school, Oxford, thirties
films, summer parks, fijords, broken statues and brief, hectic
loves, grandiose gestures, Franco's general bawling 'Viva la
Muerta! Viva! Viva!', Parisian atmospherics, 'les Soviets
partout, Laval au-poteau, Jeanne d'Arc au-poteau', burlesque,
rhetoric, tomfoolery, metamorphoses; the young warrior-poet
of the Spanish war turned into Nechayev; his hero, Benitez,
into a savage commissar; and the glories of July Paris were
followed by the murderous September days. Watteau's
Cythera was changed into the Cythera of Baudelaire: a living
grandfather became a dead one. And the foulest disease of our
time — Perish Judah! — infected them all. Elaborate set-pieces
resound: an eighteenth-century school mutiny, the felling of a
giant oak, a Grand Tour laced with personal, sometimes

private jottings, 'these choice irrelevancies and digressions, Peter, which are gorgeous almost because they *are* inessential'. Again, very Philip. Historical immediacy, Odysseus, Thor, *Führer* and *Caudillo*, lurks like a raw nerve. We both loved discussing the Franco-Prussion War, though I never dared show him my novel *Enemies*, which described it, and we exchanged *Bazaine* like a password, grinning at others' bewilderment.

Robert Nye, whom we admired, considered these works, 'talk – swift, spiky, darting, soaring about its cohesive post of strange small stories, episodes, jokes, ideas.' My friend, Ronald Hayman, demurred at one volume, at least. 'Reading the book is tantalizingly like watching a talented painter who's stopped painting because he thinks it's more important to find a way of constructing kaleidoscopes without mirrors.' Philip gave this his pirate-king smile. 'Bah!' though adding, 'still, he's an intelligent man.' He was glad of applause from Hilary Corke, Iain Hamilton, V.S. Pritchett. Stephen Spender thought it might well be one of the most remarkable poems of the century, 'Making one realize that every life has an infinite pastness crammed into a present moment of illumination.'

Philip was without conceit but he had the pride, essential to stay the course. 'I do believe most of the time that what I am doing is unique and valuable, but readers won't believe this until someone tells them so. And I can't, of course. I wouldn't mind doing so, but nobody would listen.' He would compare *Pantaloon* to Proust, *The Prelude*, and feel it 'the *Faust, Don Quixote, Iliad* or *Divine Comedy* of our time.' Reviewers avoided such comparisons, poets tended to dismiss him as a gifted amateur. Much of his later writing reminded me more of Günter Grass, likewise preoccupied with history, grotesque humour, myth, northern landscape, old horror.

Philip remained finely undeterred by massive popular and critical indifference, though I think he was glad of my postcard with its quotation from Ezra Pound: 'The best criticism of any work, to my mind the only criticism of any work of art that is of any permament value, comes from the creative writer or artist who does the next job; and *not*, not ever from the young gentlemen who make generalities about the creator.' 'Precisely,' he replied, 'and that is why a nod from Stephen, from VSP, from Nye, is so precious, and, I hope, so telling. But I should have realized that *Pantaloon* is dead against the present tide.'

This was true. Most contemporaries were either still grappling with post-Joyce challenges, or retreating from them, or totally ignoring them. 'Experiment!' Evelyn Waugh wrote, 'God forbid! Look at the results in the case of a writer like Joyce. He started off writing very well, then you can watch him going mad with vanity. He ends up as a lunatic.' Philip's detractors, who had admired his straightforward early novels and were delighted with *Friends Apart*, blamed Joyce for knocking his best talents askew, for shoving him off the familiar track. I think his friends' apathy or disdain towards his verse, as against his weekly *Observer* reviewing, must have hurt. 'For one thing, my self-confidence is a very precarious instrument — for another, alas, I do feel a certain craving for applause.' Even Ben, his closest friend, never bothered to read his books.

Finally, with four volumes of *Pantaloon* published, and some six to come, Chatto & Windus abandoned the project, a major rebuff which would have desolated me but roused not dismal self-pity but a healthy anger and injured his faith in the work not a jot. More let-downs followed, and full publication has still not been achieved.

'My private life,' he wrote from Monmouthshire, 'is, as usual, almost obscenely happy. I have become a smug, domestic animal, purring on my own hearth.' Yet a melancholy, never far from the clowning and chuckles, had deepened. Never one of their intimates, I drifted away from him and Sally, and was dismayed to hear of his undergoing electric shock treatment.

His turn to religion and would-be mysticism, which was to enable him to face death wryly but serenely, bizarre to many old cronies, is prefigured in his books and reviews; in his admiration for certain saints and teachers, for Simone Weil, Bonhoeffer and, perhaps acquired more gradually, for his father. 'The task,' he wrote, 'is not to destroy orthodox theology and replace it with a new one; but to replenish orthodoxy by a deeper perusal of its terms. Thus the Trinity has become, for me – Heaven (the Father); Earth (the Son); and every occasion of their meeting (the Holy Spirit).' The principle of rebirth, of loss and recovery, pervades his work, together with a later, more arguable element: 'If it were irrefutably demonstrated to me that there is no God and reality, above or distinct from the material world, then I would consider that human life is too terrible to be endured.' I can never think in this way, and was not to have the chance to debate this with him. In one more vain attempt at the last word I would have quoted Dick Abbeville:

I said, 'We shall need peculiar strength, unusual assiduity, to live through this ice-age of human spirit.'
'Rubbish,' he said, 'like everybody else we'll build our igloos and survive disgracefully.'

I hear his richness of voice, at once commanding and humorous, quick to size up situations, extract dry truths, unexpected alternatives, and potential, comic, poetic, or ironic. The last phase in which, not altogether incongruously, as 'Brother Philip', he regularly attended the Anglican contemplative convent at Tymawr, is described in *Part of a Journey*, a journal which the minister at his funeral believed might become a Christian classic. It depicts austere inner intellectual and moral wrestling, tortured set-backs, acknowledgements of absurdity and preventable misunderstandings, brave strivings for cohesion, acceptance, grace, yet with recognizable traits of the stormy old Bulgarian.

Dec 9   I have resolved to give up booze entirely.
Dec 10   An exception will be made, of course, at Christmas.
         At *Christmas time*.

Today, years later, in the pubs of Kersey, Hadleigh, Lindsay, Boxford, I still see that welcoming, rather ramshackle figure, impressive even when slightly unsteady, and hear the

rich voice speaking of Bazaine, Tolstoy, and unusual behaviour.

4

I was always fascinated by Counties: antique Norfolk, opulent
Kent, neat Berkshire, mighty Yorkshire, each with its dialect,
turns of speech — 'calm as a clock', 'strong enough to trot a
mouse', 'chanceways', 'eel-babby' — its flavour of sky, tree,
soil, its architecture, old tales, jokes and harbours; traditions,
cricket teams and, until mechanization, its particular harvest
stooks. In Southsea, I imagined each county surrounded by
bands of steel, scarcely visible but dangerous as the lines of
longitude and latitude which, at ebb-tide, could rip open
windjammer and dreadnought. Frontiers must entail changes
in the texture of the air, as the blind must feel, by brief change
of temperature, that they are passing a pillar box or an open
door. And within each country were further and mysterious
worlds, of tramps and gipsies with their secret signs, marks,
lore, their ghosts and legends; lands of shifting boundaries,
other angles of perception, tied very loosely to plain
geography.

In Suffolk, Celts and Romans, Danes and Saxons, Bretons,
Flemings and Dutch have carved their identities, almost
submerging me. An ancient windbreak is claimed as the oldest
human structure in Britain, older than dolmen, long barrow,
coiled terrace and stone circle. A few miles away, Illa's Place,
now Monks Eleigh, from a feudal connection with medieval
Canterbury, was earlier owned by the giant Saxon hero,
Brynoth, described in *The Battle of Maldon*:

> Thoughts should be braver, hearts bolder,
> Courage the keener, as our strength dwindles.
> Here lies our leader, all hacked down,
> Hero in dust. Long may he wail,
> That man who now thinks of fleeing the battle.

Today, in the eighties, I brood over the old gardens of

childhood: a churchyard of yews and turf in George Rothery's Henfield, the walled gardens at Hawkhurst and Chalfont St Giles. Sunswept roses at Bletsoe, the butterflies above Frank Laidlaw's petunias. Old griefs return, instants of bad behaviour, of life gone wrong and loves with forgotten names sent howling. In a drawer I find a diary of 1949, and find that I took 'B' for dinner five times in a week. Who could 'B' have been? Bill? Betty? The past turns traitor, perhaps fortunately. I can read books in a language almost forgotten, yet fitting the beams, plaster, Tudor brick and wrought iron of my cottage.

I have no disposition to sentimentalize my surroundings, despite its beauties which Constable and Gainsborough have lavished on the world. As in Devonshire, rural savagery had been relished as fiercely as in the towns. All rural England knew bloody games of shin-kicking and mass-football, cock-fights, rat-catching — two men at a table, their hands bound, competing to kill with their teeth rats released by a child. Simon Byne and Sandy McKay in 1830, fought bare-knuckled, Byne dying in the forty-seventh round. Ipswich museum exhibits the swivel-guns and iron traps, used to maim poachers. Gallows Hill so often balanced Mill Lane, and the April fields lie against an unseen backcloth of pitiless game-laws, wrongs of enclosures, tithes, atrocious hedge-births and ancient horrors. Masefield, as a child, saw the metal plate on a Herefordshire bridge stating that damage would entail seven years transportation, and, only last week, Paul Tory showed me a similar plate on a Dorset bridge. The 1381 Suffolk peasants lynched Lord Chancellor Cavendish at Lakenheath, and the men of Kent and Essex beheaded another Suffolk man, Archbishop Simon of Sudbury, Lord Treasurer of England, in the Tower. To balance this, we are told that Woodbridge secludes the head of the Lord Protector, Oliver Cromwell. Two miles from me, Maria Marten was murdered in the Red Barn by a local squire, the crime betrayed by her spectral voice, and recorded on parchment bound, after his execution, with his own skin. One of our Suffolk chroniclers, Julian Tennyson, mentions the fisherman, Joseph 'Posh' Fletcher, though barely literate, reciting his verses to Edward FitzGerald.

Man that's born of woman
Has very little time to live;
He comes up like a foremast top-sail
And down like a flying jib.

Incest, I hear, survives on remoter East Anglian farms and hamlets. Last week I read of Derbyshire police concerned with criminals who dig out badgers, to be baited at 'tournaments' by terrier dogs. Some miles from me is Breckland, which long sheltered outcast communities too violent for the authorities to resist. David Thompson, whom I have already quoted in discussing Camden Town, writes in the same book, 'In the Breckland public houses, Norfolk, until about 1950, it was the custom to offer any stranger a drink out of your mug. If he refused, as many American airmen did, he was forced outside to redeem the insult in a fight.' Here, insists local tradition, originated the legend of the Babes in the Wood and, possibly somewhere near, were the palace and grave of Boudicca, 'the Victorious', the Celtic, Icenic warrior, whom Charles Kightly suggests, 'whether as sacred queen, priestess, or inspired representative – was first and foremost the heiress of the ancient bloody and orgiastic goddess of life and death, (Andrasta), and the savagery of the rebels was the direct outcome of the Roman insult to that goddess' power.' Tramping this lonely, sometimes eerie region, ancient Celtic forest, flint-knappers' land, I find this more plausible than the Victorian belief that Boudicca lies under Parliament Hill Fields, Hampstead, or beneath Platform 10, King's Cross Station.

At Hadleigh, two miles away, the Danish king, Guthrum, is said to be buried – there is still Guthrum Street. At the treaty in 878, East Anglia passed to his rule, after he had accepted baptism from his old enemy, Alfred the Great, who became his godfather.

The dead have a reputation for remaining active. At Polstead ('Place of Pools') a ghostly rector drives a headless horse, and in 1980, a new rector and his young family were ejected by a poltergeist; his successor at the Old Rectory confirms a real though harmless presence. Polstead Church, twelfth-century, some distance from the village but deferentially close to the Big House, has a parish register containing some Mayflower names. A Hanoverian black drummer-boy haunts Blythborough. A pub at Bildeston, where a seventeenth-century magnate minted his own coin, is known for its ghosts: two Victorian children, a grey woman, a man who stands at the bar in a trilby. A gamekeeper haunts Elveden. Thetford Warren has the White Rabbit with flaring eyes, an omen of coming trouble. An Archdeacon of Sudbury is seen headless at Icklingham, on the site of his own murder. Suffolk has particular spectres: the donkey-headed, velvet-skinned Shock, visible only to those born at 4, 8, or 12 o'clock; and the white, gleaming monster, Galley Trot. In her book on East Anglian folklore, Enid Porter mentions children dragged through brambles at sunrise, against whooping-cough, and hanged by their hands to cure nose-bleeds. Live spiders were swallowed against rheumatism, and late nineteenth-century builders still mixed animal blood with mortar, for a new foundation.

At Sudbury, Dickens' 'Eatonsville', a 1706 church epitaph is: Traveller, I will relate a wondrous thing. On the day that Thomas Carter breathed his last, a Sudbury camel passed through the eye of a needle: if thou hast wealth, go and do likewise. Farewell.'

5

I lack wealth. My mother, shortly before her death, suffered a fire, without the protection of having been insured. This lost us both our mediocre savings, forcing me to rely more than ever on the impact of nearby places, people, nature. I can walk to Lavenham, all black beams and white plaster, where once the Flemish weavers brought their 'mistery' and their sexually explicit murals, and the wool dealer, Thomas Spring, financed the great perpendicular church. Arthur Mee, scourge of my childhood, wrote of this church: 'On the pier caps of the six bays of the nave are Tudor flowers and crowns of East Anglian kings . . . above, a gallery of twenty-eight standing figures, monks, pilgrims, saints, holds up the huge beam of the roof, shaped from single oak trees.' Here I can wander into the past, hung with moon-grammar and arcane symbolism. Feudal crests, carved leaves, here St Peter, there Thomas Becket, the great medieval menagerie of winged lions, dragons, tailed jesters, wild acrobats, alarmed children, tree climbers. The choir sports the *misere* carvings so numerous in old England: a peasant carrying a pig, a woman with animal head instead of legs, her man with its tail, a camel rider, a woman fiddler aped or jeered at by a cripple playing the bellows with his crutches, a stork and spoonbill tugging at a fellow's hair. Outside, old walls display the mitred *fleur de lys* of St Blaise, patron of wool-combers and healer of sore throats; and the shields, boars, *mullets* (five-pointed stars) of the manorial lords, de Vere, once rivals of the Clarences, Cavendishes, Bigods, de la Poles. More words and skills, now becoming esoteric, revive at the Guildhall: *'pargetted', 'spandrills', 'ribbon-carved'*.

History is incessant. Chelsworth was granted a charter in 962, by King Edgar. An echo from my childhood is Stifkey, from where, in the thirties, Rector Davidson, 'the prostitutes' padre', regularly tramped Paris in search of subjects. Accused of immorality with some thousand girls, he was ejected from the living, assaulted by the churchwarden; he sat fourteen hours in a barrel to raise his legal costs, was exhibited alongside a whale at Hampstead Heath Fair, was killed by his host when addressing a crowd from a lion's cage at Skegness, and was resuscitated in a London musical comedy in the seventies.

In Holy Suffolk dwelt Mrs Girling, 'The Second Appearance of Jesus', founder of the Shakers; she guaranteed them immortality, which hitherto, she explained, had been possessed by herself alone, though her death at fifty-nine may suggest error. Julian Tennyson tells of George Borrow, over at Oulton in *Suffolk Scene*:

For an hour on end he would fascinate a dinner party with some wild and wonderful tale of romance; ten minutes later he would insult his hostess to her face and march storming out of the room, to walk like a madman to some pub a dozen miles away, there to soothe his anger with three pints of ale. Footmen quaked at his mighty knock, maids trembled as they thrust a dish before him. No one could foresee his next move — a thundrous laugh, a bellow of disgust, a glare of silent and appalling fury. When one Suffolk authoress [Agnes Strickland] timidly offered to present him with twelve volumes of her book *The Queens of England*, he replied with a shout, 'For God's sake don't, Madam. I shouldn't know where to put them, or what to do with them!' and he added in a loud voice to a friend beside him, 'What a damned fool that woman is!' He used to say there were only three celebrities in the world whom he wished to meet; one was Daniel O'Connell, another was 'Lamplighter', the Derby winner; both these escaped him by their death. The third was the learned Norfolk lady, Anna Gurney, and one day he called on her at her home in North Repps. She handed him an Arabic grammar and asked him to decipher some difficult point. He tried; and while he tried, she talked to him incessantly. Exasperated, he flung down the book and ran from the house and never stopped running until he reached Old Tucker's inn at Cromer, where he ate 'five excellent sausages'.

I myself am not forward at offering my work to those better known than myself, mindful, from an early age, of Hilaire Belloc's account of Charles Kingsley being shown a book of poems, by the author. He swiftly returned it, 'Madam, there is poetry and there is verse. What you have written is not poetry, it is verse. It is not good verse, it is bad verse.'

Stories, stories. At Brandeston, Matthew Hopkins, seventeenth-century Witchfinder General, tortured the old parson, John Lowes, into confessing diabolism, then, before hanging him, forced him to read his own burial service. Here lived Charles Austin, so lavishly praised by John Stuart Mill. He was reputed to be alone in dominating Lord Macaulay in talk. 'He found Macaulay a Tory and left him a Liberal.'

A tree at Euston, they say, is the original stake thrust through the hanged body of the pirate, Chunk Harvey. A strange tale was told of Bloody Mary, at Framlingham Castle before her accession, bearing a child, half animal, which she smashed to death. One of the most alluring medieval Suffolk tales is from Woolpit, where harvesters discovered the Green Children, boy and girl, who emerged from beneath the earth, speaking an unknown language and declaring that they were from the twilit land of St Martin, and had been attracted to the brighter world by the bells of Bury St Edmunds.

My long silent walks produce their small treasure; the doubloons and pieces-of-eight I had demanded in Miss Howe's day, now transmuted to small brilliant insets of life. At Aldeburgh, Bawdsey, Orford Ness, Dunwich, the waves do their best to live up to what Virginia Woolf wrote of them. Dunwich, long broken, all of it now under the sea, once supplied 60,000 herrings a year to the Saxon kings. Feeling myself a detective reconstructing bodies from footprints, I trudge towards damp remote towers, square or rounded and the occasional spire. At Preston Church, painted on wood, is the clause, 'that the Rector for the time being sh'd yearly make or cause to be made in this Church seven sermons upon ye seven Thursdays in Lent upon pain of 20 shillings to be forfeited for the relief of the poor of this Parish'. Small beer, but I prefer small beer to no beer. The churchwarden's account book 1754, records that Sam Lygoe was paid five shillings annually for 'Whiping of the Dogs out of the Church on all Sundays and other Days upon which there is divine Service, also he is to prevent anyone sleeping in the church by waking them with a white wand.' I like to think of Sam Lygoe, doubtless as proud of his white wand as King George was of his crown.

I enjoy the medieval zig-zag lines and the crosses on the Long Melford brass of Lady Margaret Clopton and am moved by a Boxford brass showing two small shoes under a bed, denoting a child's death. I look out for the crocodile carved on a Denston cornice. St Stephen's, Ipswich, has a painted memorial to the fishmonger, Mr Lemon, and his wife who both died on 3 September 1637.

> Beneath this monument intombed lie
> The reare Remark of a Conivgal Tye

Robert & Mary who to show How neere
They did comply, how to each other deare,
One loath behind the other long to stay
(As married) Dyed together in one Day.

Present historians are tending to map the fluctuating
degrees of married love and love for children, in particular
eras. This is suggestive, though I am unconvinced that it
would be easy to research even for our own time, let alone for
the Plantagenets, Tudors, Stuarts and Hanoverians. Stoke-by-
Nayland Church was damaged by earthquake, 1884. It has an
intricate brass for Katherine Howard, which includes what I
assume is a crowned leopard, with grand, looped tail as long as
itself. Her husband, Duke of Norfolk, was killed at Bosworth:

Jockey of Norfolk, be not too bold,
For Dickon, thy master, is bought and sold.

6

A long walk is the great teacher and arbiter. I have
characters who lack plot or theme, or a plot without a theme,
sometimes a theme alone, but the walk may resolve them.
Fatigue and old inns, birds above thickets, the soundless purr
of falling leaves, flowers in a hedge, they all loosen the
imagination. In London, I write of contemporary life, though
few would class me as a modernist. Here, in Suffolk, its crisp
sunlit autumn mornings, the clear mellow afternoon, drowsy
sundown and wood smoke, little flames on piled leaves,
golden trees turning silver, lead me back to distant lives, jolt
me as old truths unfold further. Small incidents, scarcely
noticed when told, are tutored by time into significance. From
a few, hesitant words, dormant for forty years, I suddenly
realize that one of my favourite teachers, very handsome, very
suave, with a wife of exceptional beauty and charm, spent his
wedding night seated at a window catching flies. Even in
periods of apparent sterility, some hidden yeast always seems

to be working, to emerge with an image, conviction, story, unexpected, yet seldom surprising me. A novel is not a crusade, but a voyage of discovery, not least for the author. On a bench at Layham, I saw the Gwenhever for my novel *Lancelot*, 'though not beautiful, silvery, remote, as if lit by a flake of moon, brilliants on hair and arms, her smile uneasy, as if painted.' What began as an adventure story developed into Lancelot's obsession with historical truth, and how Arthur and himself will be at the mercy of prejudice, error, ignorance, and man's penchant for myth, all holding up a distorting lens to the past.

He reflects further: 'It is too often assumed that an eye-witness is competent to assess events. Yet I myself, who partook in so many august occasions, may know less of them than students centuries hence. Important questions I can fail to answer, indeed fail to identify which were important. Truth may elude all but genius, and the mistakes of genius may be illimitable and fantastic.' Celebrated teachings may be invalidated by posterity's unawareness of the traditions from which they emerged, or the tone of voice in which they were uttered. When I tested 'Love your enemies' against this, the result was disconcerting. Better, *perhaps*, to write in the dust.

From a church carving of a Wodehouse, symbol of pagan social and sexual licence, from long periods in my garden watching graduations of shadow and colour, came intimations of the unseen, questions about the reality of sacrifice, sacramental or vicious, then a story, *The Death of Robin Hood*. Later, on a bus, from Colchester, ancient Celtic capital, I saw, chalked on a barn door, '367'. In Hampstead, this would have meant nothing, but, in this landscape, old but not threadbare, it stirred a memory almost, but not quite, lost. At my destination, the only books were Gibbon, and a set of Churchill's war speeches. Gibbon was more promising, and in him I tracked it down, 367 AD, year of the so-called, never absolutely authenticated, Barbarian Conspiracy, when Roman England was overwhelmed by invaders, the country in fiercer danger than from anything until 1940. The events were factual and horrific, and in discovering them I taught myself much. The theme, however, first reflecting politicians' shallow notions of time and culture, became civilized man's equivocal attitude towards violence, destruction, loyalty, so that an armchair sophisticate like Lytton Strachey can play with the proposition that civilization loves the truth, barbarism tells it. And in the thirties I myself could vaguely accept communism, fascism, pacificism, all in the same breath, while events were actually pointing to 1940.

Suffolk, however, no less than Hampstead, has its dangers of stagnation, of savouring too long the larks, the Albertines and Paul Scarlets, the lights drooping over the tiger-lily and mingling with the phlox and woody smells. Mauberley's mottoes on sundials can be accepted too readily as a substitute for talent, a defence against hard work, an excuse for nostalgia, not creation but makebelieve. Very soon, yet again, I must depart. Also, town is where the cheques are, or should be.

'Whoever undertakes to write a biography,' Freud wrote to Arnold Zweig, 'commits himself to lies, dissimulation, hypocrisy, embellishment, even the hiding of his own inability to understand: because biographical truth is impossible, and even if one did accomplish it, it would be worthless.' Just so. Meanwhile, the job must be finished. Despite the doctors' enigmatic head-shakings I am still here. I do not know how philosophy defines luck. Logic, merit, will, are irrelevent, for then it would cease to be luck. An offshoot of personality? It certainly exists. Some have none, some too much, I myself rather more than my fair share. I looked into the gutter and picked up, if not quite a home, at least a house. I have had generous friends, more than I have mentioned here, and a fair proportion of my books have been printed, by such forbearing publishers and friends as Peter Owen. My complaints are not against life, but against myself, often behaving badly, giving less than I received. Life remains worth the living, like a fine book, written by a scoundrel, which deserves close attention. In defence against Time, I now see birthdays not as years, but as significant moments: acceptance of a book, losing virginity, surviving a bomb, seeing a Tuscan evening, feeling exhilaration on the Pennine Way, reaching the sea with Justine. With more luck, I shall reach twenty. But some of my wisest pupils – Garth McKibbin, John Atkinson – have long been dead. I shall never write a masterpiece, nor hold the Albert Hall spellbound as I sing:

> As I was a-walking the Streets of Laredo,
>   as I was a-walking Laredo one day,
> I met a young cowboy all dressed in white linen,
>   Dressed in white linen and cold as the clay.

I do not expect very much, from myself or from the world, though I would not go as far as Richard West's belief that the fall of Richard II marked the beginning of the decadence of the English nation.

As always, we advance on one front, retreat on another. There will always remain, what Camus, or Alex Comfort, has called the struggle against Death and Obedience. The more billions we spend on education and art, the less we seem to receive. I have lived to read, in the *Times Literary Supplement*, that clarity is the death of language, and to have seen London race rioters attempting to burn alive a publican and his wife, and I have heard students howling down a speaker in the name of free speech. Life is a cluster of disappointments made bearable by the challenges they establish.

Splendid strangers abound, though usually they have just departed or are late in arrival. Bits and pieces of life remain to be pursued or assessed. I have been awarded an IQ exceptionally low, have seen Hobbs and Woolley bat, Trueman and Lindwall bowl, and, with George Rothery, I saw Dexter slam Hall and Griffiths; have been offered a Swedish island, received courtesy from Ralph Richardson and seen his *Peer Gynt*. I would have liked to have bowled fast for England, rescued Graham from drowning, written Pound's *Cantos*, only better, travelled more often and more adventurously, been a better husband, and have heard Oscar Wilde lecture on 'the Secret of Botticelli' to Rocky Mountain miners. As I swing my racquet in Regent's Park I remember the vicarage lawns of long-ago Devonshire. Surrendering to the tidal pull of words, I have written too much. But there remains a Gosport, and at least one more path both from the White Horse and from the dead horses. Prayers, alas, will doubtless get answered.

Memories will change to fantasy and perhaps have already done so, together, I suppose, with possibilities of rebirth.

Index

273

275

278